NOV   1997

W9-BSL-350

Ela Area Public Library
135 S. Buesching Rd
Lake Zurich, Il. 60047

THE
DECORATIV
PAINTING
COLO
MATC
SOURCEBO

DEC , 5 1997          JAN - 5 2000

JAN - 6 1998
FEB 12 1998
                     APR 12 2000
MAR 14 1998          JUL 22 2000

MAR 30 1998

AUG 28 FEB 19 1999

MAR - 5 1999
APR 10 1999
MAY 12 1999

JUN - 1 1999

JUL 6 1999
SEP 22 1999

# THE
# DECORATIVE
# PAINTING
# COLOR
# MATCH
# SOURCEBOOK

The complete guide to finding color
matches for every top brand of paint

BOBBIE PEARCY

**NORTH LIGHT BOOKS**

CINCINNATI, OHIO

ELA AREA PUBLIC LIBRARY
135 S. Buesching Road
Lake Zurich, IL 60047

**Decorative Painting Color Match Sourcebook.** Copyright ©
1997 by Bobbie Pearcy. Manufactured in China. All rights
reserved. No part of this book may be reproduced in any form or
by any electronic or mechanical means including information
storage and retrieval systems without permission in writing from
the publisher, except by a reviewer, who may quote brief passages
in a review. Published by North Light Books, an imprint of F&W
Publications, Inc., 1507 Dana Avenue, Cincinnati, Ohio 45207.
(800) 289-0963. First edition.

Other fine North Light Books are available from your local
bookstore, art supply store or direct from the publisher.

01  00  99  98  97    5  4  3  2  1

**Library of Congress Cataloging-in-Publication Data**

Pearcy, Bobbie.
  Decorative painting color match sourcebook / by Bobbie
Pearcy.—1st ed.
     p.    cm.
  Includes index.
  ISBN 0-89134-836-0
  1. Painting.   2. Acrylic painting.   3. Color in interior
decoration.    4. Decoration and ornament.   I. Title.
TT324.P43  1997
747'94—dc21                         97-19592
                                     CIP

Edited by David Lewis
Production edited by Jennifer Lepore and Katie Carroll
Interior designed by Sandy Kent
Cover designed by Clare Finney

North Light Books are available for sales promotions, premiums
and fund-raising use. Special editions or book excerpts can also be
created to specification. For details, contact the Special Sales
Manager, F&W Publications, 1507 Dana Avenue, Cincinnati, Ohio
45207.

# Table of Contents

# Introduction

No matter which brands of acrylic paints you use, there will always be references to brands and color names you do not have available to you. Magazines and pattern books use hundreds of color names which often must be matched to complete the project as the author intended.

The *Decorative Painting Color Match Sourcebook* is designed to assist you in selecting matching colors from various brands. Where a perfect match is not available, a mix is provided. Each suggested mix includes the mixing ratio.

To add value to the sourcebook we have added gorgeous living color to each color match. This gives you a representation of an actual color swatch right from the container.

## WHAT YOU CAN LEARN BY UNDERSTANDING THE TCS NUMBER

With this book you can make thousands of color matches using only the color names. You can then find equivalent colors to use in either your favorite brand or in a brand which is available to you . . . but I encourage you to read about and reference the TCS numbers which are assigned to every paint color or mix. If you will learn how they translate to a color, you can use them to expand color selection choices available to you which will increase your painting options.

We are complimented to have artists who are now keeping their paints in TCS Color Family order. Many designers are now printing the TCS number along with the color names on their patterns. Perhaps it will become, as we intended, a reliable standard for decorative painters to understand the actual color of the paint names assigned by the different companies.

Continued Success!

Bobbie Pearcy

## HOW DID BOBBIE'S TRU-COLOR SYSTEM ORIGINATE?

As a decorative painting teacher, Bobbie Pearcy had a dilemma. How could she help her students understand the differences among the various paint colors? It can be very confusing because the major brands sometimes have different names for the same color and/or the same name for different colors. She soon discovered she was not the only one struggling with this problem.

She tried to arrange her containers in order of color value. This meant intermixing the jars, bottles and tubes of various brands. Then, she painted several swatches of one brand on the outer edge of white poster board and hand-lettered its name next to it. After many hours of work she had developed the prototype of what is known today as the Tru-Color Comparison Disc. The squares became circles of different sizes. When stacked smallest on top with a center post, she had four rings of handpainted swatches—hundreds of colors all within inches of each other.

After investing the money, time and effort to paint several discs, she tested the idea at her booth at the National Society of Tole and Decorative Painters' Annual Convention. Avid painters and painting teachers—who had been struggling with their own color matching problems—purchased all the discs available. Thus, Bobbie's Tru-Color System was born.

Bobbie's original idea has been expanded to computer software and this four-color reference book. The discs are still popular—there is more demand for them than Bobbie can meet by herself—but with a little assistance every swatch is still handpainted.

# How to Use This Book

The *Decorative Painting Color Match Sourcebook* is designed for quick access to color matches in an easy-to-use format. Each box in this book represents one specific color. It is composed of either matching colors in different brands of paint, or creating mixes to match the target color for that TCS number. This means you can use your favorite brand of paint to complete any project you choose, regardless of the brands designated in the pattern.

A Choose a color name from the table of contents (page 5), the alphabetic index (pages 86-91) or use the color bars along the sides of pages.

The color bars are grouped by color families, starting with Yellow. They represent the first color shown on the page and can in turn help you find the approximate location of a color when you are not sure of the color name, but you know, for instance, that it is a yellow color. From there, look at the color names listed in the bar; they represent the first and last color on that page.

B Turn to the listed page and TCS number or to a page where the color bar represents the color family you are looking for.

C There you will find six colors and/or mixes including your target color if you've gone the route of the alphabetic list. Manufacturer's suggested shades and highlights are located under the color name.

## A sample color box:

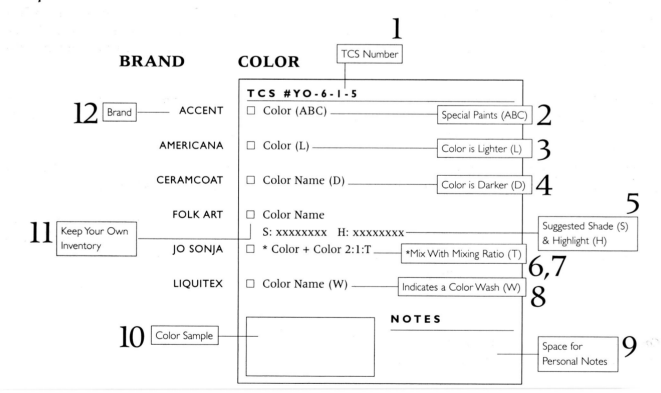

# Here's how to read the sample color box:

**1** *TCS Number.* Always located in the upper left corner. It identifies the unique color qualities which these six colors/mixes have in common.

*The TCS numbering system is designed to give you more options in your color choices.* You can find a very close color to your target color by working with the last digit of the TCS number—the value of the color. For instance, all of the colors numbered BL-6-1-1 through BL-6-1-9 are the same in hue and clarity. They differ only in value. So, if you do not have Ocean Reef Blue (TCS number BL-6-1-5) or any of its matches, look at the box before or after to find the closest color. In this case, any color or mix in TCS number BL-6-1-4 or BL-6-1-6 would work as a substitute. The hue and clarity are the same, and only the value of the color is a slight shade lighter or darker.

**2** **(A B C)** after an Accent color means it is an *Acrylic Blending Color.*

**(P P)** at the end of a Folk Art color indicates it is one of their Pure Pigment colors.

These paints, made of pure color pigments, are specially formulated for mixing your own colors. They are often used in color theory exercises.

**3** *An* **(L)** *After the Name* indicates the color is a shade lighter than the represented color. Again, this color will suffice in most cases. To darken the color to match the representative color, add a touch of a darker color in the same color family, or black, to the designated color.

**4** *A Color With a* **(D)** after it means that color is a shade darker than the represented color. In most cases this color will work as well as the color called for in the pattern. To lighten the color to match the representative color, add a touch of a lighter color in the same color family to the designated color—or you may add a touch of white.

**5** *Shades and Highlights.* Four of the six manufacturers have worked with us to create a suggested shade and highlight for each of their standard colors. For quick reference, they are printed under the color name. Please note this is only one set of many shades and highlights which could be used for each color.

**6** *Color Mixes Are Prefaced With an Asterisk (*).* Many of the colors from different brands do not perfectly match colors from other brands. When this occurs, we want you to know how to accurately match a pattern's given color, so we give you the recipe for a mix to duplicate that color. This mix is written with colors from the brand you have chosen for your color match. For instance, the color called for in the pattern: Delta Ceramcoat-Tangerine.

The sourcebook lists a mix for Jo Sonja of *Vermillion + Yellow Light 4:1. This means that by mixing four (4) parts of Jo Sonja's Vermillion with one (1) part of her Yellow Light you will have a color which matches Ceramcoat's Tangerine.

All mixes are listed with a ratio mixing formula: the first number in the formula referring to the first color in the mix, the second number corresponding with the second color, etc.

**7** *A Color Within a Mix* designated with a **(T)** after it means that adding a "touch" (lightly tip the corner of the brush in the "touch" color and add it to the color/mix) will give you a very accurate match.

Examples:  *Orange + Red (T) means add just a touch of red to the orange.

*White + Red + Orange 1:1:T means mix equal parts white and red then add a "touch" of orange.

**8** *A Color or Mix With* **(W)** at the end means that by making a wash of the color—adding a bit of medium—you can get the transparency needed to duplicate the original color of the pattern.

**9** *Personal Notes.* We have provided space for your personal notes in each match block. If you have a mix you prefer for this color, write it here.

**10** *Color Sample.* Representative color which equals all paints and mixes in this TCS box.

**11** *Record Your Inventory.* Beside each color name is a small box which you can mark to indicate you have the color(s) in your inventory.

# Understanding the TCS Color Classification System

Remember, you can match all the colors of the leading brands without reference to the TCS number. However, by understanding this number, you can add more versatility to your painting.

The TCS identifier divides the complete color spectrum into fifteen color families. All colors and mixes are identified by a two-character alphabetic abbreviation and a unique three-digit number. Each number is based on a scale of nine segments. It is helpful to familiarize yourself with the abbreviations and color class they represent.

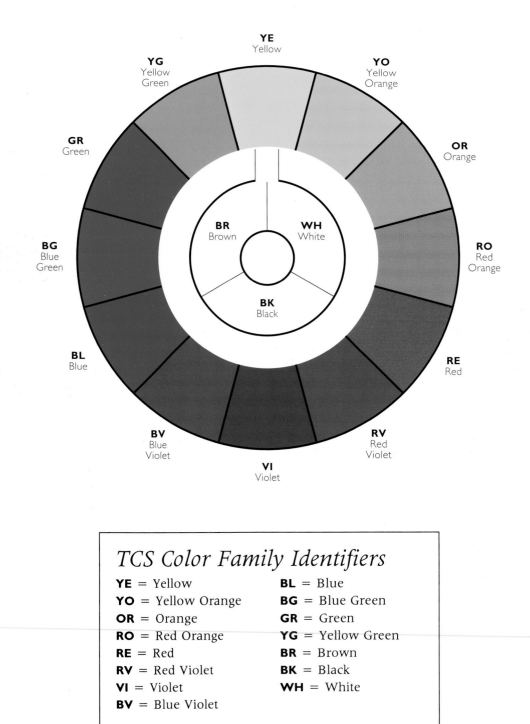

## TCS Color Family Identifiers

| | |
|---|---|
| **YE** = Yellow | **BL** = Blue |
| **YO** = Yellow Orange | **BG** = Blue Green |
| **OR** = Orange | **GR** = Green |
| **RO** = Red Orange | **YG** = Yellow Green |
| **RE** = Red | **BR** = Brown |
| **RV** = Red Violet | **BK** = Black |
| **VI** = Violet | **WH** = White |
| **BV** = Blue Violet | |

# Learn to Use the TCS Number:
# Color Family-Hue-Clarity-Value

*The individual TCS number assigned to a color identifies the following:*

TCS # BL-5-7-4
Color Family — Hue — Clarity — Value

## COLOR FAMILY

Two alpha characters which identify the color family of the color—YE (Yellow), YO (Yellow Orange), OR (Orange), etc.

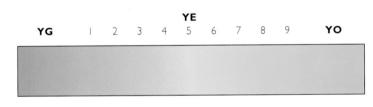

YG   | 2 3 4 5 **YE** 6 7 8 9   **YO**

## COLOR HUE

This indicates the position of a color in its color family. Each color family is segmented into nine parts. Reading clockwise from 1 (which is closer to the color on the color wheel before it) to 9 (closer to the family listed after it) with 5 being closest to the pure color of that family. Example: A yellow #8 (YE-8) would be much closer to yellow orange or a yellow with an orange cast, and a yellow #3 (YE-3) would be a yellow with a touch of green (closer to yellow green).

## COLOR CLARITY

Color clarity or intensity is identified with 1 being a very bright, clear color to 9 being a very grayed color. Adding a small amount of the complement color to a bright color will gray or mud the color. The exact opposite color on the color wheel is the complementary color: i.e., red is the complement of green. When two colors are in the same color fam-

ily, with the same hue but the clarity (second number) of one is much higher than the other, note the variance in clarity of the colors:

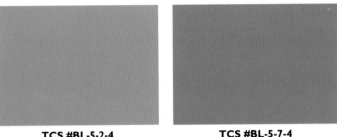

**TCS #BL-5-2-4**          **TCS #BL-5-7-4**

## COLOR VALUE

This again segmented into nine different sections to describe the relative position of the color on a gray scale where 1 is a light/pastel color and 9 is very dark. Example: White is a 1 and Black is a 9.

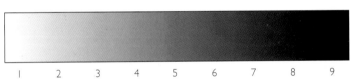

| 2 3 4 5 6 7 8 9

So, a color identified as BL-5-7-4 would indicate the color is in the blue family (BL), is a pure hue with no violet or green tones (5); is quite grayed (7); and is slightly lighter than a medium value (4). (See page 51 for all six brands of this color.)

**TCS #BL-5-7-4**

# How to Mix Acrylic Paint

I t is easy to mix acrylic paint. Just like measuring and mixing the ingredients called for in a favorite recipe, you will get accurate mixes by using the measurements of ingredients (paint) called for in a color mix. However, you do not need your measuring cups and spoons to make the measurements exact. If you can squeeze out puddles of paint of like size, you can use these to create the ratios of paint in any mix. For example, if the color is:

*Bright Red + Yellow 3:1*

Squeeze out three parts (puddles) of bright red and one part (puddle) of yellow next to each other on your palette and mix together with your palette knife or brush. The size of the puddles depends on how much of a color you need to mix.

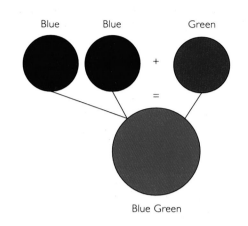

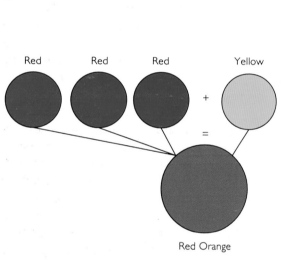

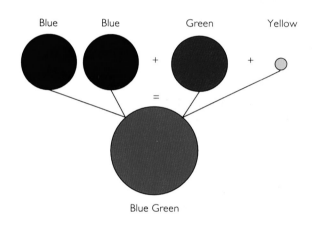

Remember the first number in the ratio refers to the first color in the mix, the second refers to the second, and so on.

When a mix calls for a touch (T) of a color, this touch of paint can be eliminated without harming the end result of the project. For example:

*Blue + Green + Yellow 2:1:T*

If you mix two puddles of blue with one puddle of green, the resulting color will be ''almost'' perfect. The purist may add just a touch of yellow to get the *exact* color the project calls for.

In creating these mixes, we start with the lighter color and add the darker or more intense color(s) a little at a time. That is because darker values will color the mix faster and there is less opportunity to pass the desired shade required. By starting with several very small puddles of the paint we need for a specific color, we add a small amount of the

darker shade to the lighter color, comparing it with the original color of the TCS number until we have a match. We paint a swatch, make note of the mixing recipe we used, then, if it is still a match when dry, we record the information. Although there are usually many mixes to match a color, we try to choose the simplest ones possible. One theory we use when mixing colors is: Any two colors can be used to mix a color between them.

Since we have already created and tested the color match recipes in this book, you can simply mix the paints in the amounts stated and get the right results.

***Please note:*** You can mix a small amount of paint with your brush. However, you must take care to keep the paint out of the ferrule (the metal part that holds the brushes in place). If paint dries underneath the ferrule, your brush will be ruined. For larger quantities of paint it is safer to use a palette knife.

## ACRYLIC PAINT MANUFACTURERS

Here are the addresses and phone numbers of the manufacturers whose products are listed in this book:

### Accent

Accent Products, Koh-I-Noor
100 North Street, Bloomsbury, NJ 08804-0068
Phone: (800) 877-3165  Fax: (800) 537-8939

### Americana

DecoArt, Inc.
P.O. Box 386, Stanford, KY 40484
Phone: (800) 367-3047  Fax: (606) 365-9739

### Ceramcoat

Delta Technical Coatings, Inc.
2550 Pellissier Place, Whittier, CA 90601-1505
Phone: (800) 423-4135  Fax: (310) 695-5157

### Folk Art

Plaid Enterprises, Inc.
1649 International Court
P.O. Box 7600, Norcross, GA 30091
Phone: (770) 923-8200  Fax: (770) 381-3404

### Jo Sonja

Chroma, Inc.
205 Bucky Drive, Lititz, PA 17543
Phone: (800) 257-8278  Fax: (717) 626-9292

### Liquitex

Binney & Smith
1100 Church Lane, P.O. Box 431, Easton, PA 18044
Phone: (800) 272-9652  Fax: (610) 559-9007

## How Are These Color Matches Made?

The *Decorative Painting Color Match Sourcebook* and TCS Color Match Software (see page 93) require thousands of color comparisons. We strive for accuracy so that you can have confidence in these conversions. They are not created by casual viewing of the bottle or jar and are matched only when dry. Here is the process:

First, viewing the handpainted swatches from the Tru-Color Comparison Discs, Bobbie identifies the color family and judges the hue, clarity and value of each color. These colors are grouped as matches and organized based on their relationship to each other.

Then, each color is handpainted on a TCS Color Card. Where there is not a perfect match between brands, a mix is created. They are painted beside the target color and then viewed in different lighting conditions. The mixes are tweaked to most closely duplicate the original color and best mixing ratios are assigned.

All the cards are placed in one of the fifteen color groups or families. Finally, the TCS number evaluation begins. They can now be assigned a numeric value based on their relationship with each other. The most pure Hues of each color family is assigned a 5, then all the color matches are placed in order 1 through 9 as they compare with the most pure color in the family. A like process is performed for Clarity and Value and a 1 through 9 number is assigned. This then becomes the final TCS number for that set of matches.

As more colors are added, each will be a assigned a TCS Number which will place it in its proper relationship to other colors. This enables you to easily determine where these colors appear in the full color spectrum.

# Using the Color Match Project Planner

O n the project planner:
- List the colors named in the pattern, along with brand.
- Locate these colors in the alphabetic index and note the page and TCS number of each color.
- Turn to the listed page and TCS number.

- You have a choice of six matching colors and/or mixes including your original color. Check your personal inventory boxes to determine if you have the color needed. Any color or mix in that TCS number box can be substituted for the original color.

## *For example:*

## COLOR MATCH PROJECT PLANNER

**PROJECT NAME** *Kit Kat (a wall hung broom holder)*    **SUBJECT** *Animals*

**PROJECT SOURCE (OR DESIGNING ARTIST)** *a pattern packet by Jane Doe*

| BRAND | COLOR REQUESTED | PAGE # | TCS # | COLOR MATCH |
|---|---|---|---|---|
| Folk Art | Settler's Blue | 42 | BL-5-7-4 | Ceramcoat Cape Cod |
| Folk Art | Denim Blue | 43 | BL-5-7-8 | Ceramcoat Nightfall |
| Folk Art | Poppy Red | 22 | RE-3-2-6 | Jo Sonja Rose Pk. + Vermillion 3:1 |
| Ceramcoat | Golden Brown | 61 | BR-1-2-4 | In Inventory |
| | | | | |

## COLOR MATCH PROJECT PLANNER

**PROJECT NAME** _____    **SUBJECT** _____

**PROJECT SOURCE (OR DESIGNING ARTIST)** _____

| BRAND | COLOR REQUESTED | PAGE # | TCS # | COLOR MATCH |
|---|---|---|---|---|
| | | | | |
| | | | | |
| | | | | |
| | | | | |
| | | | | |
| | | | | |
| | | | | |
| | | | | |
| | | | | |
| | | | | |
| | | | | |
| | | | | |
| | | | | |
| | | | | |
| | | | | |

# COLOR MATCH PROJECT PLANNER

**PROJECT NAME** _____ **SUBJECT** _____

**PROJECT SOURCE (OR DESIGNING ARTIST)** _____

| BRAND | COLOR REQUESTED | PAGE # | TCS # | COLOR MATCH |
|-------|-----------------|--------|-------|-------------|
|  |  |  |  |  |
|  |  |  |  |  |
|  |  |  |  |  |
|  |  |  |  |  |
|  |  |  |  |  |
|  |  |  |  |  |
|  |  |  |  |  |
|  |  |  |  |  |
|  |  |  |  |  |
|  |  |  |  |  |
|  |  |  |  |  |
|  |  |  |  |  |
|  |  |  |  |  |
|  |  |  |  |  |
|  |  |  |  |  |

# COLOR MATCH PROJECT PLANNER

**PROJECT NAME** _____ **SUBJECT** _____

**PROJECT SOURCE (OR DESIGNING ARTIST)** _____

| BRAND | COLOR REQUESTED | PAGE # | TCS # | COLOR MATCH |
|-------|-----------------|--------|-------|-------------|
|  |  |  |  |  |
|  |  |  |  |  |
|  |  |  |  |  |
|  |  |  |  |  |
|  |  |  |  |  |
|  |  |  |  |  |
|  |  |  |  |  |
|  |  |  |  |  |
|  |  |  |  |  |
|  |  |  |  |  |
|  |  |  |  |  |
|  |  |  |  |  |
|  |  |  |  |  |
|  |  |  |  |  |
|  |  |  |  |  |

# BRAND    COLOR    COLOR

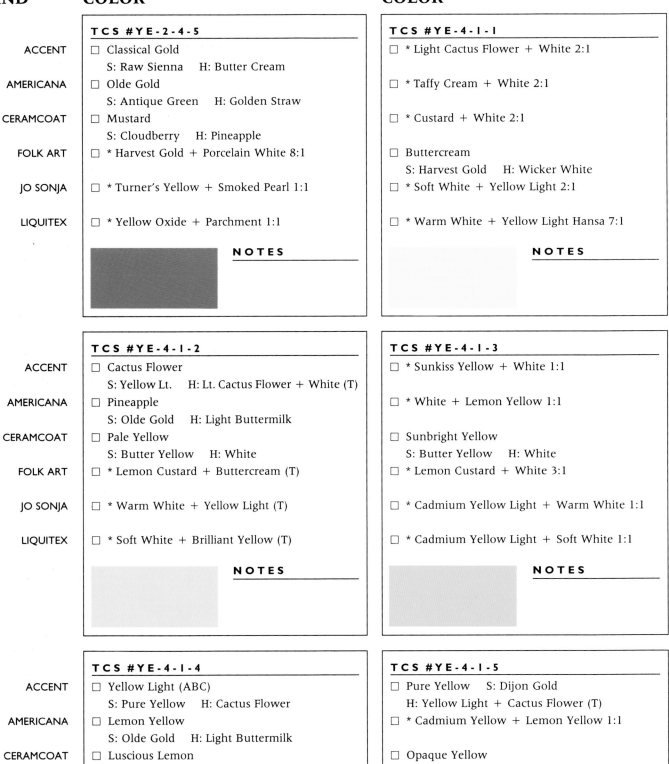

## TCS #YE-2-4-5

| BRAND | |
|---|---|
| ACCENT | ☐ Classical Gold<br>S: Raw Sienna    H: Butter Cream |
| AMERICANA | ☐ Olde Gold<br>S: Antique Green    H: Golden Straw |
| CERAMCOAT | ☐ Mustard<br>S: Cloudberry    H: Pineapple |
| FOLK ART | ☐ * Harvest Gold + Porcelain White 8:1 |
| JO SONJA | ☐ * Turner's Yellow + Smoked Pearl 1:1 |
| LIQUITEX | ☐ * Yellow Oxide + Parchment 1:1 |

**NOTES**

## TCS #YE-4-1-1

| | |
|---|---|
| ☐ * Light Cactus Flower + White 2:1 |
| ☐ * Taffy Cream + White 2:1 |
| ☐ * Custard + White 2:1 |
| ☐ Buttercream<br>S: Harvest Gold    H: Wicker White |
| ☐ * Soft White + Yellow Light 2:1 |
| ☐ * Warm White + Yellow Light Hansa 7:1 |

**NOTES**

## TCS #YE-4-1-2

| ACCENT | ☐ Cactus Flower<br>S: Yellow Lt.    H: Lt. Cactus Flower + White (T) |
|---|---|
| AMERICANA | ☐ Pineapple<br>S: Olde Gold    H: Light Buttermilk |
| CERAMCOAT | ☐ Pale Yellow<br>S: Butter Yellow    H: White |
| FOLK ART | ☐ * Lemon Custard + Buttercream (T) |
| JO SONJA | ☐ * Warm White + Yellow Light (T) |
| LIQUITEX | ☐ * Soft White + Brilliant Yellow (T) |

**NOTES**

## TCS #YE-4-1-3

| | |
|---|---|
| ☐ * Sunkiss Yellow + White 1:1 |
| ☐ * White + Lemon Yellow 1:1 |
| ☐ Sunbright Yellow<br>S: Butter Yellow    H: White |
| ☐ * Lemon Custard + White 3:1 |
| ☐ * Cadmium Yellow Light + Warm White 1:1 |
| ☐ * Cadmium Yellow Light + Soft White 1:1 |

**NOTES**

## TCS #YE-4-1-4

| ACCENT | ☐ Yellow Light (ABC)<br>S: Pure Yellow    H: Cactus Flower |
|---|---|
| AMERICANA | ☐ Lemon Yellow<br>S: Olde Gold    H: Light Buttermilk |
| CERAMCOAT | ☐ Luscious Lemon<br>S: Yellow    H: Pale Yellow |
| FOLK ART | ☐ Lemon Custard<br>S: Harvest Gold    H: White |
| JO SONJA | ☐ Cadmium Yellow Light |
| LIQUITEX | ☐ Yellow Light Hansa |

**NOTES**

## TCS #YE-4-1-5

| | |
|---|---|
| ☐ Pure Yellow    S: Dijon Gold<br>H: Yellow Light + Cactus Flower (T) |
| ☐ * Cadmium Yellow + Lemon Yellow 1:1 |
| ☐ Opaque Yellow<br>S: Antique Gold    H: Pale Yellow |
| ☐ Yellow Medium (PP) |
| ☐ Cadmium Yellow Mid. (D) |
| ☐ Yellow Medium Azo |

**NOTES**

| BRAND | COLOR | COLOR |
|-------|-------|-------|

**TCS #YE-5-1-5**

ACCENT
☐ Yellow Light (L)

AMERICANA
☐ Yellow Light
    S: Raw Sienna   H: Pineapple

CERAMCOAT
☐ Bright Yellow
    S: Empire Gold   H: Pale Yellow

FOLK ART
☐ Yellow Light (PP)

JO SONJA
☐ Yellow Light

LIQUITEX
☐ Cadmium Yellow Light

**NOTES**

---

**TCS #YE-5-1-6**

ACCENT
☐ Sunkiss Yellow
    S: Dijon Gold   H: Mellow Yellow

AMERICANA
☐ Cadmium Yellow
    S: Terra Cotta   H: Pineapple

CERAMCOAT
☐ * Bright Yellow + Yellow 1:1

FOLK ART
☐ Sunny Yellow
    S: Harvest Gold   H: White

JO SONJA
☐ Cadmium Yellow Mid

LIQUITEX
☐ Brilliant Yellow / Cadmium Yellow Medium Hue

**NOTES**

---

**TCS #YE-5-1-7**

ACCENT
☐ * Pure Yellow + Dijon Gold 3:1

AMERICANA
☐ Primary Yellow
    S: Antique Gold   H: Pineapple

CERAMCOAT
☐ Yellow
    S: Pigskin   H: Custard

FOLK ART
☐ School Bus Yellow
    S: Butterscotch   H: Warm White

JO SONJA
☐ Cadmium Yellow Medium (L)

LIQUITEX
☐ Cadmium Yellow Medium

**NOTES**

---

**TCS #YE-5-2-3**

ACCENT
☐ Mellow Yellow
    S: Sunsational Yellow   H: Light Cactus Flower

AMERICANA
☐ * Pineapple + Lemon Yellow (T)

CERAMCOAT
☐ Pineapple Yellow
    S: Antique Gold   H: White

FOLK ART
☐ * Lemon Custard + White 1:1

JO SONJA
☐ * Yellow Light + Warm White 1:1

LIQUITEX
☐ * Yellow Hansa Light + Soft White 1:1

**NOTES**

---

**TCS #YE-5-4-5**

ACCENT
☐ * Golden Harvest + White 1:1

AMERICANA
☐ * True Ochre + White 1:1

CERAMCOAT
☐ Butter Yellow
    S: Pigskin   H: Ivory

FOLK ART
☐ * Yellow Ochre + White 1:1

JO SONJA
☐ * Turner's Yellow + White 3:1

LIQUITEX
☐ * Turner's Yellow + White 3:1

**NOTES**

---

**TCS #YE-5-5-2**

ACCENT
☐ * White + Dijon Gold 2:1

AMERICANA
☐ * White + Golden Straw 2:1

CERAMCOAT
☐ * White + Straw 2:1

FOLK ART
☐ Sunflower
    S: Harvest Gold   H: Buttercream

JO SONJA
☐ * White + Turner's Yellow 4:1

LIQUITEX
☐ * White + Yellow Oxide 3:1

**NOTES**

## BRAND    COLOR    COLOR

| | TCS #YE-5-5-5 | TCS #YE-6-2-2 |
|---|---|---|
| ACCENT | ☐ * Dijon Gold + White 1:1 | ☐ Light Cactus Flower    S: Yellow Light<br>H: White Wash + Light Cactus Flower 1:1 |
| AMERICANA | ☐ Golden Straw<br>S: Honey Brown    H: Moon Yellow | ☐ Taffy Cream<br>S: Golden Straw    H: White |
| CERAMCOAT | ☐ Straw<br>S: Golden Brown    H: Ivory | ☐ Custard<br>S: Butter Yellow    H: White |
| FOLK ART | ☐ Buttercup<br>S: Harvest Gold    H: White | ☐ Lemonade<br>S: Harvest Gold    H: White |
| JO SONJA | ☐ * Opal + Turner's Yellow 5:1 | ☐ * White + Yellow Light 3:1 |
| LIQUITEX | ☐ * Yellow Oxide + White 1:1 | ☐ * White + Hansa Yellow 4:1 |

NOTES

NOTES

| | TCS #YE-6-2-4 | TCS #YE-6-2-6 |
|---|---|---|
| ACCENT | ☐ Sunsational Yellow<br>S: Dijon Gold    H: Mellow Yellow | ☐ Dijon Gold<br>S: Golden Ochre    H: Pure Yellow |
| AMERICANA | ☐ * Cadmium Yellow + White 1:1 | ☐ Marigold<br>S: Raw Sienna    H: Golden Straw |
| CERAMCOAT | ☐ Crocus Yellow<br>S: Antique Gold    H: Light Ivory | ☐ Empire Gold<br>S: Mocha Brown    H: Crocus Yellow |
| FOLK ART | ☐ * White + School Bus Yellow 3:1 | ☐ * Yellow Med. + Pure Orange (T) |
| JO SONJA | ☐ * White + Turner's Yellow 3:1 | ☐ Turner's Yellow |
| LIQUITEX | ☐ * White + Turner's Yellow 3:1 | ☐ Turner's Yellow |

NOTES

NOTES

| | TCS #YE-6-4-5 | TCS #YE-6-4-7 |
|---|---|---|
| ACCENT | ☐ Golden Harvest<br>S: Golden Ochre    H: Sunsational Yellow | ☐ Yellow Ochre (ABC)<br>S: Golden Oxide    H: Golden Harvest |
| AMERICANA | ☐ Antique Gold<br>S: Raw Sienna    H: Golden Straw | ☐ True Ochre<br>S: Burnt Umber    H: Golden Straw |
| CERAMCOAT | ☐ Antique Gold<br>S: Raw Sienna    H: Ivory | ☐ Antique Gold (L) |
| FOLK ART | ☐ Harvest Gold<br>S: English Mustard    H: Lemonade | ☐ Yellow Ochre (PP) |
| JO SONJA | ☐ Yellow Oxide (D) | ☐ Yellow Oxide |
| LIQUITEX | ☐ Yellow Oxide (D) | ☐ Yellow Oxide |

NOTES

NOTES

# BRAND          COLOR                                   COLOR

## TCS #YE-6-4-8

ACCENT
☐ * Yellow Ochre + Tumbleweed 3:1

AMERICANA
☐ * True Ochre + Raw Sienna (T)

CERAMCOAT
☐ Pigskin
S: Autumn Brown    H: Butter Yellow

FOLK ART
☐ Yellow Ochre (PP) (L)

JO SONJA
☐ * Yellow Oxide + Raw Sienna (T)

LIQUITEX
☐ * Yellow Oxide + Raw Siena (T)

**NOTES**

## TCS #YE-7-7-3

☐ Butter Cream
S: Yellow Ochre    H: Adobe Wash
☐ Moon Yellow
S: Honey Brown    H: Taffy
☐ Old Parchment
S: Spice Tan    H: Light Ivory
☐ Moon Yellow
S: English Mustard    H: White
☐ * Warm White + Yellow Oxide 2:1

☐ * Soft White + Yellow Oxide 2:1

**NOTES**

## TCS #YE-7-7-4

ACCENT
☐ Devonshire Cream    S: Yellow Ochre
H: Adobe Wash + Devonshire Cream (T)

AMERICANA
☐ Moon Yellow (L)

CERAMCOAT
☐ Maple Sugar Tan
S: Burnt Sienna    H: Ivory

FOLK ART
☐ Buttercrunch
S: English Mustard    H: White

JO SONJA
☐ * Yellow Oxide + Warm White 1:1

LIQUITEX
☐ * Yellow Oxide + Soft White 1:1

**NOTES**

## TCS #YE-7-7-6

☐ * Devonshire Cream + Tumbleweed 6:1

☐ Yellow Ochre
S: Honey Brown    H: Moon Yellow
☐ * Old Parchment + Spice Tan 5:1

☐ * Moon Yellow + Teddy Bear Tan 6:1

☐ * Warm White + Yellow Oxide + Fawn 10:1:T

☐ * Soft White + Yellow Ox. + Unbleached Tit.
10:1:1

**NOTES**

## TCS #YO-2-1-3

ACCENT
☐ Golden Oxide
S: Tumbleweed    H: Yellow Ochre

AMERICANA
☐ * Antique Gold + Raw Sienna (T)

CERAMCOAT
☐ * Antique Gold + Raw Sienna (T)

FOLK ART
☐ Trans. Oxide Yellow (PP)

JO SONJA
☐ * Turner's Yellow + Raw Sienna (T)

LIQUITEX
☐ * Turner's Yellow + Raw Siena (T)

**NOTES**

## TCS #YO-5-1-4

☐ * Pure Yellow + True Orange 3:1

☐ Tangerine
S: Terra Cotta    H: Lemon Yellow
☐ * Yellow + Bittersweet 3:1

☐ * Yellow Medium + Pure Orange 3:1

☐ * Cadmium Yellow + Vermillion 12:1

☐ Yellow Orange Azo

**NOTES**

**BRAND**  **COLOR**  **COLOR**

### TCS #YO-6-1-1

| | |
|---|---|
| ACCENT | ☐ * Light Tumbleweed + Peaches n' Cream (T) |
| AMERICANA | ☐ * Sand + Medium Flesh (T) |
| CERAMCOAT | ☐ Western Sunset Yellow<br>S: Mocha Brown    H: Putty |
| FOLK ART | ☐ * Wicker White + Peach Cobbler 3:1 |
| JO SONJA | ☐ * Warm White + Yellow Oxide + Vermillion 10:1:T |
| LIQUITEX | ☐ * Soft White + Brilliant Orange 8:1 |

**NOTES**

### TCS #YO-6-1-3

| | |
|---|---|
| ☐ * True Orange + Cactus Flower 2:1 |
| ☐ * Tangerine + Moon Yellow 2:1 |
| ☐ Calypso Orange<br>S: Dark Goldenrod    H: Western Sunset Yellow |
| ☐ * Tangerine + White 4:1 |
| ☐ * Cad Yellow Light + Vermillion 8:1 |
| ☐ * Yellow Orang Azo + Soft White + Apricot 2:2:1 |

**NOTES**

### TCS #YO-6-1-5

| | |
|---|---|
| ACCENT | ☐ * True Orange + Pure Yellow 2:1 |
| AMERICANA | ☐ * Tangerine + Pumpkin (T) |
| CERAMCOAT | ☐ * Yellow + Pumpkin 1:1 |
| FOLK ART | ☐ Tangerine<br>S: Earthenware    H: Sunny Yellow |
| JO SONJA | ☐ * Cadmium Yellow Mid + Vermillion 8:1 |
| LIQUITEX | ☐ * Yellow Orange Azo + Brilliant Orange 2:1 |

**NOTES**

### TCS #OR-4-1-5

| | |
|---|---|
| ☐ True Orange<br>S: Vermillion    H: Pure Yellow |
| ☐ * Tangerine + Cadmium Orange (T) |
| ☐ Bittersweet Orange<br>S: Terra Cotta    H: Yellow |
| ☐ Glazed Carrots<br>S: Rusty Nail    H: White |
| ☐ * Cadmium Yellow Mid. + Cadmium Scarlet 2:1 |
| ☐ Brilliant Orange / Cad. Orange Hue |

**NOTES**

### TCS #OR-4-2-1

| | |
|---|---|
| ACCENT | ☐ Blonde    S: Light Peaches n' Cream<br>H: Blonde + White Wash (T) |
| AMERICANA | ☐ * Sand + Toffee 5:1 |
| CERAMCOAT | ☐ Queen Anne's Lace<br>S: Rosetta    H: White |
| FOLK ART | ☐ * Georgia Peach + Taffy 1:1 |
| JO SONJA | ☐ * Warm White + Yellow Oxide + Vermillion 12:1:T |
| LIQUITEX | ☐ * Soft White + Apricot 6:1 |

**NOTES**

### TCS #OR-4-7-4

| | |
|---|---|
| ☐ * Golden Oxide + True Orange 3:1 |
| ☐ * Tangerine + Terra Cotta 2:1 |
| ☐ Dark Goldenrod<br>S: Terra Cotta    H: Calypso Orange |
| ☐ Butterscotch<br>S: Molasses    H: White |
| ☐ * Turner's Yellow + Gold Oxide 8:1 |
| ☐ * Cadmium Orange + Raw Siena 4:1 |

**NOTES**

## BRAND     COLOR        COLOR

**TCS #OR-4-7-6**

| ACCENT | ☐ * Sedona Clay + True Orange 1:1 |
| AMERICANA | ☐ * Terra Cotta + Burnt Orange 3:1 |
| CERAMCOAT | ☐ Terra Cotta<br>S: Brown Iron Oxide    H: Island Coral |
| FOLK ART | ☐ * Pumpkin Pie + Golden Harvest 2:1 |
| JO SONJA | ☐ Gold Oxide (D) |
| LIQUITEX | ☐ * Raw Siena + Cadmium Orange 3:1 |

**NOTES**

**TCS #OR-4-7-8**

| ACCENT | ☐ * Tumbleweed + Sedona Clay 1:1 |
| AMERICANA | ☐ * Burnt Orange + Burnt Sienna (T) |
| CERAMCOAT | ☐ * Mocha Brown + Raw Sienna 1:1 |
| FOLK ART | ☐ Pecan Pie (Disc.) or * Persimmon + Buckskin Brown 1:1 |
| JO SONJA | ☐ Gold Oxide |
| LIQUITEX | ☐ * Raw Siena + Red Oxide 6:1 |

**NOTES**

**TCS #OR-4-7-9**

| ACCENT | ☐ * Sedona Clay + Tumbleweed 2:1 |
| AMERICANA | ☐ * Burnt Orange + Burnt Sienna 5:1 |
| CERAMCOAT | ☐ Cinnamon<br>S: Sonoma    H: Santa Fe Rose |
| FOLK ART | ☐ * Teddy Bear Brown + Persimmon 1:1 |
| JO SONJA | ☐ * Gold Oxide + Red Earth 1:1 |
| LIQUITEX | ☐ * Raw Sienna + Red Oxide 1:1 |

**NOTES**

**TCS #OR-5-1-5**

| ACCENT | ☐ * True Orange + Razzle Red (T) |
| AMERICANA | ☐ Pumpkin<br>S: Burnt Sienna    H: Cadmium Yellow |
| CERAMCOAT | ☐ Pumpkin<br>S: Georgia Clay    H: Yellow |
| FOLK ART | ☐ Pure Orange (PP) |
| JO SONJA | ☐ * Vermillion + Yellow Light 3:1 |
| LIQUITEX | ☐ Cadmium Orange |

**NOTES**

**TCS #OR-5-2-1**

| ACCENT | ☐ * Blonde + White 1:1 |
| AMERICANA | ☐ * Buttermilk + Flesh 3:1 |
| CERAMCOAT | ☐ Putty<br>S: Dresden Flesh    H: White |
| FOLK ART | ☐ * Taffy + Georgia Peach 1:1 |
| JO SONJA | ☐ * Warm White + Provincial Beige (T) |
| LIQUITEX | ☐ * Soft White + Unbleached Titanium (T) |

**NOTES**

**TCS #OR-5-3-4**

| ACCENT | ☐ * Apricot Stone + Light Flesh 1:1 |
| AMERICANA | ☐ * Peaches 'n Cream + Flesh Tone 1:1 |
| CERAMCOAT | ☐ Island Coral<br>S: Desert Sun Orange    H: Putty |
| FOLK ART | ☐ Peach Cobbler<br>S: Cinnamon    H: Taffy |
| JO SONJA | ☐ * White + Gold Oxide 4:1 |
| LIQUITEX | ☐ Apricot |

**NOTES**

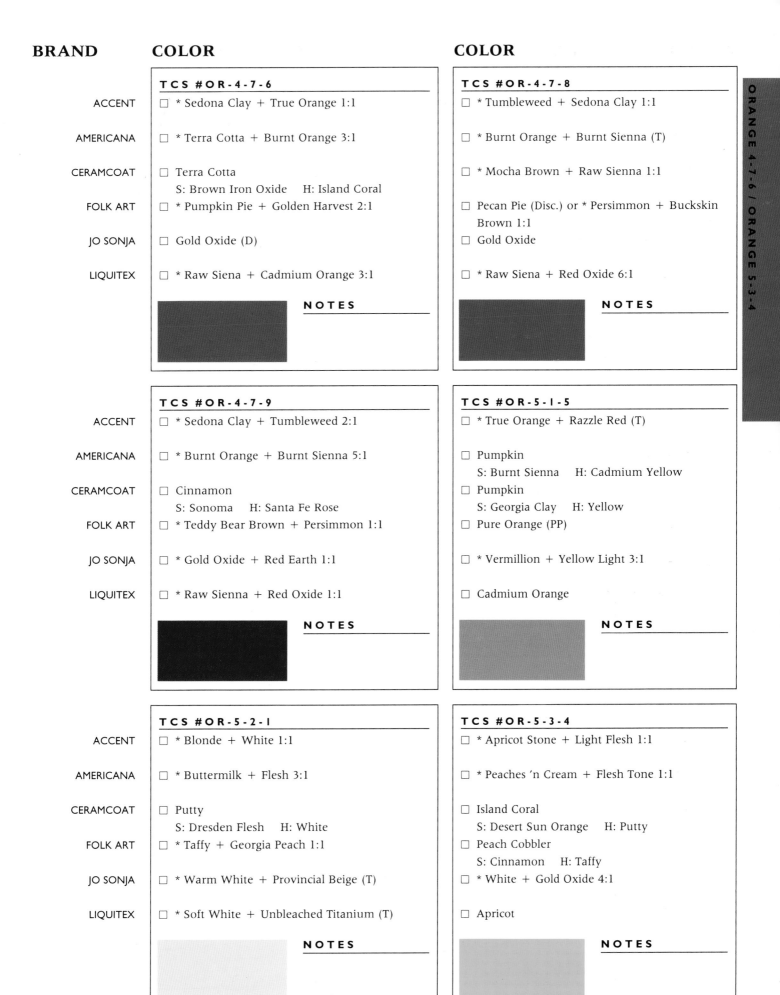

# BRAND     COLOR                          COLOR

## TCS #OR-5-7-3

| ACCENT | ☐ * Adobe Wash + Victorian Mauve 6:1 |
| AMERICANA | ☐ * Sand + Flesh Tone 1:1 |
| CERAMCOAT | ☐ Dresden Flesh<br>S: Light Chocolate   H: Putty |
| FOLK ART | ☐ * Almond Parfait + Dusty Peach 1:1 |
| JO SONJA | ☐ * Warm White + Provincial Beige 12:1 |
| LIQUITEX | ☐ * Unbleached Titanium + Apricot 10:1 |

**NOTES**

## TCS #OR-5-9-6

| ACCENT | ☐ * Sedona Clay + White 1:1 |
| AMERICANA | ☐ * Peaches 'n Cream + Burnt Orange 3:1 |
| CERAMCOAT | ☐ Desert Sun Orange<br>S: Burnt Sienna   H: Rosetta |
| FOLK ART | ☐ * Cinnamon + White 2:1 |
| JO SONJA | ☐ * Warm White + Gold Oxide 4:1 |
| LIQUITEX | ☐ * Soft White + Red Oxide 5:1 |

**NOTES**

## TCS #OR-5-9-7

| ACCENT | ☐ * Sedona Clay + White 2:1 |
| AMERICANA | ☐ * Burnt Orange + Medium Flesh 5:1 |
| CERAMCOAT | ☐ Santa Fe Rose<br>S: Cinnamon   H: Medium Flesh |
| FOLK ART | ☐ Terra Cotta<br>S: Earthenware   H: Peach Cobbler |
| JO SONJA | ☐ * Warm White + Red Earth 2:1 |
| LIQUITEX | ☐ * Soft White + Red Oxide 2:1 |

**NOTES**

## TCS #OR-5-9-8

| ACCENT | ☐ * Sedona Clay + White (T) |
| AMERICANA | ☐ * Burnt Orange + Medium Flesh 3:1 |
| CERAMCOAT | ☐ Cayenne<br>S: Brown Iron Oxide   H: Fleshtone |
| FOLK ART | ☐ Cinnamon<br>S: Molasses   H: Georgia Peach |
| JO SONJA | ☐ * Burnt Sienna + White 1:1 |
| LIQUITEX | ☐ * Burnt Siena + White 1:1 |

**NOTES**

## TCS #OR-6-3-1

| ACCENT | ☐ Light Flesh (D) |
| AMERICANA | ☐ * White + Flesh Tone (T) |
| CERAMCOAT | ☐ Santa's Flesh<br>S: Normandy Rose   H: White |
| FOLK ART | ☐ Georgia Peach<br>S: Peach Perfection   H: White |
| JO SONJA | ☐ * Warm White + Gold Oxide (T) |
| LIQUITEX | ☐ * Soft White + Apricot (T) |

**NOTES**

## TCS #OR-6-3-2

| ACCENT | ☐ Light Flesh   S: Medium Flesh<br>H: Adobe Wash + Light Flesh 1:1 |
| AMERICANA | ☐ * Flesh Tone + White 1:1 |
| CERAMCOAT | ☐ Santa's Flesh (L) |
| FOLK ART | ☐ Dusty Peach<br>S: Portrait Dark   H: White |
| JO SONJA | ☐ * Warm White + Gold Oxide 14:1 |
| LIQUITEX | ☐ * Soft White + Apricot 12:1 |

**NOTES**

| BRAND | COLOR | COLOR |
|---|---|---|

**TCS #OR-6-3-3**

ACCENT
☐ Light Peaches n' Cream
    S: Peaches n' Cream    H: Lt. Flesh

AMERICANA
☐ * Flesh Tone + Medium Flesh 1:1

CERAMCOAT
☐ * Fleshtone + Medium Flesh 1:1

FOLK ART
☐ Skintone
    S: Portrait Dark    H: Portrait Light

JO SONJA
☐ * Warm White + Gold Oxide 12:1

LIQUITEX
☐ * Soft White + Apricot + Lt. Port. Pink 4:1:T

**NOTES**

---

**TCS #OR-6-3-4**

☐ Medium Flesh
    S: Dark Flesh    H: Light Flesh
☐ Flesh Tone
    S: Sable Brown    H: Hi-Lite Flesh
☐ Fleshtone
    S: Desert Sun Orange    H: Santa's Flesh
☐ * Dusty Peach + Apricot Cream (T)

☐ * Warm White + Gold Oxide 8:1

☐ * Soft White + Apricot + Lt. Port. Pink 3:1:T

**NOTES**

---

**TCS #OR-6-3-5**

ACCENT
☐ Peaches n' Cream
    S: Dark Flesh    H: Light Peaches n' Cream

AMERICANA
☐ Medium Flesh
    S: Light Cinnamon    H: Peaches 'n Cream

CERAMCOAT
☐ Medium Flesh
    S: Dark Flesh    H: Fleshtone

FOLK ART
☐ Apricot Cream
    S: Portrait Dark    H: Portrait Light

JO SONJA
☐ * Coral + Raw Sienna + Warm White 1:1:1

LIQUITEX
☐ * Soft White + Apricot + Lt. Port. Pink 1:1:T

**NOTES**

---

**TCS #OR-6-3-6**

☐ * English Marmalade + Sedona Clay 3:1

☐ * Medium Flesh + Burnt Orange (T)

☐ Caucasian Flesh
    S: Red Iron Oxide    H: Fleshtone
☐ * Peach Cobbler + Cinnamon (T)

☐ * Warm White + Red Earth + Turner's Yellow 8:1:1
☐ * Sandalwood + Lt. Portrait Pink + Raw Siena 1:1:1

**NOTES**

---

**TCS #OR-6-3-7**

ACCENT
☐ Dark Flesh
    S: Sedona Clay    H: Medium Flesh

AMERICANA
☐ Shading Flesh (D)

CERAMCOAT
☐ * Dark Flesh + Normandy Rose 1:1

FOLK ART
☐ Portrait Dark (D)

JO SONJA
☐ * White + Red Earth + Turner's Yellow 7:1:1

LIQUITEX
☐ * Deep Portrait Pink + Light Portrait Pink 3:1

**NOTES**

---

**TCS #OR-6-3-8**

☐ * Sedona Clay + White 1:1

☐ Shading Flesh
    S: Light Cinnamon    H: Base Flesh
☐ Dark Flesh
    S: Sonoma    H: Rosetta
☐ Portrait Dark
    S: Dark Brown    H: Peach Perfection
☐ * Opal + Gold Oxide + Napthol Red Lt. 4:2:1

☐ Deep Portrait Pink

**NOTES**

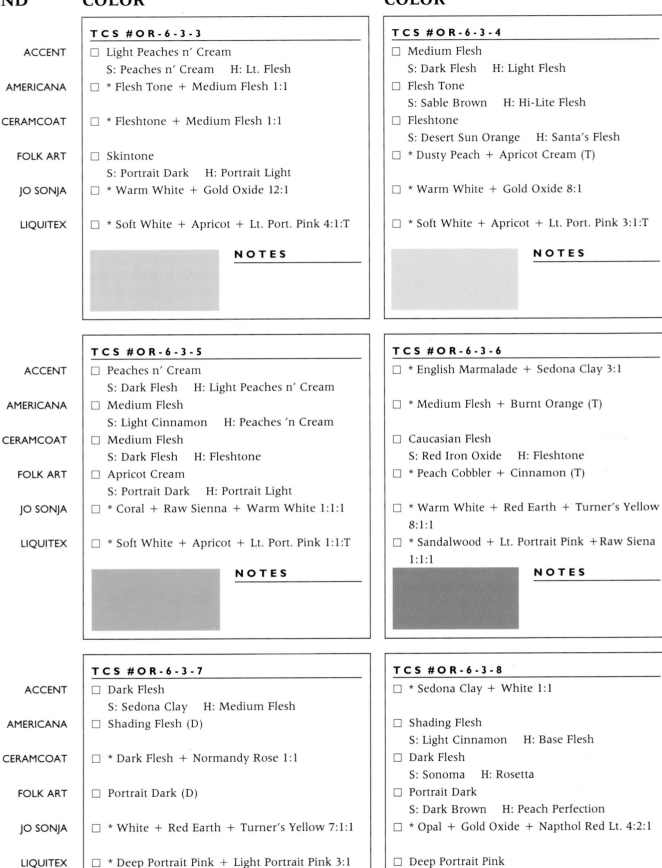

# BRAND                COLOR                                    COLOR

## T C S # O R - 6 - 7 - 2

ACCENT
☐ * Victorian Mauve + Cool Neutral 1:1

AMERICANA
☐ Base Flesh
    S: Shading Flesh    H: Hi-Lite Flesh

CERAMCOAT
☐ Normandy Rose (D)

FOLK ART
☐ Portrait Medium
    S: Portrait Dark    H: Georgia Peach

JO SONJA
☐ * Opal + Burnt Sienna 10:1

LIQUITEX
☐ * White + Deep Portrait Pink 2:1

**N O T E S**

## T C S # O R - 6 - 7 - 3

ACCENT
☐ Victorian Mauve (D)

AMERICANA
☐ Dusty Rose
    S: Red Iron Oxide    H: Dusty Rose + White 1:1

CERAMCOAT
☐ Normandy Rose
    S: Sonoma    H: Dresden Flesh

FOLK ART
☐ Sachet Rose (Disc.) or Port. Medium + Spice Pink 4:1

JO SONJA
☐ * Opal + Burnt Sienna 8:1

LIQUITEX
☐ * Deep Portrait Pink + White 1:1

**N O T E S**

## T C S # O R - 6 - 7 - 4

ACCENT
☐ Victorian Mauve    S: Vict. Mauve + Dark Flesh 1:1    H: Vict. Mauve + White Wash 1:1

AMERICANA
☐ * Cashmere Beige + Mauve 4:1

CERAMCOAT
☐ Misty Mauve
    S: Rose Mist    H: Pink Frosting

FOLK ART
☐ * Portrait Medium + Spice Pink 3:1

JO SONJA
☐ * Opal + Burnt Sienna 6:1

LIQUITEX
☐ Sandalwood

**N O T E S**

## T C S # O R - 6 - 7 - 7

ACCENT
☐ * Dark Flesh + Light Roseberry 1:1

AMERICANA
☐ * Medium Flesh + Gooseberry 1:1

CERAMCOAT
☐ * Rose Cloud + Caucasian Flesh 1:1

FOLK ART
☐ Spice Pink
    S: Dark Brown    H: Dusty Peach

JO SONJA
☐ * Opal + Burnt Sienna + Rose Pink 1:1:T

LIQUITEX
☐ * Sandalwood + Light Portrait Pink 2:1

**N O T E S**

## T C S # R O - 1 - 3 - 5

ACCENT
☐ English Marmalade
    S: Vermillion    H: Sunkiss Yellow

AMERICANA
☐ * Pumpkin + Cadmium Orange (T)

CERAMCOAT
☐ * Orange + Sunbright Yellow + White 1:1:1

FOLK ART
☐ Cameo Coral (Disc.) or * Peach Perfection + Pure Orange 2:1

JO SONJA
☐ * White + Vermillion 3:1

LIQUITEX
☐ * Cad. Red Light + Yellow Lt. Hansa + White 1:1:1

**N O T E S**

## T C S # R O - 2 - 3 - 3

ACCENT
☐ Apricot Stone
    S: Sedona Clay    H: Peaches n' Cream

AMERICANA
☐ * Peaches 'n Cream + Dusty Rose (T)

CERAMCOAT
☐ Rosetta Pink
    S: Adobe Pink    H: Santa's Flesh

FOLK ART
☐ Peach Perfection
    S: Cinnamon    H: Georgia Peach

JO SONJA
☐ * Warm White + Norwegian Orange 5:1

LIQUITEX
☐ * Light Portrait Pink + Raw Siena (T)

**N O T E S**

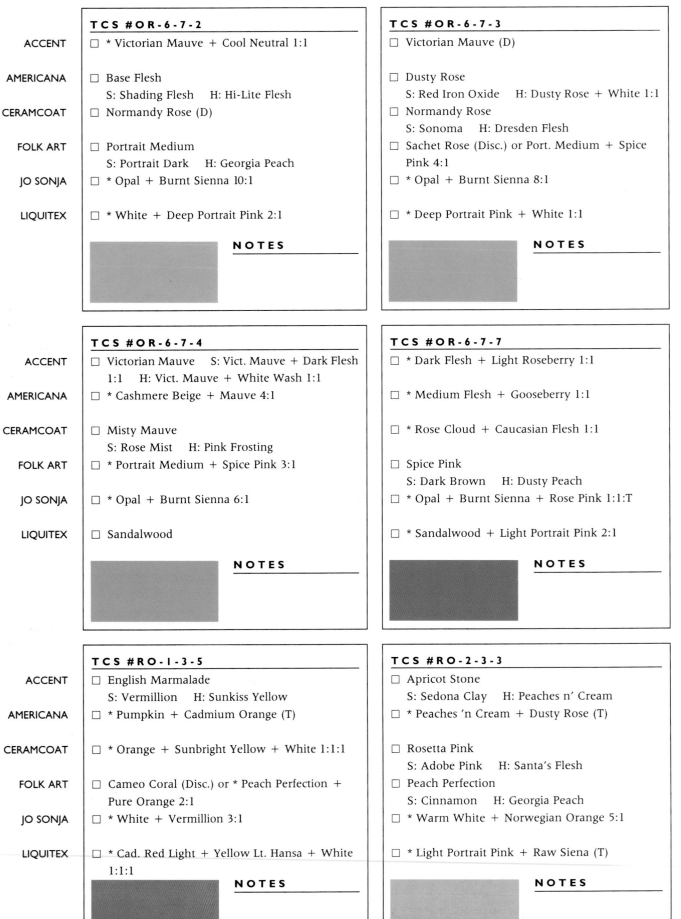

| BRAND | COLOR | COLOR |
|---|---|---|

**TCS #RO-3-3-3**

ACCENT ☐ * Coral Blush + Cactus Flower 1:1

AMERICANA ☐ Peaches 'n Cream    S: Light Cinnamon
H: Peaches 'n Cream + White 1:1

CERAMCOAT ☐ * Pink Angel + White 6:1

FOLK ART ☐ * Peach Cobbler + Salmon 8:1

JO SONJA ☐ * Warm White + Vermillion 5:1

LIQUITEX ☐ * Apricot + Light Portrait Pink 1:1

**NOTES**

**TCS #RO-5-1-4**

☐ * True Orange + Vermillion 2:1

☐ * Cadmium Orange + Pumpkin 1:1

☐ * Tangerine + Pumpkin 1:1

☐ Pure Orange
S: Molasses    H: Tangerine
☐ * Cadmium Yellow Mid. + Vermillion 1:1

☐ * Cadmium Orange + Scarlet 1:1

**NOTES**

**TCS #RO-5-1-6**

ACCENT ☐ * True Orange + Pure Red (T)

AMERICANA ☐ Tangelo Orange
S: Oxblood    H: Cadmium Yellow
CERAMCOAT ☐ Tangerine
S: Red Iron Oxide    H: Yellow
FOLK ART ☐ Autumn Leaves
S: Rusty Nail    H: Taffy
JO SONJA ☐ * Vermillion + Yellow Light 4:1

LIQUITEX ☐ * Scarlet + Brilliant Yellow 1:1

**NOTES**

**TCS #RO-5-1-7**

☐ Vermillion (ABC)
S: Pennsylvania Clay    H: Sunkiss Yellow
☐ Cadmium Orange
S: Georgia Clay    H: Pumpkin
☐ Orange
S: Tomato Spice    H: Bittersweet
☐ Red Orange
S: Huckleberry    H: White
☐ Vermillion

☐ Scarlet

**NOTES**

**TCS #RO-5-1-8**

ACCENT ☐ * Vermillion + Napthol Red Light 1:1

AMERICANA ☐ * Cadmium Orange + Cadmium Red 1:1

CERAMCOAT ☐ * Tangerine + Napthol Crimson 1:1

FOLK ART ☐ Pimento (Disc.) or * Autumn Leaves + Calico Red 1:1

JO SONJA ☐ Vermillion (L)

LIQUITEX ☐ Cadmium Red Light

**NOTES**

**TCS #RO-5-3-1**

☐ * Light Flesh + Pink Blossom 4:1

☐ * Flesh + Flesh Tone 8:1

☐ * Santa's Flesh + Pink Frosting 1:1

☐ Victorian Rose
S: Cherokee Rose    H: Warm White
☐ * White + Norwegian Orange 15:1

☐ * Pale Portrait Pink + Apricot 10:1

**NOTES**

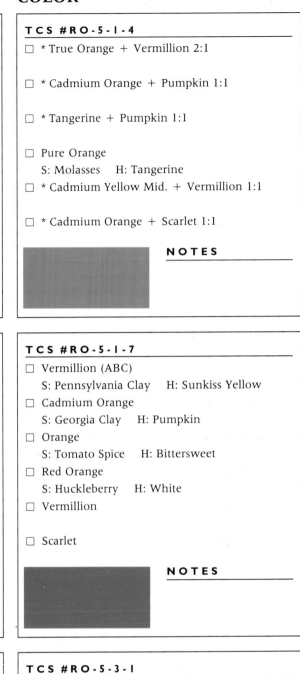

RED ORANGE 3-3-3 / RED ORANGE 5-3-1

25

## BRAND            COLOR                                    COLOR

### TCS #RO-5-3-2

| ACCENT | ☐ * Pink Blossom + Warm Neutral 1:1 |
| AMERICANA | ☐ * White + Gooseberry 3:1 |
| CERAMCOAT | ☐ Indiana Rose |
|  | S: Antique Rose    H: Pink Frosting |
| FOLK ART | ☐ Rose Blush |
|  | S: Rose Garden    H: White |
| JO SONJA | ☐ * Smoked Pearl + Rose Pink 4:1 |
| LIQUITEX | ☐ * Light Portrait Pink + Unbleached Titanium 1:1 |

**NOTES**

### TCS #RO-5-3-3

| ACCENT | ☐ * Peaches n' Cream + Cottage Rose (T) |
| AMERICANA | ☐ * Dusty Rose + White 1:1 |
| CERAMCOAT | ☐ Pink Angel |
|  | S: Adobe Pink    H: Santa's Flesh |
| FOLK ART | ☐ Promenade(D) |
| JO SONJA | ☐ * Warm White + Norwegian Orange (T) |
| LIQUITEX | ☐ * Light Portrait Pink + Apricot 1:1 |

**NOTES**

### TCS #RO-5-3-4

| ACCENT | ☐ * Coral Blush + Peaches n' Cream 1:1 |
| AMERICANA | ☐ * Coral Rose + Peaches 'n Cream 1:1 |
| CERAMCOAT | ☐ * Coral + Rosetta 1:1 |
| FOLK ART | ☐ Promenade |
|  | S: Dark Brown    H: Georgia Peach |
| JO SONJA | ☐ * Warm White + Norwegian Orange 4:1 |
| LIQUITEX | ☐ * White + Red Oxide 3:1 |

**NOTES**

### TCS #RO-5-4-4

| ACCENT | ☐ Sedona Clay (D) |
| AMERICANA | ☐ Burnt Orange (D) |
| CERAMCOAT | ☐ Georgia Clay |
|  | S: Red Iron Oxide    H: Bittersweet |
| FOLK ART | ☐ Persimmon |
|  | S: Molasses    H: Warm White |
| JO SONJA | ☐ * Norwegian Orange + Vermillion 2:1 |
| LIQUITEX | ☐ * Brilliant Orange + Red Oxide 3:1 |

**NOTES**

### TCS #RO-5-4-5

| ACCENT | ☐ Sedona Clay |
|  | S: Burnt Sienna (ABC)    H: Dark Flesh |
| AMERICANA | ☐ Burnt Orange |
|  | S: Burnt Sienna    H: Cadmium Orange |
| CERAMCOAT | ☐ * Georgia Clay + Burnt Sienna (T) |
| FOLK ART | ☐ Pumpkin Pie (Disc.) or * Persimmon + Dk. Portrait 3:1 |
| JO SONJA | ☐ * Norwegian Orange + Vermillion 3:1 |
| LIQUITEX | ☐ * Brilliant Orange + Red Oxide 2:1 |

**NOTES**

### TCS #RO-5-4-7

| ACCENT | ☐ Pennsylvania Clay |
|  | S: Burnt Sienna (ABC)    H: Vermillion |
| AMERICANA | ☐ Oxblood |
|  | S: Antique Maroon    H: Cadmium Orange |
| CERAMCOAT | ☐ * Cayenne + Red Iron Oxide 3:1 |
| FOLK ART | ☐ Sunset Orange (Disc.) or * Persimmon + Rusty Nail 6:1 |
| JO SONJA | ☐ * Norwegian Orange + Burnt Sienna (T) |
| LIQUITEX | ☐ * Red Oxide + Raw Siena 3:1 |

**NOTES**

| BRAND | COLOR | COLOR |
|---|---|---|

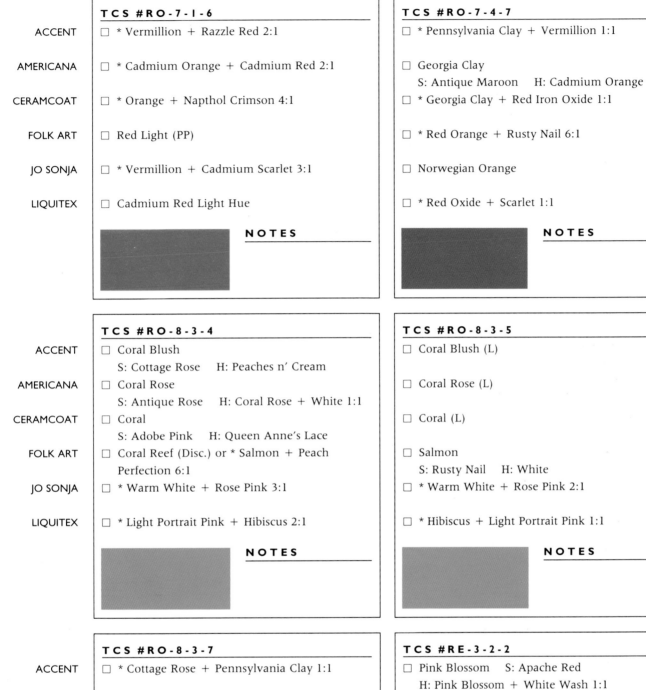

**TCS #RO-7-1-6**

| ACCENT | □ * Vermillion + Razzle Red 2:1 |
| AMERICANA | □ * Cadmium Orange + Cadmium Red 2:1 |
| CERAMCOAT | □ * Orange + Napthol Crimson 4:1 |
| FOLK ART | □ Red Light (PP) |
| JO SONJA | □ * Vermillion + Cadmium Scarlet 3:1 |
| LIQUITEX | □ Cadmium Red Light Hue |

**NOTES**

**TCS #RO-7-4-7**

| ACCENT | □ * Pennsylvania Clay + Vermillion 1:1 |
| AMERICANA | □ Georgia Clay<br>S: Antique Maroon    H: Cadmium Orange |
| CERAMCOAT | □ * Georgia Clay + Red Iron Oxide 1:1 |
| FOLK ART | □ * Red Orange + Rusty Nail 6:1 |
| JO SONJA | □ Norwegian Orange |
| LIQUITEX | □ * Red Oxide + Scarlet 1:1 |

**NOTES**

**TCS #RO-8-3-4**

| ACCENT | □ Coral Blush<br>S: Cottage Rose    H: Peaches n' Cream |
| AMERICANA | □ Coral Rose<br>S: Antique Rose    H: Coral Rose + White 1:1 |
| CERAMCOAT | □ Coral<br>S: Adobe Pink    H: Queen Anne's Lace |
| FOLK ART | □ Coral Reef (Disc.) or * Salmon + Peach Perfection 6:1 |
| JO SONJA | □ * Warm White + Rose Pink 3:1 |
| LIQUITEX | □ * Light Portrait Pink + Hibiscus 2:1 |

**NOTES**

**TCS #RO-8-3-5**

| ACCENT | □ Coral Blush (L) |
| AMERICANA | □ Coral Rose (L) |
| CERAMCOAT | □ Coral (L) |
| FOLK ART | □ Salmon<br>S: Rusty Nail    H: White |
| JO SONJA | □ * Warm White + Rose Pink 2:1 |
| LIQUITEX | □ * Hibiscus + Light Portrait Pink 1:1 |

**NOTES**

**TCS #RO-8-3-7**

| ACCENT | □ * Cottage Rose + Pennsylvania Clay 1:1 |
| AMERICANA | □ Antique Rose<br>S: Tomato Red    H: Coral Rose |
| CERAMCOAT | □ Adobe Red<br>S: Red Iron Oxide    H: Coral |
| FOLK ART | □ Gingersnap (Disc.) or * Salmon + Dark Portrait 5:1 |
| JO SONJA | □ * Warm White + Rose Pink + Gold Oxide 1:1:1 |
| LIQUITEX | □ * Soft White + Red Oxide + Napthol Crimson 2:1:1 |

**NOTES**

**TCS #RE-3-2-2**

| ACCENT | □ Pink Blossom    S: Apache Red<br>H: Pink Blossom + White Wash 1:1 |
| AMERICANA | □ * Spice Pink + Flesh Tone 1:1 |
| CERAMCOAT | □ * Indiana Rose + Pink Frosting 1:1 |
| FOLK ART | □ * White + Strawberry Pink 3:1 |
| JO SONJA | □ * Opal + Rose Pink (T) |
| LIQUITEX | □ Pale Portrait Pink |

**NOTES**

27

# BRAND COLOR COLOR

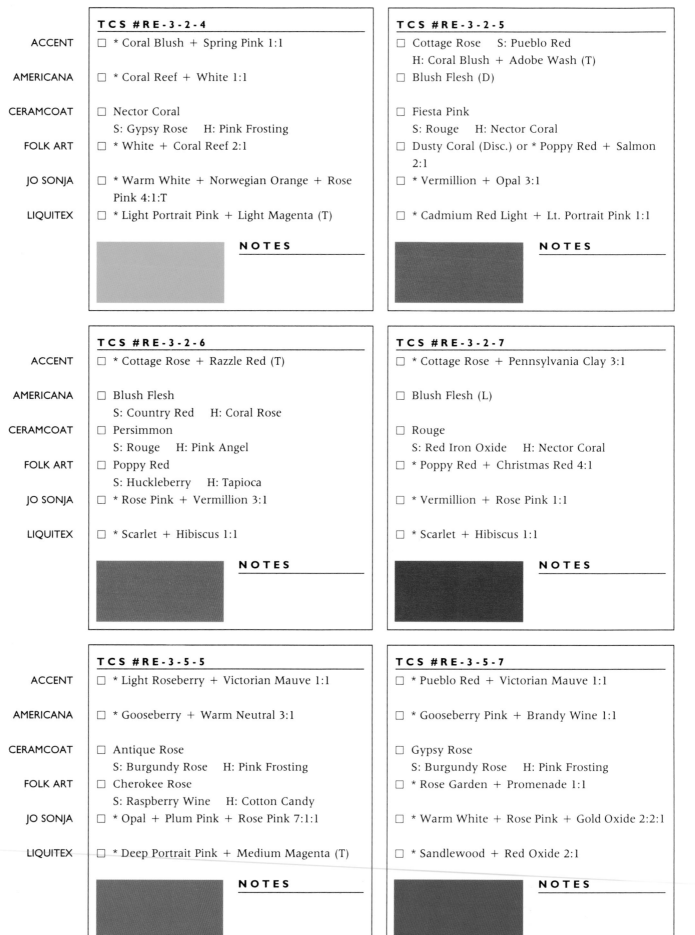

**TCS #RE-3-2-4**

ACCENT     ☐ * Coral Blush + Spring Pink 1:1

AMERICANA     ☐ * Coral Reef + White 1:1

CERAMCOAT     ☐ Nector Coral
S: Gypsy Rose   H: Pink Frosting

FOLK ART     ☐ * White + Coral Reef 2:1

JO SONJA     ☐ * Warm White + Norwegian Orange + Rose Pink 4:1:T

LIQUITEX     ☐ * Light Portrait Pink + Light Magenta (T)

**NOTES**

**TCS #RE-3-2-5**

ACCENT     ☐ Cottage Rose    S: Pueblo Red
H: Coral Blush + Adobe Wash (T)

AMERICANA     ☐ Blush Flesh (D)

CERAMCOAT     ☐ Fiesta Pink
S: Rouge   H: Nector Coral

FOLK ART     ☐ Dusty Coral (Disc.) or * Poppy Red + Salmon 2:1

JO SONJA     ☐ * Vermillion + Opal 3:1

LIQUITEX     ☐ * Cadmium Red Light + Lt. Portrait Pink 1:1

**NOTES**

**TCS #RE-3-2-6**

ACCENT     ☐ * Cottage Rose + Razzle Red (T)

AMERICANA     ☐ Blush Flesh
S: Country Red   H: Coral Rose

CERAMCOAT     ☐ Persimmon
S: Rouge   H: Pink Angel

FOLK ART     ☐ Poppy Red
S: Huckleberry   H: Tapioca

JO SONJA     ☐ * Rose Pink + Vermillion 3:1

LIQUITEX     ☐ * Scarlet + Hibiscus 1:1

**NOTES**

**TCS #RE-3-2-7**

ACCENT     ☐ * Cottage Rose + Pennsylvania Clay 3:1

AMERICANA     ☐ Blush Flesh (L)

CERAMCOAT     ☐ Rouge
S: Red Iron Oxide   H: Nector Coral

FOLK ART     ☐ * Poppy Red + Christmas Red 4:1

JO SONJA     ☐ * Vermillion + Rose Pink 1:1

LIQUITEX     ☐ * Scarlet + Hibiscus 1:1

**NOTES**

**TCS #RE-3-5-5**

ACCENT     ☐ * Light Roseberry + Victorian Mauve 1:1

AMERICANA     ☐ * Gooseberry + Warm Neutral 3:1

CERAMCOAT     ☐ Antique Rose
S: Burgundy Rose   H: Pink Frosting

FOLK ART     ☐ Cherokee Rose
S: Raspberry Wine   H: Cotton Candy

JO SONJA     ☐ * Opal + Plum Pink + Rose Pink 7:1:1

LIQUITEX     ☐ * Deep Portrait Pink + Medium Magenta (T)

**NOTES**

**TCS #RE-3-5-7**

ACCENT     ☐ * Pueblo Red + Victorian Mauve 1:1

AMERICANA     ☐ * Gooseberry Pink + Brandy Wine 1:1

CERAMCOAT     ☐ Gypsy Rose
S: Burgundy Rose   H: Pink Frosting

FOLK ART     ☐ * Rose Garden + Promenade 1:1

JO SONJA     ☐ * Warm White + Rose Pink + Gold Oxide 2:2:1

LIQUITEX     ☐ * Sandlewood + Red Oxide 2:1

**NOTES**

**TCS #RE-4-1-5**

| | |
|---|---|
| ACCENT | ☐ * Vermillion + Napthol Red Light 1:1 |
| AMERICANA | ☐ Brilliant Red<br>S: Napa Red    H: Cadmium Orange |
| CERAMCOAT | ☐ * Napthol Crimson + Orange 1:1 |
| FOLK ART | ☐ * Christmas Red + Red Light 3:1 |
| JO SONJA | ☐ Cadmium Scarlet |
| LIQUITEX | ☐ * Cadmium Red Light + Cadmium Red Medium 4:1 |

NOTES

**TCS #RE-4-1-6**

| | |
|---|---|
| ACCENT | ☐ Napthol Red Light (ABC)<br>S: Crimson    H: Vermillion |
| AMERICANA | ☐ Cadmium Red<br>S: Deep Burgundy    H: Coral Rose |
| CERAMCOAT | ☐ * Bright Red + Napthol Crimson 1:1 |
| FOLK ART | ☐ * Red Light + Napthol Crimson 1:1 |
| JO SONJA | ☐ Napthol Red Light |
| LIQUITEX | ☐ * Cadmium Red Light + Cadmium Red Med. 2:1 |

NOTES

**TCS #RE-4-2-5**

| | |
|---|---|
| ACCENT | ☐ * Pure Red + Pueblo Red 4:1 |
| AMERICANA | ☐ Country Red<br>S: Antique Maroon    H: Antique Rose |
| CERAMCOAT | ☐ Tomato Spice (D) |
| FOLK ART | ☐ * Red Light + Red Clay 2:1 |
| JO SONJA | ☐ * Napthol Red Light + Raw Umber 8:1 |
| LIQUITEX | ☐ Napthol Red Light |

NOTES

**TCS #RE-4-2-6**

| | |
|---|---|
| ACCENT | ☐ * Pure Red + Pueblo Red 2:1 |
| AMERICANA | ☐ Tomato Red<br>S: Napa Red    H: Cadmium Red |
| CERAMCOAT | ☐ Tomato Spice<br>S: Candy Bar Brown    H: Fiesta Pink |
| FOLK ART | ☐ * Red Light + Red Clay 1:1 |
| JO SONJA | ☐ * Napthol Red Light + Raw Umber 5:1 |
| LIQUITEX | ☐ Napthol Red Light (L) |

NOTES

**TCS #RE-4-2-7**

| | |
|---|---|
| ACCENT | ☐ Pueblo Red<br>S: Barn Red    H: Pueblo Red + Adobe Wash 1:1 |
| AMERICANA | ☐ Crimson Tide<br>S: Black Plum    H: Brilliant Red |
| CERAMCOAT | ☐ Tomato Spice (L) |
| FOLK ART | ☐ Barnyard Red<br>S: Chocolate Fudge    H: Dusty Peach |
| JO SONJA | ☐ * Rose Pink + Burgundy 3:1 |
| LIQUITEX | ☐ * Hibiscus + Burgundy 3:1 |

NOTES

**TCS #RE-4-3-1**

| | |
|---|---|
| ACCENT | ☐ * White + Pink Blossom 2:1 |
| AMERICANA | ☐ Hi-Lite Flesh<br>S: Base Flesh    H: White |
| CERAMCOAT | ☐ Pink Frosting<br>S: Hydrangea    H: White |
| FOLK ART | ☐ Cotton Candy<br>S: Rose Chiffon    H: White |
| JO SONJA | ☐ * Warm White + Rose Pink (T) |
| LIQUITEX | ☐ * Pale Portrait Pink + White 1:1 |

NOTES

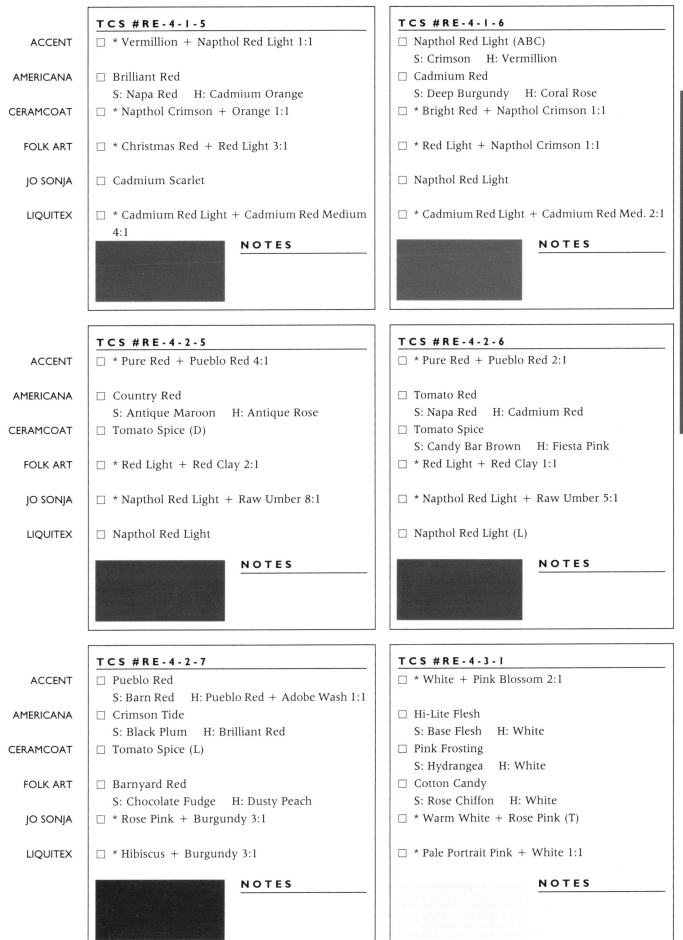

RED 4-3-3 / RED 4-4-1

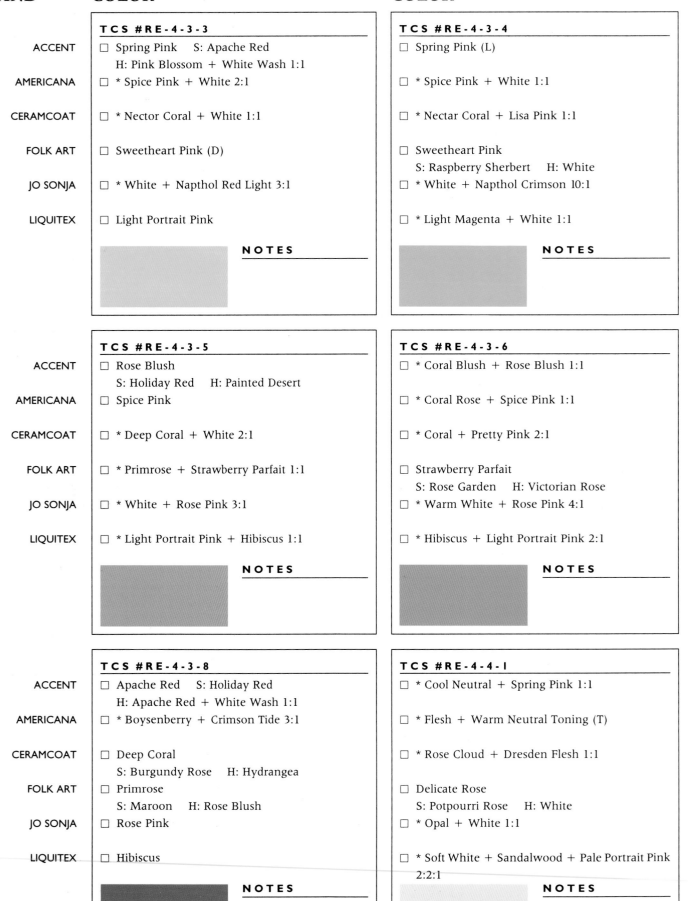

### TCS #RE-4-3-3

ACCENT
☐ Spring Pink    S: Apache Red
   H: Pink Blossom + White Wash 1:1

AMERICANA
☐ * Spice Pink + White 2:1

CERAMCOAT
☐ * Nector Coral + White 1:1

FOLK ART
☐ Sweetheart Pink (D)

JO SONJA
☐ * White + Napthol Red Light 3:1

LIQUITEX
☐ Light Portrait Pink

**NOTES**

### TCS #RE-4-3-4

☐ Spring Pink (L)

☐ * Spice Pink + White 1:1

☐ * Nectar Coral + Lisa Pink 1:1

☐ Sweetheart Pink
   S: Raspberry Sherbert    H: White
☐ * White + Napthol Crimson 10:1

☐ * Light Magenta + White 1:1

**NOTES**

### TCS #RE-4-3-5

ACCENT
☐ Rose Blush
   S: Holiday Red    H: Painted Desert

AMERICANA
☐ Spice Pink

CERAMCOAT
☐ * Deep Coral + White 2:1

FOLK ART
☐ * Primrose + Strawberry Parfait 1:1

JO SONJA
☐ * White + Rose Pink 3:1

LIQUITEX
☐ * Light Portrait Pink + Hibiscus 1:1

**NOTES**

### TCS #RE-4-3-6

☐ * Coral Blush + Rose Blush 1:1

☐ * Coral Rose + Spice Pink 1:1

☐ * Coral + Pretty Pink 2:1

☐ Strawberry Parfait
   S: Rose Garden    H: Victorian Rose
☐ * Warm White + Rose Pink 4:1

☐ * Hibiscus + Light Portrait Pink 2:1

**NOTES**

### TCS #RE-4-3-8

ACCENT
☐ Apache Red    S: Holiday Red
   H: Apache Red + White Wash 1:1

AMERICANA
☐ * Boysenberry + Crimson Tide 3:1

CERAMCOAT
☐ Deep Coral
   S: Burgundy Rose    H: Hydrangea

FOLK ART
☐ Primrose
   S: Maroon    H: Rose Blush

JO SONJA
☐ Rose Pink

LIQUITEX
☐ Hibiscus

**NOTES**

### TCS #RE-4-4-1

☐ * Cool Neutral + Spring Pink 1:1

☐ * Flesh + Warm Neutral Toning (T)

☐ * Rose Cloud + Dresden Flesh 1:1

☐ Delicate Rose
   S: Potpourri Rose    H: White
☐ * Opal + White 1:1

☐ * Soft White + Sandalwood + Pale Portrait Pink
   2:2:1

**NOTES**

**TCS #RE-4-4-3**

| | |
|---|---|
| ACCENT | ☐ * Cool Neutral + Light Roseberry 2:1 |
| AMERICANA | ☐ * White + Mauve 4:1 |
| CERAMCOAT | ☐ Rose Cloud<br>S: Rose Mist    H: Pink Frosting |
| FOLK ART | ☐ * Berries 'n Cream + Victorian Rose 3:1 |
| JO SONJA | ☐ * Opal + Plum Pink 5:1 |
| LIQUITEX | ☐ * Pale Portrait Pink + Venetian Rose 2:1 |

**NOTES**

**TCS #RE-4-4-5**

| | |
|---|---|
| ACCENT | ☐ * Light Roseberry + Victorian Mauve 2:1 |
| AMERICANA | ☐ Gooseberry Pink    S: Crimson Tide<br>H: Gooseberry Pink + White 1:1 |
| CERAMCOAT | ☐ * Antique Rose + Sachet 1:1 |
| FOLK ART | ☐ Rose Chiffon<br>S: Raspberry Wine    H: Cotton Candy |
| JO SONJA | ☐ * Opal + Plum Pink + Indian Red Oxide 5:1:T |
| LIQUITEX | ☐ * Venetian Rose + Light Portrait Pink 2:1 |

**NOTES**

**TCS #RE-4-6-5**

| | |
|---|---|
| ACCENT | ☐ Barn Red<br>S: Fingerberry Red    H: Pennsylvania Clay |
| AMERICANA | ☐ Red Iron Oxide<br>S: Antique Maroon    H: Burnt Orange |
| CERAMCOAT | ☐ Red Iron Oxide<br>S: Candy Bar Brown    H: Coral |
| FOLK ART | ☐ Rusty Nail<br>S: Chocolate Fudge    H: Taffy |
| JO SONJA | ☐ Red Earth |
| LIQUITEX | ☐ Red Oxide |

**NOTES**

**TCS #RE-4-6-7**

| | |
|---|---|
| ACCENT | ☐ * Pure Red + Barn Red 1:1 |
| AMERICANA | ☐ * Country Red + Brandy Wine (T) |
| CERAMCOAT | ☐ * Burgundy Rose + Red Iron Oxide 2:1 |
| FOLK ART | ☐ Apple Spice<br>S: Raspberry Wine    H: Victorian Rose |
| JO SONJA | ☐ * Red Earth + Burgundy 1:1 |
| LIQUITEX | ☐ * Red Oxide + Burgundy 1:1 |

**NOTES**

**TCS #RE-4-6-8**

| | |
|---|---|
| ACCENT | ☐ * Barn Red + Fingerberry 2:1 |
| AMERICANA | ☐ Brandy Wine<br>S: Antique Maroon    H: Antique Rose |
| CERAMCOAT | ☐ Burgundy Rose<br>S: Midnight    H: Antique Rose |
| FOLK ART | ☐ Huckleberry<br>S: Dark Brown    H: Delicate Rose |
| JO SONJA | ☐ * Norwegian Orange + Indian Red Oxide 4:1 |
| LIQUITEX | ☐ * Red Oxide + Burnt Siena 1:1 |

**NOTES**

**TCS #RE-5-1-1**

| | |
|---|---|
| ACCENT | ☐ * White + Bordeaux 12:1 |
| AMERICANA | ☐ * White + Flesh 2:1 |
| CERAMCOAT | ☐ * White + Napthol Red Light 15:1 |
| FOLK ART | ☐ Portrait Light<br>S: Portrait Medium    H: White |
| JO SONJA | ☐ * Warm White + Napthol Crimson 12:1 |
| LIQUITEX | ☐ * Soft White + Pale Portrait Pink 4:1 |

**NOTES**

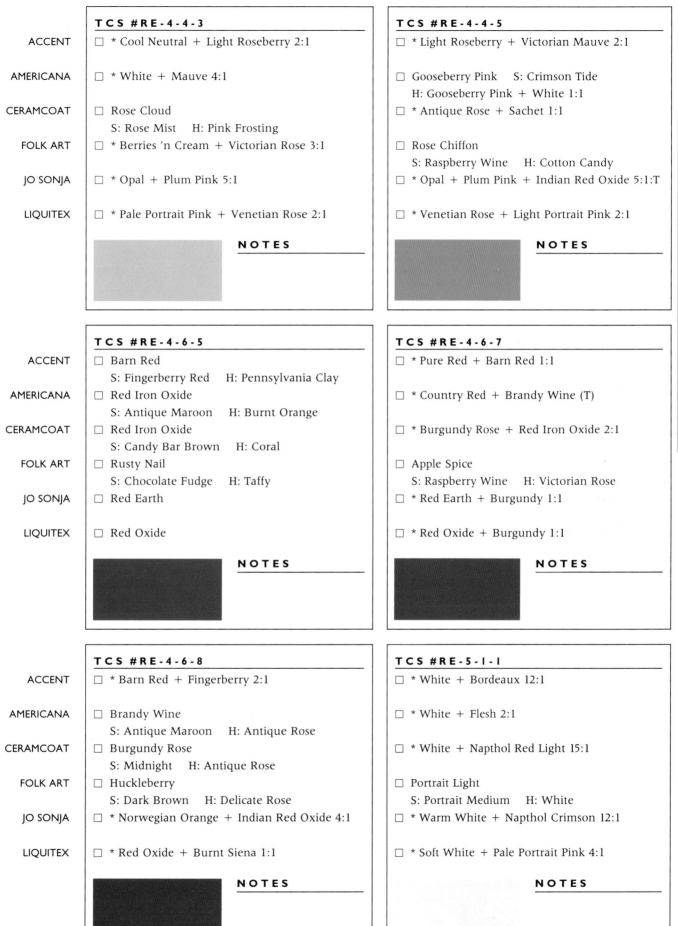

# BRAND          COLOR                                    COLOR

---

**TCS #RE-5-1-4**

ACCENT
☐ * Napthol Red Light + Jo Sonja Red 1:1

AMERICANA
☐ Calico Red
   S: Deep Burgundy    H: Blush

CERAMCOAT
☐ Opaque Red
   S: Black Cherry    H: Red Orange

FOLK ART
☐ * Christmas Red + Red Light 1:1

JO SONJA
☐ * Napthol Red Light + Napthol Crimson 3:1

LIQUITEX
☐ * Cadmium Red Light + Cadmium Red Medium
   2:1

**NOTES**

---

**TCS #RE-5-1-5**

☐ Razzle Red
   S: Crimson    H: Vermillion
☐ Napthol Red
   S: Napa Red    H: Blush
☐ Napthol Crimson
   S: Black Cherry    H: Tangerine
☐ Christmas Red
   S: Raspberry Wine    H: Vanilla Cream
☐ * Cadmium Scarlet + Napthol Crimson (T)

☐ * Scarlet + Cadmium Red Medium Hue 1:1

**NOTES**

---

**TCS #RE-5-1-6**

ACCENT
☐ Razzle Red (L)

AMERICANA
☐ Cherry Red
   S: Napa Red    H: Blush

CERAMCOAT
☐ Bright Red
   S: Black Cherry    H: Tangerine

FOLK ART
☐ Lipstick Red
   S: Cherry Royale    H: Red Orange

JO SONJA
☐ * Napthol Red Light + Napthol Crimson 1:1

LIQUITEX
☐ Cadmium Red Medium Hue / Lacquer Red

**NOTES**

---

**TCS #RE-5-2-5**

☐ * Painted Desert + Pure Red 2:1

☐ * Baby Pink + Calico Red 2:1

☐ Pretty Pink
   S: Berry Red    H: Pink Frosting
☐ * White + Hot Pink + Poppy Red 2:2:1

☐ * White + Napthol Crimson + Trans. Magenta
   2:1:T

☐ * White + Napthol Crimson + Raspberry 2:1:T

**NOTES**

---

**TCS #RE-5-5-5**

ACCENT
☐ * Pueblo Red + Barn Red (T)

AMERICANA
☐ * Crimson Tide + Country Red (T)

CERAMCOAT
☐ * Tomato Spice + Burgundy Rose 6:1

FOLK ART
☐ Brick Red
   S: Raspberry Wine    H: White

JO SONJA
☐ * Red Earth + Rose Pink 1:1

LIQUITEX
☐ * Red Oxide + Hibiscus 1:1

**NOTES**

---

**TCS #RE-5-5-7**

☐ * Barn Red + Pure Red 2:1

☐ * Country Red + Brandy Wine 1:1

☐ * Burgundy Rose + Red Iron Oxide 1:1

☐ Red Clay
   S: Huckleberry    H: Victorian Rose
☐ * Red Earth + Burgundy (T)

☐ * Red Oxide + Burgundy (T)

**NOTES**

# BRAND          COLOR                              COLOR

## TCS #RE-5-5-8

| ACCENT | ☐ * Barn Red + Fingerberry (T) |
|---|---|
| AMERICANA | ☐ Antique Maroon<br>S: Black Plum    H: Santa Red |
| CERAMCOAT | ☐ Candy Bar Brown<br>S: Black    H: Gypsy Rose |
| FOLK ART | ☐ Chocolate Cherry (Disc.) or * Red Clay + Huckleberry 3:1 |
| JO SONJA | ☐ * Burgundy + Indian Red Oxide 6:1 |
| LIQUITEX | ☐ * Burgundy + Burnt Umber 4:1 |

**NOTES**

## TCS #RE-5-6-9

| ACCENT | ☐ Fingerberry Red<br>S: Raw Umber    H: Barn Red |
|---|---|
| AMERICANA | ☐ Rookwood Red<br>S: Black Plum    H: Cherry Red |
| CERAMCOAT | ☐ Sonoma Wine<br>S: Black    H: Gypsy Rose |
| FOLK ART | ☐ Brownie (Disc.) or * Huckleberry + Molasses 1:1 |
| JO SONJA | ☐ Indian Red Oxide |
| LIQUITEX | ☐ * Burgundy + Burnt Umber 2:1 |

**NOTES**

## TCS #RE-5-8-5

| ACCENT | ☐ * Burnt Sienna + Antique White 1:1 |
|---|---|
| AMERICANA | ☐ French Mocha<br>S: Antique Maroon    H: Warm Neutral |
| CERAMCOAT | ☐ * Dark Flesh + Cinnamon 3:1 |
| FOLK ART | ☐ * Spice Pink + Teddy Bear Brown 1:1 |
| JO SONJA | ☐ * Burnt Sienna + Smoked Pearl + Ind. Red Oxide 2:2:1 |
| LIQUITEX | ☐ * Venetian Rose + Burnt Siena 1:1 |

**NOTES**

## TCS #RE-6-1-5

| ACCENT | ☐ Jo Sonja Red<br>S: Crimson    H: Vermillion |
|---|---|
| AMERICANA | ☐ True Red<br>S: Rookwood Red    H: Cadmium Orange |
| CERAMCOAT | ☐ Fire Red<br>S: Mendocino Red    H: Pumpkin |
| FOLK ART | ☐ * Christmas Red + Calico Red 1:1 |
| JO SONJA | ☐ * Napthol Red Light + Napthol Crimson 2:1 |
| LIQUITEX | ☐ * Cadmium Red Medium + Cadmium Red Light 1:1 |

**NOTES**

## TCS #RE-6-1-6

| ACCENT | ☐ Pure Red<br>S: Crimson    H: Vermillion |
|---|---|
| AMERICANA | ☐ Berry Red<br>S: Napa Red    H: Cadmium Red |
| CERAMCOAT | ☐ Cardinal Red<br>S: Black Cherry    H: Tangerine |
| FOLK ART | ☐ Engine Red<br>S: Cherry Royale    H: Red Orange |
| JO SONJA | ☐ * Napthol Crimson + Napthol Red Light 1:1 |
| LIQUITEX | ☐ Cadmium Red Medium |

**NOTES**

## TCS #RE-6-2-1

| ACCENT | ☐ * White + Painted Desert (T) |
|---|---|
| AMERICANA | ☐ * White + Spice Pink (T) |
| CERAMCOAT | ☐ * White + Hydrangea (T) |
| FOLK ART | ☐ Rose White<br>S: Baby Pink    H: White |
| JO SONJA | ☐ * White + Napthol Red Crimson (T) |
| LIQUITEX | ☐ * White + Light Magenta (T) |

**NOTES**

RED 6-2-3 / RED 6-3-2

## TCS #RE-6-2-3

| BRAND | |
|---|---|
| ACCENT | ☐ Painted Desert<br>　　S: Rose Blush　H: Painted Desert + White 1:1 |
| AMERICANA | ☐ * White + Spice Pink 3:1 |
| CERAMCOAT | ☐ Hydrangea Pink<br>　　S: Fuchsia　H: Pink Frosting |
| FOLK ART | ☐ * White + Calico Red 7:1 |
| JO SONJA | ☐ * White + Napthol Red Light 7:1 |
| LIQUITEX | ☐ * Light Magenta + White 1:1 |

**NOTES**

## TCS #RE-6-2-4

| | |
|---|---|
| ☐ Painted Desert (L) | |
| ☐ * Baby Pink + Spice Pink (T) | |
| ☐ Lisa Pink<br>　　S: Mendocino Red　H: Pink Frosting | |
| ☐ * White + Calico Red 4:1 | |
| ☐ * White + Napthol Red Light 4:1 | |
| ☐ Light Magenta | |

**NOTES**

## TCS #RE-6-2-6

| BRAND | |
|---|---|
| ACCENT | ☐ Crimson (D) |
| AMERICANA | ☐ Primary Red<br>　　S: Napa Red　H: Tangelo Orange |
| CERAMCOAT | ☐ Napthol Red Light<br>　　S: Black Cherry　H: Tangerine |
| FOLK ART | ☐ Calico Red<br>　　S: Raspberry Wine　H: Vanilla Cream |
| JO SONJA | ☐ Napthol Crimson (D) |
| LIQUITEX | ☐ Napthol Crimson (D) |

**NOTES**

## TCS #RE-6-2-7

| | |
|---|---|
| ☐ Crimson (ABC)<br>　　S: Burgundy　H: Rose Blush | |
| ☐ Santa Red<br>　　S: Napa Red　H: Cadmium Red | |
| ☐ Tompte Red<br>　　S: Black Cherry　H: Hydrangea | |
| ☐ Napthol Crimson (PP) | |
| ☐ Napthol Crimson | |
| ☐ Napthol Crimson | |

**NOTES**

## TCS #RE-6-2-8

| BRAND | |
|---|---|
| ACCENT | ☐ Crimson (L) |
| AMERICANA | ☐ * Country Red + Berry Red 1:1 |
| CERAMCOAT | ☐ Tompte Red (L) |
| FOLK ART | ☐ Crimson<br>　　S: Cherry Royale　H: Baby Pink |
| JO SONJA | ☐ Napthol Crimson (L) |
| LIQUITEX | ☐ Alizarine Crimson Perm. Hue |

**NOTES**

## TCS #RE-6-3-2

| | |
|---|---|
| ☐ * White + Holiday Red 5:1 | |
| ☐ Baby Pink<br>　　S: Royal Fuchsia　H: Baby Pink + White 1:1 | |
| ☐ * Hydrangea Pink + Fuchsia (T) | |
| ☐ Baby Pink<br>　　S: Pink　H: White | |
| ☐ * White + Napthol Crimson 6:1 | |
| ☐ * White + Napthol Crimson 6:1 | |

**NOTES**

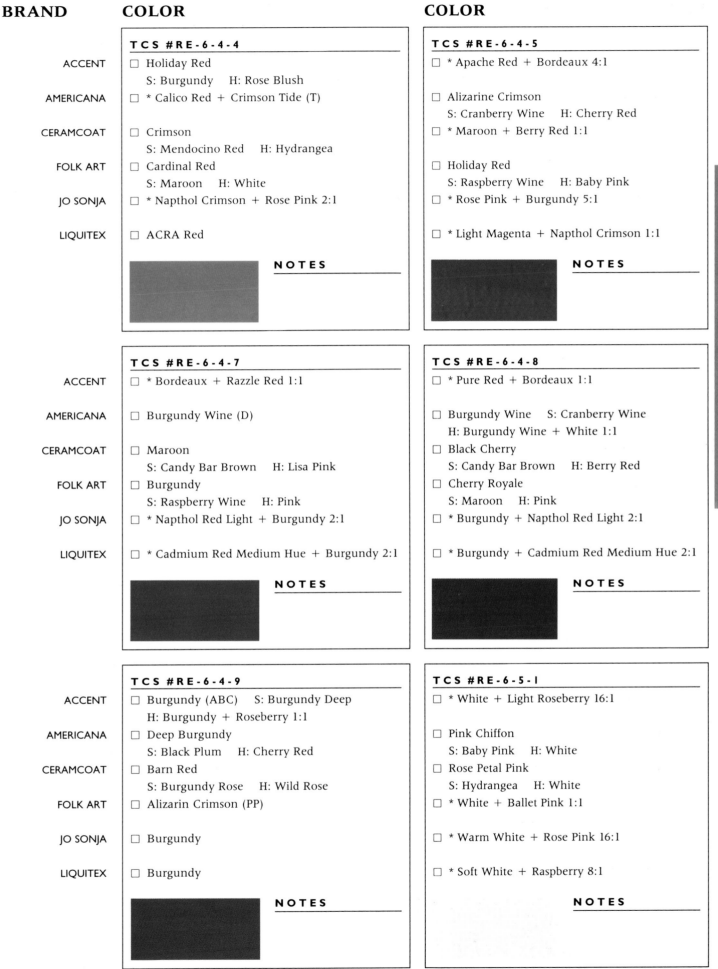

---

**TCS #RE-6-4-4**

ACCENT
- ☐ Holiday Red
  S: Burgundy    H: Rose Blush

AMERICANA
- ☐ * Calico Red + Crimson Tide (T)

CERAMCOAT
- ☐ Crimson
  S: Mendocino Red    H: Hydrangea

FOLK ART
- ☐ Cardinal Red
  S: Maroon    H: White

JO SONJA
- ☐ * Napthol Crimson + Rose Pink 2:1

LIQUITEX
- ☐ ACRA Red

**NOTES**

---

**TCS #RE-6-4-5**

- ☐ * Apache Red + Bordeaux 4:1

- ☐ Alizarine Crimson
  S: Cranberry Wine    H: Cherry Red
- ☐ * Maroon + Berry Red 1:1

- ☐ Holiday Red
  S: Raspberry Wine    H: Baby Pink
- ☐ * Rose Pink + Burgundy 5:1

- ☐ * Light Magenta + Napthol Crimson 1:1

**NOTES**

---

**TCS #RE-6-4-7**

ACCENT
- ☐ * Bordeaux + Razzle Red 1:1

AMERICANA
- ☐ Burgundy Wine (D)

CERAMCOAT
- ☐ Maroon
  S: Candy Bar Brown    H: Lisa Pink

FOLK ART
- ☐ Burgundy
  S: Raspberry Wine    H: Pink

JO SONJA
- ☐ * Napthol Red Light + Burgundy 2:1

LIQUITEX
- ☐ * Cadmium Red Medium Hue + Burgundy 2:1

**NOTES**

---

**TCS #RE-6-4-8**

- ☐ * Pure Red + Bordeaux 1:1

- ☐ Burgundy Wine    S: Cranberry Wine
  H: Burgundy Wine + White 1:1
- ☐ Black Cherry
  S: Candy Bar Brown    H: Berry Red
- ☐ Cherry Royale
  S: Maroon    H: Pink
- ☐ * Burgundy + Napthol Red Light 2:1

- ☐ * Burgundy + Cadmium Red Medium Hue 2:1

**NOTES**

---

**TCS #RE-6-4-9**

ACCENT
- ☐ Burgundy (ABC)    S: Burgundy Deep
  H: Burgundy + Roseberry 1:1

AMERICANA
- ☐ Deep Burgundy
  S: Black Plum    H: Cherry Red

CERAMCOAT
- ☐ Barn Red
  S: Burgundy Rose    H: Wild Rose

FOLK ART
- ☐ Alizarin Crimson (PP)

JO SONJA
- ☐ Burgundy

LIQUITEX
- ☐ Burgundy

**NOTES**

---

**TCS #RE-6-5-1**

- ☐ * White + Light Roseberry 16:1

- ☐ Pink Chiffon
  S: Baby Pink    H: White
- ☐ Rose Petal Pink
  S: Hydrangea    H: White
- ☐ * White + Ballet Pink 1:1

- ☐ * Warm White + Rose Pink 16:1

- ☐ * Soft White + Raspberry 8:1

**NOTES**

## BRAND          COLOR                                    COLOR

### TCS #RE-6-5-2

| ACCENT | ☐ * White + Light Roseberry 12:1 |
| AMERICANA | ☐ * White + Raspberry 4:1 |
| CERAMCOAT | ☐ * Pink Quartz + White 2:1 |
| FOLK ART | ☐ Ballet Pink<br>S: Rose Crimson    H: Rose White |
| JO SONJA | ☐ * Opal + Rose Pink 12:1 |
| LIQUITEX | ☐ * Soft White + Raspberry 6:1 |

**NOTES**

### TCS #RE-6-5-3

| ACCENT | ☐ * White + Bordeaux 6:1 |
| AMERICANA | ☐ * White + Raspberry 3:1 |
| CERAMCOAT | ☐ Pink Quartz<br>S: Black Cherry    H: Pink Frosting |
| FOLK ART | ☐ * Raspberry Sherbert + White 1:1 |
| JO SONJA | ☐ * Opal + Plum Pink 10:1 |
| LIQUITEX | ☐ * Soft White + Raspberry 4:1 |

**NOTES**

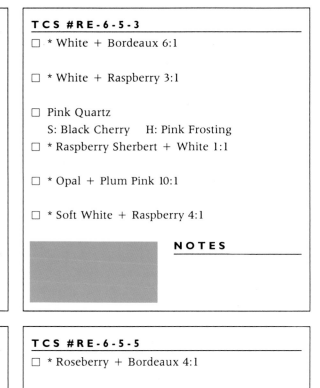

### TCS #RE-6-5-4

| ACCENT | ☐ * White + Bordeaux 2:1 |
| AMERICANA | ☐ * Raspberry + White 1:1 |
| CERAMCOAT | ☐ * Pink Quartz + Dusty Mauve 4:1 |
| FOLK ART | ☐ Rose Pink<br>S: Maroon    H: Spring Rose |
| JO SONJA | ☐ * Opal + Plum Pink 7:1 |
| LIQUITEX | ☐ * Soft White + Dark Victorian Rose 3:1 |

**NOTES**

### TCS #RE-6-5-5

| ACCENT | ☐ * Roseberry + Bordeaux 4:1 |
| AMERICANA | ☐ Raspberry<br>S: Cranberry Wine    H: Spice Pink |
| CERAMCOAT | ☐ Wild Rose<br>S: Barn Red    H: Rose Cloud |
| FOLK ART | ☐ Raspberry Sherbert<br>S: Maroon    H: Sweetheart Pink |
| JO SONJA | ☐ * Opal + Plum Pink 1:1 |
| LIQUITEX | ☐ * White + Dark Victorian Rose 1:1 |

**NOTES**

### TCS #RE-6-5-7

| ACCENT | ☐ * Pueblo Red + Roseberry 3:1 |
| AMERICANA | ☐ Antique Mauve<br>S: Rookwood Red    H: Mauve |
| CERAMCOAT | ☐ Dusty Mauve<br>S: Sonoma    H: Rose Cloud |
| FOLK ART | ☐ Rose Garden<br>S: Raspberry Wine    H: Spring Rose |
| JO SONJA | ☐ Plum Pink |
| LIQUITEX | ☐ * Dark Victorian Rose + White 2:1 |

**NOTES**

### TCS #RE-6-5-8

| ACCENT | ☐ * Bordeaux + Barn Red 1:1 |
| AMERICANA | ☐ Cranberry Wine<br>S: Black Plum    H: Boysenberry |
| CERAMCOAT | ☐ * Black Cherry + Burgundy Rose (T) |
| FOLK ART | ☐ Maroon<br>S: Licorice    H: Baby Pink |
| JO SONJA | ☐ * Plum Pink + Burgundy 3:1 |
| LIQUITEX | ☐ Dark Victorian Rose |

**NOTES**

| BRAND | COLOR | COLOR |
|---|---|---|

**TCS #RE-6-7-2**

ACCENT — ☐ * Light Roseberry + White 1:1

AMERICANA — ☐ * White + Mauve 3:1

CERAMCOAT — ☐ * Sachet + White 1:1

FOLK ART — ☐ Spring Rose
S: Rose Garden    H: White

JO SONJA — ☐ * Opal + Plum Pink 6:1

LIQUITEX — ☐ * Pale Portrait Pink + Venetian Rose 4:1

**NOTES**

**TCS #RE-6-7-4**

☐ Light Roseberry
S: Roseberry    H: Light Roseberry + White 1:1
☐ French Mauve
S: Antique Mauve    H: Pink Chiffon
☐ Sachet Pink
S: Rose Mist    H: Pink Frosting
☐ Berries 'n Cream
S: Rose Garden    H: Cotton Candy
☐ * Opal + Plum Pink 3:1

☐ * Pale Portrait Pink + Venetian Rose 1:1

**NOTES**

**TCS #RE-6-7-5**

ACCENT — ☐ Roseberry
S: Burgundy    H: Light Roseberry

AMERICANA — ☐ Mauve
S: Cranberry Wine    H: Mauve + White 1:1

CERAMCOAT — ☐ Bouquet Pink
S: Sonoma    H: Rose Cloud

FOLK ART — ☐ Potpourri Rose
S: Raspberry Wine    H: Delicate Rose

JO SONJA — ☐ * Opal + Plum Pink 2:1

LIQUITEX — ☐ Venetian Rose

**NOTES**

**TCS #RE-6-7-7**

☐ Roseberry (L)

☐ * Mauve + Cranberry Wine 2:1

☐ Rose Mist
S: Sonoma    H: Sachet
☐ * Rose Garden + Potpourri Rose 1:1

☐ * Plum Pink + Indian Red Oxide 4:1

☐ * Venetian Rose + Dark Victorian Rose 4:1

**NOTES**

**TCS #RE-7-2-5**

ACCENT — ☐ * Holiday Red + Apache Red 1:1

AMERICANA — ☐ * True Red + Boysenberry Pink 1:1

CERAMCOAT — ☐ Berry Red
S: Black Cherry    H: Hydrangea

FOLK ART — ☐ * Cardinal Red + Pink (T)

JO SONJA — ☐ * Napthol Crimson + Trans. Magenta 1:1

LIQUITEX — ☐ * Napthol Crimson + Hibiscus 1:1

**NOTES**

**TCS #RE-7-2-9**

☐ Bordeaux (L)

☐ Black Plum
S: Soft Black    H: Plum
☐ * Sweetheart Blush + Candy Bar 3:1

☐ Burnt Carmine (PP)

☐ * Burgundy + Trans. Magenta 1:1

☐ Maroon

**NOTES**

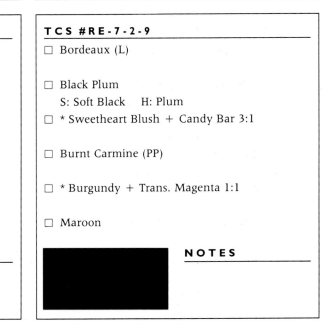

## BRAND    COLOR    COLOR

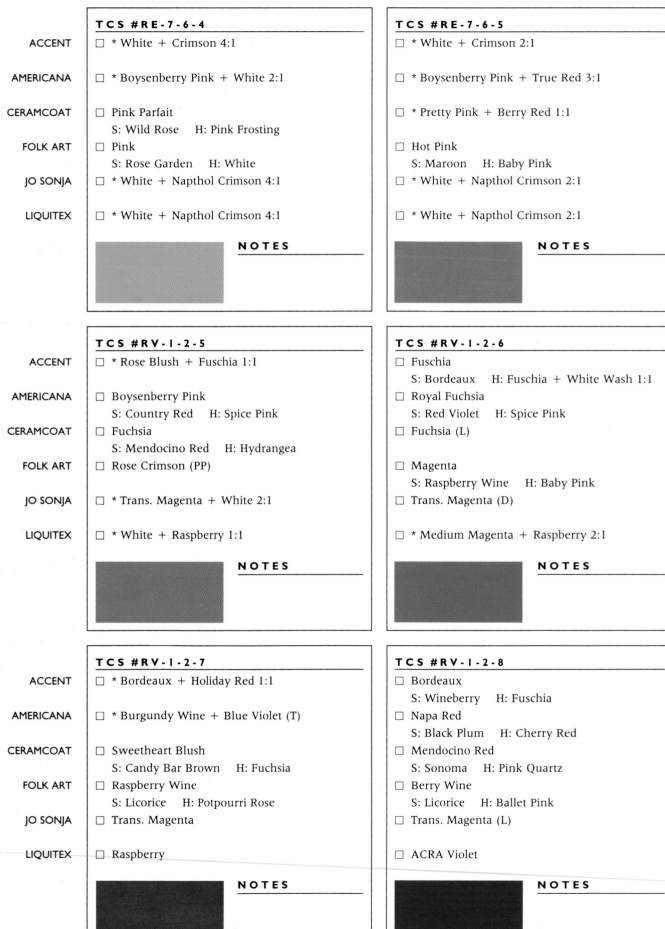

### TCS #RE-7-6-4

| | |
|---|---|
| ACCENT | ☐ * White + Crimson 4:1 |
| AMERICANA | ☐ * Boysenberry Pink + White 2:1 |
| CERAMCOAT | ☐ Pink Parfait<br>S: Wild Rose    H: Pink Frosting |
| FOLK ART | ☐ Pink<br>S: Rose Garden    H: White |
| JO SONJA | ☐ * White + Napthol Crimson 4:1 |
| LIQUITEX | ☐ * White + Napthol Crimson 4:1 |

**NOTES**

### TCS #RE-7-6-5

| | |
|---|---|
| ☐ * White + Crimson 2:1 |
| ☐ * Boysenberry Pink + True Red 3:1 |
| ☐ * Pretty Pink + Berry Red 1:1 |
| ☐ Hot Pink<br>S: Maroon    H: Baby Pink |
| ☐ * White + Napthol Crimson 2:1 |
| ☐ * White + Napthol Crimson 2:1 |

**NOTES**

### TCS #RV-1-2-5

| | |
|---|---|
| ACCENT | ☐ * Rose Blush + Fuschia 1:1 |
| AMERICANA | ☐ Boysenberry Pink<br>S: Country Red    H: Spice Pink |
| CERAMCOAT | ☐ Fuchsia<br>S: Mendocino Red    H: Hydrangea |
| FOLK ART | ☐ Rose Crimson (PP) |
| JO SONJA | ☐ * Trans. Magenta + White 2:1 |
| LIQUITEX | ☐ * White + Raspberry 1:1 |

**NOTES**

### TCS #RV-1-2-6

| | |
|---|---|
| ☐ Fuschia<br>S: Bordeaux    H: Fuschia + White Wash 1:1 |
| ☐ Royal Fuchsia<br>S: Red Violet    H: Spice Pink |
| ☐ Fuchsia (L) |
| ☐ Magenta<br>S: Raspberry Wine    H: Baby Pink |
| ☐ Trans. Magenta (D) |
| ☐ * Medium Magenta + Raspberry 2:1 |

**NOTES**

### TCS #RV-1-2-7

| | |
|---|---|
| ACCENT | ☐ * Bordeaux + Holiday Red 1:1 |
| AMERICANA | ☐ * Burgundy Wine + Blue Violet (T) |
| CERAMCOAT | ☐ Sweetheart Blush<br>S: Candy Bar Brown    H: Fuchsia |
| FOLK ART | ☐ Raspberry Wine<br>S: Licorice    H: Potpourri Rose |
| JO SONJA | ☐ Trans. Magenta |
| LIQUITEX | ☐ Raspberry |

**NOTES**

### TCS #RV-1-2-8

| | |
|---|---|
| ☐ Bordeaux<br>S: Wineberry    H: Fuschia |
| ☐ Napa Red<br>S: Black Plum    H: Cherry Red |
| ☐ Mendocino Red<br>S: Sonoma    H: Pink Quartz |
| ☐ Berry Wine<br>S: Licorice    H: Ballet Pink |
| ☐ Trans. Magenta (L) |
| ☐ ACRA Violet |

**NOTES**

## BRAND                COLOR

COLOR

### TCS #RV-1-4-6

ACCENT
☐ * Bordeaux + Roseberry 4:1

AMERICANA
☐ * Royal Fuchsia + Napa Red 1:1

CERAMCOAT
☐ Raspberry
　　S: Black Cherry　　H: Tangerine

FOLK ART
☐ * Cherry Royale + Pink 2:1

JO SONJA
☐ * Plum Pink + Rose Pink 3:1

LIQUITEX
☐ * Burgundy + Medium Magenta 3:1

NOTES

### TCS #RV-2-2-8

☐ Burgundy Deep
　　S: Wineberry　　H: Burgundy + Roseberry (T)
☐ Red Violet
　　S: Black Plum　　H: Fuchsia
☐ * Mendocino + Grape 4:1

☐ Fuchsia
　　S: Raspberry Wine　　H: Baby Pink
☐ * Trans. Magenta + Burgundy 2:1

☐ * Burgundy + Raspberry 1:1

NOTES

### TCS #RV-2-4-6

ACCENT
☐ * Fuschia + Painted Desert 8:1

AMERICANA
☐ * Royal Fuchsia + Orchid 6:1

CERAMCOAT
☐ * Royal Fuchsia + White 8:1

FOLK ART
☐ * Fuchsia + White 8:1

JO SONJA
☐ * Trans. Magenta + Amethyst 8:1

LIQUITEX
☐ Medium Magenta

NOTES

### TCS #RV-2-4-7

☐ * Burgundy Deep + Fuschia 4:1

☐ * Royal Fuchsia + Plum 8:1

☐ Royal Fuchsia
　　S: Mulberry　　H: Pink Quartz
☐ * Fuchsia + Hot Pink 8:1

☐ * Trans. Magenta + Burgundy + Opal 2:2:1

☐ * Medium Magenta + ACRA Violet 2:1

NOTES

### TCS #RV-2-4-8

ACCENT
☐ * Burgundy Deep + Egg Plant 6:1

AMERICANA
☐ * Napa Red + Royal Fuchsia + Diox. Purple
　　2:1:1

CERAMCOAT
☐ Mulberry
　　S: Black　　H: Royal Fuchsia

FOLK ART
☐ * Berry Wine + Purple Passion 4:1

JO SONJA
☐ * Trans. Magenta + Plum Pink 1:1

LIQUITEX
☐ * Burgundy + Twilight + White 6:1:1

NOTES

### TCS #RV-3-2-4

☐ * Wild Hyacinth + Fuschia 3:1

☐ * Orchid + Royal Fuchsia 5:1

☐ Lilac Dust
　　S: Grape　　H: Lilac Dust + White 1:1
☐ * Orchid + Fuchsia 4:1

☐ * Opal + Amethyst + Trans. Magenta 1:1:1

☐ * White + Medium Magenta + Prism Violet
　　5:2:1

NOTES

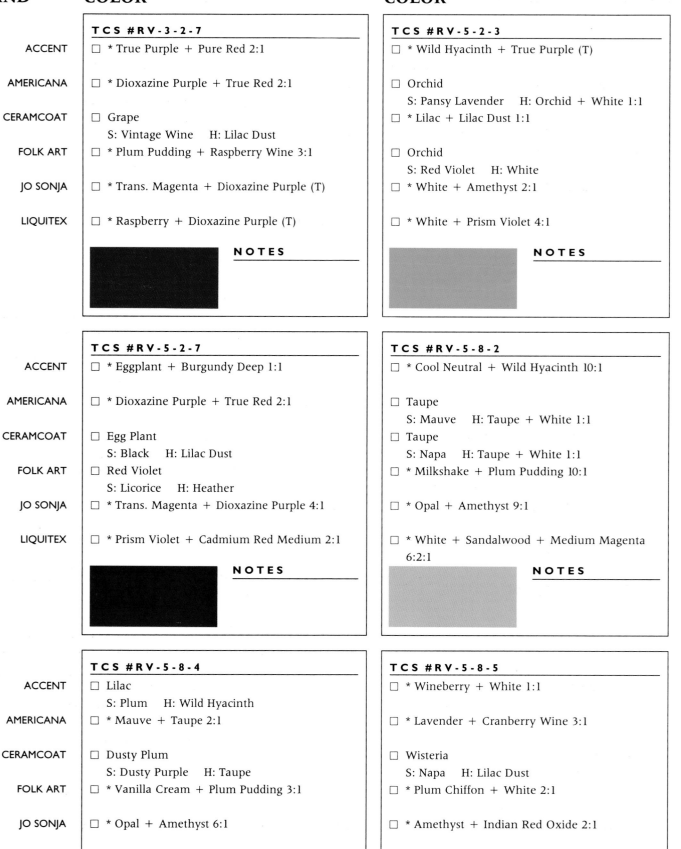

**TCS #RV-3-2-7**

ACCENT     ☐ * True Purple + Pure Red 2:1

AMERICANA     ☐ * Dioxazine Purple + True Red 2:1

CERAMCOAT     ☐ Grape
       S: Vintage Wine    H: Lilac Dust

FOLK ART     ☐ * Plum Pudding + Raspberry Wine 3:1

JO SONJA     ☐ * Trans. Magenta + Dioxazine Purple (T)

LIQUITEX     ☐ * Raspberry + Dioxazine Purple (T)

**NOTES**

**TCS #RV-5-2-3**

ACCENT     ☐ * Wild Hyacinth + True Purple (T)

AMERICANA     ☐ Orchid
       S: Pansy Lavender    H: Orchid + White 1:1
    ☐ * Lilac + Lilac Dust 1:1

FOLK ART     ☐ Orchid
       S: Red Violet    H: White
    ☐ * White + Amethyst 2:1

LIQUITEX     ☐ * White + Prism Violet 4:1

**NOTES**

**TCS #RV-5-2-7**

ACCENT     ☐ * Eggplant + Burgundy Deep 1:1

AMERICANA     ☐ * Dioxazine Purple + True Red 2:1

CERAMCOAT     ☐ Egg Plant
       S: Black    H: Lilac Dust

FOLK ART     ☐ Red Violet
       S: Licorice    H: Heather

JO SONJA     ☐ * Trans. Magenta + Dioxazine Purple 4:1

LIQUITEX     ☐ * Prism Violet + Cadmium Red Medium 2:1

**NOTES**

**TCS #RV-5-8-2**

ACCENT     ☐ * Cool Neutral + Wild Hyacinth 10:1

AMERICANA     ☐ Taupe
       S: Mauve    H: Taupe + White 1:1
    ☐ Taupe
       S: Napa    H: Taupe + White 1:1
    ☐ * Milkshake + Plum Pudding 10:1

JO SONJA     ☐ * Opal + Amethyst 9:1

LIQUITEX     ☐ * White + Sandalwood + Medium Magenta
       6:2:1

**NOTES**

**TCS #RV-5-8-4**

ACCENT     ☐ Lilac
       S: Plum    H: Wild Hyacinth

AMERICANA     ☐ * Mauve + Taupe 2:1

CERAMCOAT     ☐ Dusty Plum
       S: Dusty Purple    H: Taupe

FOLK ART     ☐ * Vanilla Cream + Plum Pudding 3:1

JO SONJA     ☐ * Opal + Amethyst 6:1

LIQUITEX     ☐ * Medium Magenta + Light Violet +
       Sandalwood 3:3:1

**NOTES**

**TCS #RV-5-8-5**

ACCENT     ☐ * Wineberry + White 1:1

AMERICANA     ☐ * Lavender + Cranberry Wine 3:1

CERAMCOAT     ☐ Wisteria
       S: Napa    H: Lilac Dust

FOLK ART     ☐ * Plum Chiffon + White 2:1

JO SONJA     ☐ * Amethyst + Indian Red Oxide 2:1

LIQUITEX     ☐ * Medium Magenta + Prism Violet 3:1

**NOTES**

| BRAND | COLOR | COLOR |
|---|---|---|

**TCS #RV-5-8-8**

| ACCENT | ☐ Wineberry |
|---|---|
| | S: Eggplant    H: Wild Heather |
| AMERICANA | ☐ * Cranberry Wine + Dioxazine Purple 3:1 |
| CERAMCOAT | ☐ Dusty Purple |
| | S: Vintage Wine + Black 3:1    H: Dusty Plum |
| FOLK ART | ☐ Purple Passion |
| | S: Licorice    H: Orchid |
| JO SONJA | ☐ * Amethyst + Indian Red Oxide 2:1 |
| LIQUITEX | ☐ * Cadmium Red Medium Hue + Prism Violet 3:1 |

**NOTES**

**TCS #RV-5-8-9**

| ACCENT | ☐ Plum |
|---|---|
| | S: Dioxazine Purple    H: Lilac |
| AMERICANA | ☐ Plum |
| | S: Black Plum    H: Fuchsia |
| CERAMCOAT | ☐ Dusty Purple (L) |
| FOLK ART | ☐ Plum Pudding |
| | S: Licorice    H: Heather |
| JO SONJA | ☐ * Indian Red Oxide + Amethyst 1:1 |
| LIQUITEX | ☐ * Wisteria + Black 10:1 |

**NOTES**

**TCS #RV-5-9-8**

| ACCENT | ☐ * Wineberry + White 5:1 |
|---|---|
| AMERICANA | ☐ * Cranberry Wine + Dioxazine Purple 1:1 |
| CERAMCOAT | ☐ Napa Wine |
| | S: Vintage Wine    H: Dusty Plum |
| FOLK ART | ☐ Plum Chiffon |
| | S: Licorice    H: Orchid |
| JO SONJA | ☐ * Amethyst + Indian Red Oxide 1:1 |
| LIQUITEX | ☐ * Medium Magenta + Prism Violet 5:1 |

**NOTES**

**TCS #RV-9-2-3**

| ACCENT | ☐ Wild Hyacinth    S: Wild Heather    H: Wild Hyacinth + White Wash 1:1 |
|---|---|
| AMERICANA | ☐ * Orchid + Lavender 4:1 |
| CERAMCOAT | ☐ Lilac |
| | S: Wisteria    H: Ice Storm |
| FOLK ART | ☐ * Heather + Sweetheart Pink 1:1 |
| JO SONJA | ☐ Amethyst |
| LIQUITEX | ☐ * White + Prism Violet 2:1 |

**NOTES**

**TCS #RV-9-2-5**

| ACCENT | ☐ * Eggplant + White 1:1 |
|---|---|
| AMERICANA | ☐ * Lavender + Orchid 1:1 |
| CERAMCOAT | ☐ * Vintage Wine + White 1:1 |
| FOLK ART | ☐ Heather |
| | S: Purple Passion    H: Orchid |
| JO SONJA | ☐ * Amethyst + Dioxazine Purple 8:1 |
| LIQUITEX | ☐ * Prism Violet + White 1:1 |

**NOTES**

**TCS #RV-9-2-8**

| ACCENT | ☐ Purple Canyon |
|---|---|
| | S: Eggplant    H: Wild Heather |
| AMERICANA | ☐ Pansy Lavender |
| | S: Royal Purple    H: Orchid |
| CERAMCOAT | ☐ Vintage Wine |
| | S: Black    H: Lilac |
| FOLK ART | ☐ * Red Violet + Dioxazine Purple 3:1 |
| JO SONJA | ☐ * Amethyst + Dioxazine Purple 3:2 |
| LIQUITEX | ☐ Prism Violet |

**NOTES**

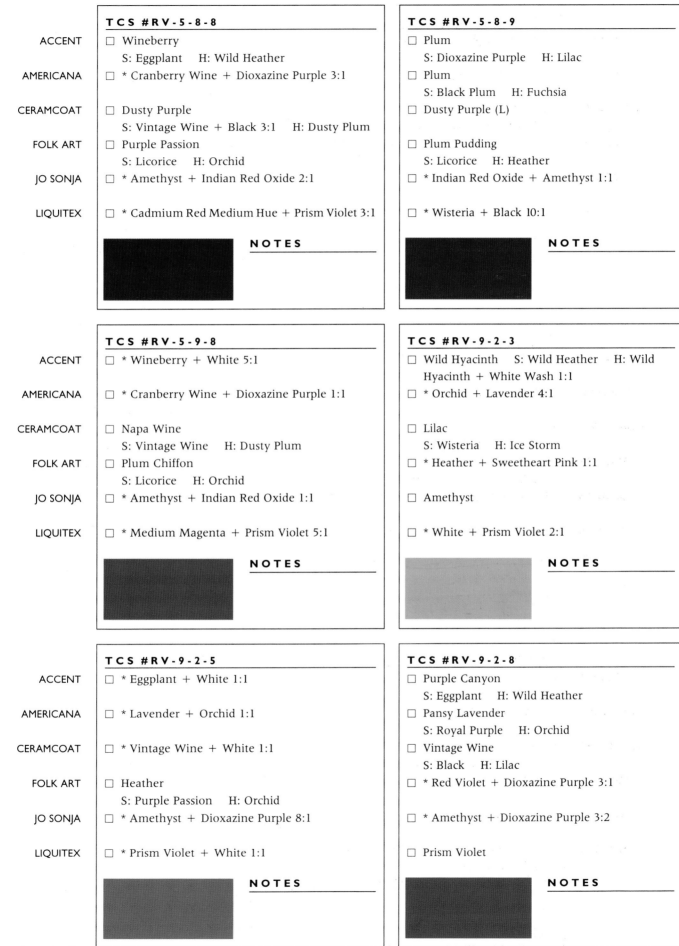

**RED VIOLET 9-2-9 / VIOLET 5-1-4**

## TCS #RV-9-2-9

| BRAND | COLOR |
|---|---|
| ACCENT | ☐ Eggplant<br>S: Dioxazine Purple   H: Wild Heather |
| AMERICANA | ☐ Royal Purple<br>S: Dioxazine Purple   H: Pansy Lavender |
| CERAMCOAT | ☐ Vintage Wine (L) |
| FOLK ART | ☐ * Dioxazine Purple + Heather 2:1 |
| JO SONJA | ☐ * Amethyst + Dioxazine Purple 1:1 |
| LIQUITEX | ☐ Wisteria |

NOTES

## TCS #RV-9-6-1

| BRAND | COLOR |
|---|---|
| ACCENT | ☐ * April Showers + Wild Hyacinth 12:1 |
| AMERICANA | ☐ * Grey Sky + Orchid 2:1 |
| CERAMCOAT | ☐ Ice Storm Violet<br>S: Lavender   H: White |
| FOLK ART | ☐ * Gray Mist + Orchid 10:1 |
| JO SONJA | ☐ * Warm White + Amethyst 12:1 |
| LIQUITEX | ☐ * Soft White + Perm. Light Violet 4:1 |

NOTES

## TCS #RV-9-6-5

| BRAND | COLOR |
|---|---|
| ACCENT | ☐ * Wild Hyacinth + True Purple + Soft Grey 4:1:1 |
| AMERICANA | ☐ Summer Lilac<br>S: Pansy Lavender   H: Lilac |
| CERAMCOAT | ☐ * Lilac + Lavender 3:1 |
| FOLK ART | ☐ * Purple Lilac + Orchid 4:1 |
| JO SONJA | ☐ * White + Amethyst + French Blue 3:2:T |
| LIQUITEX | ☐ * Light Violet + Prism Violet 2:1 |

NOTES

## TCS #VI-4-1-7

| BRAND | COLOR |
|---|---|
| ACCENT | ☐ * True Purple + Pure Red (T) |
| AMERICANA | ☐ * Dioxazine Purple + Cadmium Red (T) |
| CERAMCOAT | ☐ * Purple + Napthol Red Light (T) |
| FOLK ART | ☐ Violet Pansy<br>S: Licorice   H: Purple Lilac |
| JO SONJA | ☐ * Diox. Purple + White + Nap. Crimson 1:1:T |
| LIQUITEX | ☐ * Dioxazine Purple + Ultramarine Blue 1:1 |

NOTES

## TCS #VI-5-1-2

| BRAND | COLOR |
|---|---|
| ACCENT | ☐ * White + Wild Heather 6:1 |
| AMERICANA | ☐ Lilac<br>S: Orchid   H: Lilac + White 1:1 |
| CERAMCOAT | ☐ * White + Lilac 6:1 |
| FOLK ART | ☐ * White + Heather 6:1 |
| JO SONJA | ☐ * White + Dioxazine Purple 12:1 |
| LIQUITEX | ☐ * White + Dioxazine Purple 12:1 |

NOTES

## TCS #VI-5-1-4

| BRAND | COLOR |
|---|---|
| ACCENT | ☐ Wild Heather<br>S: Purple Canyon   H: Wild Hyacinth |
| AMERICANA | ☐ * Lavender + White 2:1 |
| CERAMCOAT | ☐ G.P. Purple<br>S: Purple   H: Ice Storm Violet |
| FOLK ART | ☐ Lavender (D) |
| JO SONJA | ☐ * Amethyst + Prussian Blue (T) |
| LIQUITEX | ☐ Light Violet |

NOTES

# BRAND     COLOR        COLOR

## TCS #VI-5-1-5

| BRAND | COLOR |
|---|---|
| ACCENT | ☐ Wild Heather (L) |
| AMERICANA | ☐ Lavender<br>S: Dioxazine Purple    H: Lavender + White 1:1 |
| CERAMCOAT | ☐ * Purple + White 2:1 |
| FOLK ART | ☐ Lavender<br>S: Red Violet    H: Lavender Sachet |
| JO SONJA | ☐ * Diox. Purple + White 1:1 |
| LIQUITEX | ☐ Brilliant Purple |

**NOTES**

## TCS #VI-5-1-7

| BRAND | COLOR |
|---|---|
| ACCENT | ☐ True Purple<br>S: Dioxazine Purple    H: Wild Heather |
| AMERICANA | ☐ Dioxazine Purple<br>S: Payne's Grey    H: Lavender |
| CERAMCOAT | ☐ Purple<br>S: Vintage Wine    H: G.P. Purple |
| FOLK ART | ☐ Purple<br>S: Licorice    H: Lavender |
| JO SONJA | ☐ Dioxazine Purple (D) |
| LIQUITEX | ☐ Dioxazine Purple (D) |

**NOTES**

## TCS #VI-5-1-9

| BRAND | COLOR |
|---|---|
| ACCENT | ☐ Dioxazine Purple (ABC)    S: Diox. Purple + Black 1:1    H: Wild Heather + Diox. Purple (T) |
| AMERICANA | ☐ * Dioxazine Purple + Prussian Blue (T) |
| CERAMCOAT | ☐ * Purple + Midnight (T) |
| FOLK ART | ☐ Dioxazine Purple (PP) |
| JO SONJA | ☐ Dioxazine Purple |
| LIQUITEX | ☐ Dioxazine Purple |

**NOTES**

## TCS #VI-5-8-5

| BRAND | COLOR |
|---|---|
| ACCENT | ☐ * Wild Heather + April Showers 2:1 |
| AMERICANA | ☐ * Lavender + Neutral Gray 3:1 |
| CERAMCOAT | ☐ Lavender<br>S: Vintage Wine    H: Ice Storm Violet |
| FOLK ART | ☐ Purple Lilac<br>S: Violet Pansy    H: Lavender Sachet |
| JO SONJA | ☐ * Amethyst + Nimbus Grey 4:1 |
| LIQUITEX | ☐ * Brilliant Purple + Mixing Gray 3:1 |

**NOTES**

## TCS #VI-9-6-6

| BRAND | COLOR |
|---|---|
| ACCENT | ☐ * Wild Hyacinth + Purple Canyon + Soldier Blue 2:1:1 |
| AMERICANA | ☐ Violet Haze<br>S: Dioxazine Purple    H: Lilac |
| CERAMCOAT | ☐ * Purple Dusk + Hammered Iron 6:1 |
| FOLK ART | ☐ * Periwinkle + Slate Blue 3:1 |
| JO SONJA | ☐ * White + French Blue + Diox. Purple 2:1:1 |
| LIQUITEX | ☐ * French Gray/Blue + Prism Violet 2:1 |

**NOTES**

## TCS #BV-2-6-1

| BRAND | COLOR |
|---|---|
| ACCENT | ☐ * April Showers + Wild Heather 12:1 |
| AMERICANA | ☐ * Grey Sky + Lilac 2:1 |
| CERAMCOAT | ☐ * White + Lavender 8:1 |
| FOLK ART | ☐ Lavender Sachet<br>S: Periwinkle    H: White |
| JO SONJA | ☐ * Warm White + Dioxazine Purple 12:1 |
| LIQUITEX | ☐ * Soft White + Brilliant Purple 10:1 |

**NOTES**

43

## BRAND          COLOR                                    COLOR

### TCS #BV-5-2-4

| | |
|---|---|
| ACCENT | ☐ * Monet Blue + Bluebonnet 2:1 |
| AMERICANA | ☐ * Country Blue + Lavender 4:1 |
| CERAMCOAT | ☐ Bahama Purple<br>S: Purple Dusk    H: White |
| FOLK ART | ☐ * Light Periwinkle + Lavender 4:1 |
| JO SONJA | ☐ * White + Diox. Purple + Storm Blue 6:1:1 |
| LIQUITEX | ☐ * Light Blue Violet + Brilliant Purple 4:1 |

**NOTES**

### TCS #BV-5-2-8

| | |
|---|---|
| ☐ * True Purple + Ultramarine Blue Dp. 1:1 |
| ☐ * Dioxazine Purple + Ultra Blue Deep 1:1 |
| ☐ * Purple + Navy Blue 1:1 |
| ☐ Night Sky<br>S: Licorice    H: Light Periwinkle |
| ☐ * Dioxazine Purple + Ultra Blue Deep 1:1 |
| ☐ * Dioxazine Purple + Ultramarine Blue 1:1 |

**NOTES**

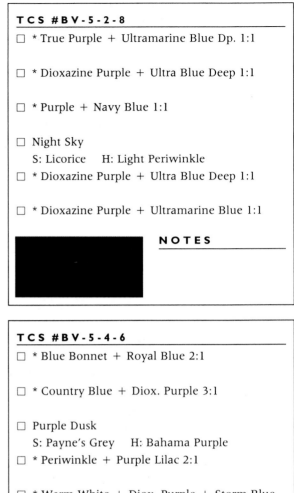

### TCS #BV-5-4-4

| | |
|---|---|
| ACCENT | ☐ Blue Bonnet    S: Royal Blue<br>H: Blue Bonnet + White Wash (T) |
| AMERICANA | ☐ * Country Blue + Orchid 1:1 |
| CERAMCOAT | ☐ * Lilac + Blue Jay 3:1 |
| FOLK ART | ☐ * Coastal Blue + Heather 2:1 |
| JO SONJA | ☐ * Amethyst + Prussian Blue + White 3:1:1 |
| LIQUITEX | ☐ * Light Blue Violet + Permanent Light Violet 1:1 |

**NOTES**

### TCS #BV-5-4-6

| | |
|---|---|
| ☐ * Blue Bonnet + Royal Blue 2:1 |
| ☐ * Country Blue + Diox. Purple 3:1 |
| ☐ Purple Dusk<br>S: Payne's Grey    H: Bahama Purple |
| ☐ * Periwinkle + Purple Lilac 2:1 |
| ☐ * Warm White + Diox. Purple + Storm Blue 2:2:1 |
| ☐ * Brilliant Purple + Twilight 4:1 |

**NOTES**

### TCS #BV-5-4-8

| | |
|---|---|
| ACCENT | ☐ * Royal Blue + Wild Hyacinth 1:1 |
| AMERICANA | ☐ * Uniform Blue + Orchid 1:1 |
| CERAMCOAT | ☐ * Liberty Blue + Purple 1:1 |
| FOLK ART | ☐ Periwinkle<br>S: Blue Ink    H: Light Periwinkle |
| JO SONJA | ☐ * Amethyst + Prussian Blue 4:1 |
| LIQUITEX | ☐ * Brilliant Purple + Twilight 2:1 |

**NOTES**

### TCS #BV-6-8-3

| | |
|---|---|
| ☐ * April Showers + Light Stoneware Blue 1:1 |
| ☐ * French Gray/Blue + Ice Blue 1:1 |
| ☐ * Dolphin + Ice Storm 2:1 |
| ☐ Whipped Berry<br>S: Slate Blue    H: Icy White |
| ☐ * Warm White + Sapphire + Amethyst 8:2:1 |
| ☐ * Soft White + French Gray/Blue 1:1 |

**NOTES**

| BRAND | COLOR | COLOR |
|---|---|---|

**TCS #BV-7-8-3**

| ACCENT | ☐ * Blue Bonnet + April Showers 1:1 |
| AMERICANA | ☐ * Flesh + Country Blue 3:1 |
| CERAMCOAT | ☐ Lavender Lace<br>S: Heritage Blue     H: Ice Storm Violet |
| FOLK ART | ☐ * Cotton Candy + Porcelain Blue 1:1 |
| JO SONJA | ☐ * Warm White + Sapphire + Dioxazine Purple 8:2:1 |
| LIQUITEX | ☐ * White + French Gray/Blue + Perm. Lt. Violet 1:1:T |

**NOTES**

**TCS #BV-8-3-3**

| ACCENT | ☐ * Monet Blue + White 2:1 |
| AMERICANA | ☐ * Country Blue + White 2:1 |
| CERAMCOAT | ☐ * Periwinkle + White 2:1 |
| FOLK ART | ☐ Baby Blue<br>S: French Blue     H: White<br>☐ * White + Storm Blue 15:1 |
| JO SONJA | ☐ * White + Twilight 12:1 |

**NOTES**

**TCS #BV-8-3-4**

| ACCENT | ☐ Monet Blue     S: Ultramarine Blue Deep<br>H: Monet Blue + White Wash 1:1 |
| AMERICANA | ☐ Country Blue<br>S: Sapphire     H: Country Blue + White 1:1 |
| CERAMCOAT | ☐ Periwinkle Blue     S: Navy Blue<br>H: Chambray Blue |
| FOLK ART | ☐ Light Periwinkle<br>S: Blue Ink     H: White |
| JO SONJA | ☐ * White + Sapphire Blue + Amethyst 2:2:1 |
| LIQUITEX | ☐ Light Blue Violet |

**NOTES**

**TCS #BV-8-3-6**

| ACCENT | ☐ * Ultra Blue Deep + White 4:1 |
| AMERICANA | ☐ * Blue Violet + White 1:1 |
| CERAMCOAT | ☐ Blue Lagoon<br>S: Opaque Blue     H: Blue Heaven |
| FOLK ART | ☐ * Ultramarine Blue + White 2:1 |
| JO SONJA | ☐ * Ultra Blue Deep + White 4:1 |
| LIQUITEX | ☐ * Ultramarine Blue + White 4:1 |

**NOTES**

**TCS #BV-9-1-8**

| ACCENT | ☐ * Pure Blue + Dioxazine Purple 12:1 |
| AMERICANA | ☐ Blue Violet<br>S: Payne's Grey     H: Blue Violet + White 1:1 |
| CERAMCOAT | ☐ Ultra Blue<br>S: Navy Blue     H: Blue Mist |
| FOLK ART | ☐ * Ultramarine + Dioxazine Purple 12:1 |
| JO SONJA | ☐ * Ultra Blue Deep + Dioxazine Purple 12:1 |
| LIQUITEX | ☐ Brilliant Blue Purple |

**NOTES**

**TCS #BV-9-6-7**

| ACCENT | ☐ Royal Blue<br>S: Windsor Blue     H: Clear Blue |
| AMERICANA | ☐ * Blue Violet + Prussian Blue 5:1 |
| CERAMCOAT | ☐ * Copen Blue + Purple 4:1 |
| FOLK ART | ☐ Sterling Blue<br>S: Blue Ink     H: Baby Blue |
| JO SONJA | ☐ * Sapphire + Dioxazine Purple 6:1 |
| LIQUITEX | ☐ * Twilight + White 3:1 |

**NOTES**

# BRAND          COLOR                                    COLOR

### TCS #BV-9-6-8

| ACCENT | ☐ Royal Blue (L) |
| AMERICANA | ☐ * Prussian Blue + Blue Violet 4:1 |
| CERAMCOAT | ☐ * Prussian Blue + Purple 1:1 |
| FOLK ART | ☐ Midnight   S: Licorice   H: White |
| JO SONJA | ☐ * Storm Blue + Dioxazine Purple 1:1 |
| LIQUITEX | ☐ Twilight |

**NOTES**

### TCS #BV-9-6-9

| ACCENT | ☐ * Royal Blue + Liberty Blue 2:1 |
| AMERICANA | ☐ * Navy + Dioxazine Purple 3:1 |
| CERAMCOAT | ☐ * Midnight Blue + Periwinkle Blue 2:1 |
| FOLK ART | ☐ Blue Ink   S: Licorice   H: Periwinkle |
| JO SONJA | ☐ * Pthalo Blue + Dioxazine Purple 5:1 |
| LIQUITEX | ☐ Twilight (L) |

**NOTES**

### TCS #BL-3-3-2

| ACCENT | ☐ Indian Sky   S: Sapphire   H: White Wash |
| AMERICANA | ☐ * White + Country Blue 6:1 |
| CERAMCOAT | ☐ * White + Periwinkle Blue 5:1 |
| FOLK ART | ☐ * White + Porcelain Blue 6:1 |
| JO SONJA | ☐ * White + Ultra Blue Deep 8:1 |
| LIQUITEX | ☐ * White + Light Blue Violet 5:1 |

**NOTES**

### TCS #BL-3-3-5

| ACCENT | ☐ * Sapphire + White 1:1 |
| AMERICANA | ☐ * Sapphire + White 1:1 |
| CERAMCOAT | ☐ * Liberty Blue + White 1:1 |
| FOLK ART | ☐ French Blue   S: Midnight   H: Icy White |
| JO SONJA | ☐ * Sapphire + White 1:1 |
| LIQUITEX | ☐ * White + Swedish Blue + French Gray/Blue 2:1:1 |

**NOTES**

### TCS #BL-3-8-8

| ACCENT | ☐ * Soldier Blue + Payne's Grey 5:1 |
| AMERICANA | ☐ * Uniform Blue + Charcoal Grey 5:1 |
| CERAMCOAT | ☐ Heritage Blue   S: Charcoal   H: Tide Pool |
| FOLK ART | ☐ * Heartland Blue + Charcoal Grey 4:1 |
| JO SONJA | ☐ * French Blue + Plum Pink 4:1 |
| LIQUITEX | ☐ * Twilight + Neutral Gray 5:1 |

**NOTES**

### TCS #BL-4-2-6

| ACCENT | ☐ * Ultra Blue Deep + White 4:1 |
| AMERICANA | ☐ Sapphire   S: True Blue   H: Sapphire + White 1:1 |
| CERAMCOAT | ☐ * Ultra Blue + Pthalo Blue 3:1 |
| FOLK ART | ☐ * True Blue + Light Blue 4:1 |
| JO SONJA | ☐ * Ultra Blue Deep + White 4:1 |
| LIQUITEX | ☐ * Swedish Blue + Ultramarine 3:1 |

**NOTES**

| BRAND | COLOR | | COLOR |
|---|---|---|---|

## TCS #BL-4-5-5

| | |
|---|---|
| ACCENT | ☐ * Paradise Blue + Royal Blue 3:1 |
| AMERICANA | ☐ * Sapphire + Blue Violet 4:1 |
| CERAMCOAT | ☐ Denim Blue <br> S: Navy Blue    H: Blue Mist |
| FOLK ART | ☐ Paisley Blue (D) |
| JO SONJA | ☐ * Sapphire + Ultra Blue 1:1 |
| LIQUITEX | ☐ * Brilliant Blue Purple + White 1:1 |

**NOTES**

## TCS #BL-4-5-6

| | |
|---|---|
| ACCENT | ☐ Sapphire (ABC) <br> S: Royal Blue    H: Sapphire + White Wash 1:1 |
| AMERICANA | ☐ * Sapphire + Williamsburg Blue 4:1 |
| CERAMCOAT | ☐ Liberty Blue <br> S: Nightfall Blue    H: Lavender Lace |
| FOLK ART | ☐ Paisley Blue <br> S: Heartland Blue    H: Light Blue |
| JO SONJA | ☐ Sapphire |
| LIQUITEX | ☐ * Swedish Blue + French Gray/Blue 1:1 |

**NOTES**

## TCS #BL-4-8-4

| | |
|---|---|
| ACCENT | ☐ Blue Smoke <br> S: Stoneware Blue    H: Indian Sky |
| AMERICANA | ☐ Light French Blue <br> S: French Grey/Blue    H: Ice Blue |
| CERAMCOAT | ☐ Dolphin Grey <br> S: Adriatic Blue    H: Lavender Lace |
| FOLK ART | ☐ Amish Blue (D) |
| JO SONJA | ☐ * White + French Blue 3:1 |
| LIQUITEX | ☐ * White + French Gray/Blue 2:1 |

**NOTES**

## TCS #BL-4-8-5

| | |
|---|---|
| ACCENT | ☐ * Light Stoneware Blue + April Showers (T) |
| AMERICANA | ☐ * White + French Grey/Blue 2:1 |
| CERAMCOAT | ☐ Dolphin Grey (L) |
| FOLK ART | ☐ Amish Blue <br> S: Denim Blue    H: Lavender Sachet |
| JO SONJA | ☐ * White + French Blue 2:1 |
| LIQUITEX | ☐ * White + French Gray/Blue 1:1 |

**NOTES**

## TCS #BL-4-8-8

| | |
|---|---|
| ACCENT | ☐ * Soldier Blue + Payne's Grey 4:1 |
| AMERICANA | ☐ * Uniform Blue + Charcoal Grey 3:1 |
| CERAMCOAT | ☐ Adriatic Blue <br> S: Black    H: Dolphin Grey |
| FOLK ART | ☐ Slate Blue <br> S: Indigo    H: Lavender Sachet |
| JO SONJA | ☐ * French Blue + Sapphire 2:1 |
| LIQUITEX | ☐ * French Gray/Blue + Payne's Gray 3:1 |

**NOTES**

## TCS #BL-4-9-2

| | |
|---|---|
| ACCENT | ☐ * April Showers + Light Stoneware 3:1 |
| AMERICANA | ☐ Ice Blue <br> S: Blue/Grey Mist    H: Ice Blue + White 1:1 |
| CERAMCOAT | ☐ * Blue Wisp + Drizzle Grey 1:1 |
| FOLK ART | ☐ * Teal Blue + Dove Gray 1:1 |
| JO SONJA | ☐ * Warm White + Payne's Grey 12:1 |
| LIQUITEX | ☐ * Soft White + Payne's Gray 12:1 |

**NOTES**

# BRAND          COLOR                                          COLOR

## T C S  # B L - 4 - 9 - 5

ACCENT
- ☐ * April Showers + Chesapeake Blue 1:1

AMERICANA
- ☐ Blue/Grey Mist
  S: Payne's Grey    H: Ice Blue

CERAMCOAT
- ☐ * Bridgeport + Adriatic (T)

FOLK ART
- ☐ Blue Gray Dust (Disc.) or * Amish Blue + Medium Gray 4:1

JO SONJA
- ☐ * Nimbus Gray + Storm Blue + Gold Oxide 1:T:T

LIQUITEX
- ☐ * Baltic Blue + Unbleached Titanium 1:1

**NOTES**

## T C S  # B L - 4 - 9 - 8

ACCENT
- ☐ * Soldier Blue + Black 4:1

AMERICANA
- ☐ * French Grey/Blue + Black 4:1

CERAMCOAT
- ☐ Fjord Blue
  S: Payne's Grey    H: Tide Pool

FOLK ART
- ☐ Oxford Blue (Disc.) or * Amish Blue + Charcoal 4:1

JO SONJA
- ☐ * French Blue + Black 4:1

LIQUITEX
- ☐ * French Gray/Blue + Black 4:1

**NOTES**

## T C S  # B L - 4 - 9 - 9

ACCENT
- ☐ * Liberty Blue + Payne's Gray (T)

AMERICANA
- ☐ * Prussian Blue + Black (T)

CERAMCOAT
- ☐ Dark Night Blue
  S: Black    H: Dolphin Gray

FOLK ART
- ☐ Payne's Gray (PP)

JO SONJA
- ☐ Storm Blue

LIQUITEX
- ☐ * French Gray/Blue + Payne's Gray 6:1

**NOTES**

## T C S  # B L - 5 - 1 - 1

ACCENT
- ☐ * White + April Showers 12:1

AMERICANA
- ☐ * White + Dove Grey 10:1

CERAMCOAT
- ☐ * White + Drizzle Grey 12:1

FOLK ART
- ☐ Winter White
  S: Baby Blue    H: None
- ☐ * White + Nimbus Grey (T)

LIQUITEX
- ☐ * White + Neutral Gray (T)

**NOTES**

## T C S  # B L - 5 - 1 - 5

ACCENT
- ☐ Ultramarine Blue
  S: Windsor Blue    H: Larkspur Blue

AMERICANA
- ☐ Primary Blue
  S: Deep Midnight    H: Baby Blue

CERAMCOAT
- ☐ Phthalo Blue
  S: Midnight    H: Blue Jay

FOLK ART
- ☐ True Blue
  S: Midnight    H: French Blue

JO SONJA
- ☐ Ultramarine Blue

LIQUITEX
- ☐ Phthalo Blue

**NOTES**

## T C S  # B L - 5 - 1 - 6

ACCENT
- ☐ Pure Blue    S: Pure Blue + Black 2:1
  H: Pure Blue + White Wash (T)

AMERICANA
- ☐ True Blue
  S: Prussian Blue    H: True Blue + White 1:1

CERAMCOAT
- ☐ * Ultra Blue + Navy 1:1

FOLK ART
- ☐ Ultramarine Blue (PP)

JO SONJA
- ☐ Ultramarine Blue Deep

LIQUITEX
- ☐ Ultramarine Blue

**NOTES**

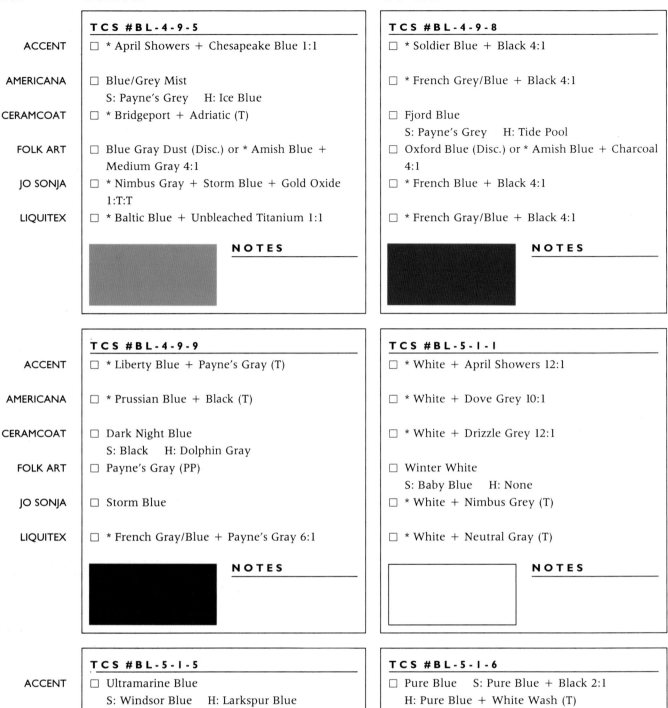

| BRAND | COLOR | COLOR |
|---|---|---|

# BRAND COLOR COLOR

## TCS #BL-5-1-9

| BRAND | |
|---|---|
| ACCENT | ☐ Midnight Blue<br>S: Black    H: Monet Blue |
| AMERICANA | ☐ * Prussian Blue + Ultra Blue Deep 2:1 |
| CERAMCOAT | ☐ * Midnight Blue + Pthalo Blue 2:1 |
| FOLK ART | ☐ Navy Blue<br>S: Licorice    H: Settler's Blue |
| JO SONJA | ☐ * Storm Blue + Ultra Blue 2:1 |
| LIQUITEX | ☐ * Navy + Ultramarine Blue 2:1 |

NOTES

## TCS #BL-5-2-2

| BRAND | |
|---|---|
| ACCENT | ☐ * White + Ultramarine Blue Deep 4:1 |
| AMERICANA | ☐ Baby Blue<br>S: Sapphire    H: Baby Blue + White 1:1 |
| CERAMCOAT | ☐ Blue Heaven<br>S: Copen Blue    H: Blue Mist |
| FOLK ART | ☐ Light Blue<br>S: Blueberry Pie    H: Paisley Blue |
| JO SONJA | ☐ * White + Sapphire 6:1 |
| LIQUITEX | ☐ * White + Phthalo Blue + Neutral Gray 6:1:1 |

NOTES

## TCS #BL-5-2-4

| BRAND | |
|---|---|
| ACCENT | ☐ * Clear Blue + White 1:1 |
| AMERICANA | ☐ * True Blue + White 1:1 |
| CERAMCOAT | ☐ Blue Jay<br>S: Manganese Blue    H: Blue Mist |
| FOLK ART | ☐ * Blue Ribbon + White 1:1 |
| JO SONJA | ☐ * White + Pthalo Blue 3:1 |
| LIQUITEX | ☐ * White + Phthalo Blue 3:1 |

NOTES

## TCS #BL-5-2-5

| BRAND | |
|---|---|
| ACCENT | ☐ * Ultramarine Blue + Pure Blue 1:1 |
| AMERICANA | ☐ Ultra Blue Deep (D) |
| CERAMCOAT | ☐ Opaque Blue<br>S: Payne's Grey    H: Blue Jay |
| FOLK ART | ☐ Brilliant Blue<br>S: Midnight    H: Light Periwinkle |
| JO SONJA | ☐ * Pthalo Blue + Ultramarine Blue 1:1 |
| LIQUITEX | ☐ * Phthalo Blue + Ultramarine 1:1 |

NOTES

## TCS #BL-5-2-6

| BRAND | |
|---|---|
| ACCENT | ☐ * Ultramarine Blue + Windsor Blue 1:1 |
| AMERICANA | ☐ Ultra Blue Deep<br>S: Payne's Grey    H: Sapphire |
| CERAMCOAT | ☐ Navy Blue<br>S: Navy + Black 3:1    H: Blue Jay |
| FOLK ART | ☐ * Ultramarine + Midnight 3:1 |
| JO SONJA | ☐ Pthalo Blue |
| LIQUITEX | ☐ Prussian Blue |

NOTES

## TCS #BL-5-2-7

| BRAND | |
|---|---|
| ACCENT | ☐ * Windsor Blue + Liberty Blue 1:1 |
| AMERICANA | ☐ Prussian Blue<br>S: Payne's Grey    H: Sapphire |
| CERAMCOAT | ☐ * Navy Blue + Midnight 4:1 |
| FOLK ART | ☐ Prussian Blue (PP) |
| JO SONJA | ☐ Prussian Blue Hue |
| LIQUITEX | ☐ Navy |

NOTES

## TCS #BL-5-2-8

|  |  |
|---|---|
| ACCENT | ☐ Liberty Blue<br>S: Black    H: Stoneware Blue |
| AMERICANA | ☐ Deep Midnight Blue<br>S: Payne's Grey    H: Uniform Blue |
| CERAMCOAT | ☐ Midnight Blue<br>S: Black    H: Bonnie Blue |
| FOLK ART | ☐ Indigo<br>S: Licorice    H: Prussian Blue |
| JO SONJA | ☐ Prussian Blue Hue (L) |
| LIQUITEX | ☐ * Phthalo Blue + Payne's Gray 1:1 |

**NOTES**

## TCS #BL-5-2-9

|  |  |
|---|---|
| ACCENT | ☐ Payne's Grey (ABC)<br>S: Black    H: Payne's Grey + April Showers 1:1 |
| AMERICANA | ☐ Payne's Grey<br>S: Lamp (Ebony) Black    H: Uniform Blue |
| CERAMCOAT | ☐ Payne's Grey<br>S: Black    H: Dolphin Grey |
| FOLK ART | ☐ * Payne's Gray + Prussian Blue (T) |
| JO SONJA | ☐ Payne's Grey |
| LIQUITEX | ☐ Payne's Gray |

**NOTES**

## TCS #BL-5-5-3

|  |  |
|---|---|
| ACCENT | ☐ * Light Stoneware + Soft Blue + White 1:1:1 |
| AMERICANA | ☐ Winter Blue<br>S: Sapphire    H: Blue Chiffon |
| CERAMCOAT | ☐ Wedgewood Blue<br>S: Manganese Blue    H: Blue Mist |
| FOLK ART | ☐ * Bluebell + White 1:1 |
| JO SONJA | ☐ * Smoked Pearl + Sapphire (T) |
| LIQUITEX | ☐ * White + French Gray/Blue 3:1 |

**NOTES**

## TCS #BL-5-5-5

|  |  |
|---|---|
| ACCENT | ☐ * Light Stoneware + Larkspur 1:1 |
| AMERICANA | ☐ * Williamsburg Blue + White (T) |
| CERAMCOAT | ☐ Bonnie Blue<br>S: Midnight Blue    H: Blue Mist |
| FOLK ART | ☐ Bluebell<br>S: Bavarian Blue    H: Icy White |
| JO SONJA | ☐ * Nimbus Grey + Sapphire 2:1 |
| LIQUITEX | ☐ * Cerulean Blue Hue + White + French Gray/<br>Blue 1:1:T |

**NOTES**

## TCS #BL-5-5-6

|  |  |
|---|---|
| ACCENT | ☐ * Soft Blue + Stoneware Blue 1:1 |
| AMERICANA | ☐ * Blue/Grey Mist + Victorian Blue 1:1 |
| CERAMCOAT | ☐ * Blue Haze + Cape Cod Blue 1:1 |
| FOLK ART | ☐ Prairie Blue<br>S: Indigo    H: Icy White |
| JO SONJA | ☐ * Warm White + Sapphire + Burnt Sienna<br>6:2:1 |
| LIQUITEX | ☐ * French Gray/Blue + Baltic Blue 3:1 |

**NOTES**

## TCS #BL-5-7-2

|  |  |
|---|---|
| ACCENT | ☐ * Light Stoneware + White 2:1 |
| AMERICANA | ☐ * White + French Grey/Blue 5:1 |
| CERAMCOAT | ☐ Chambray Blue<br>S: Tide Pool Blue    H: White |
| FOLK ART | ☐ * Porcelain Blue + White 2:1 |
| JO SONJA | ☐ * White + French Blue 3:1 |
| LIQUITEX | ☐ * White + French Gray/Blue 3:1 |

**NOTES**

## BRAND        COLOR        COLOR

### TCS #BL-5-7-3

| | |
|---|---|
| ACCENT | ☐ Light Stoneware Blue<br>S: Stoneware Blue    H: Indian Sky |
| AMERICANA | ☐ * French Grey/Blue + White 2:1 |
| CERAMCOAT | ☐ Tide Pool Blue<br>S: Heritage Blue    H: Lavender Lace |
| FOLK ART | ☐ Porcelain Blue<br>S: Denim Blue    H: White |
| JO SONJA | ☐ * French Blue + White 2:1 |
| LIQUITEX | ☐ * French Gray/Blue + White 2:1 |

**NOTES**

### TCS #BL-5-7-4

| | |
|---|---|
| ACCENT | ☐ Stoneware Blue<br>S: Soldier Blue    H: Light Stoneware Blue |
| AMERICANA | ☐ French Grey/Blue<br>S: Uniform Blue    H: Country Blue |
| CERAMCOAT | ☐ Cape Cod Blue<br>S: Nightfall    H: Lavender Lace |
| FOLK ART | ☐ Settler's Blue<br>S: Denim Blue    H: Icy White |
| JO SONJA | ☐ * White + French Blue 2:1 |
| LIQUITEX | ☐ French Gray/Blue |

**NOTES**

### TCS #BL-5-7-5

| | |
|---|---|
| ACCENT | ☐ Stoneware Blue (L) |
| AMERICANA | ☐ Williamsburg Blue<br>S: Uniform Blue    H: Country Blue |
| CERAMCOAT | ☐ Williamsburg Blue<br>S: Nightfall Blue    H: Chambray Blue |
| FOLK ART | ☐ Settler's Blue (L) |
| JO SONJA | ☐ * Warm White + Prussian Blue + Ultra Blue +<br>Black 36:2:1:1 |
| LIQUITEX | ☐ French Gray/Blue (L) |

**NOTES**

### TCS #BL-5-7-7

| | |
|---|---|
| ACCENT | ☐ * Soldier Blue + Windsor Blue 1:1 |
| AMERICANA | ☐ Uniform Blue<br>S: Deep Midnight Blue    H: French Grey/Blue |
| CERAMCOAT | ☐ * Cape Cod + Prussian Blue 3:1 |
| FOLK ART | ☐ Heartland Blue<br>S: Licorice    H: Paisley Blue |
| JO SONJA | ☐ French Blue (D) |
| LIQUITEX | ☐ * French Gray/Blue + Twilight 1:1 |

**NOTES**

### TCS #BL-5-7-8

| | |
|---|---|
| ACCENT | ☐ Soldier Blue<br>S: Payne's Grey (ABC)    H: Stoneware Blue |
| AMERICANA | ☐ Uniform Blue (L) |
| CERAMCOAT | ☐ Nightfall Blue<br>S: Nightfall Blue + Black 3:1    H: Tide Pool |
| FOLK ART | ☐ Denim Blue<br>S: Licorice    H: White |
| JO SONJA | ☐ French Blue |
| LIQUITEX | ☐ * French Gray/Blue + Payne's Gray 4:1 |

**NOTES**

### TCS #BL-6-1-1

| | |
|---|---|
| ACCENT | ☐ * White + Monet Blue 7:1 |
| AMERICANA | ☐ * White + Baby Blue 3:1 |
| CERAMCOAT | ☐ * Blue Mist + White 1:1 |
| FOLK ART | ☐ Icy White<br>S: Any cool color    H: White |
| JO SONJA | ☐ * White + Pthalo Blue 12:1 |
| LIQUITEX | ☐ * White + Phthalo Blue 12:1 |

**NOTES**

## BRAND          COLOR                                    COLOR

### TCS #BL-6-1-2

| ACCENT | ☐ * White + Monet Blue 4:1 |
| AMERICANA | ☐ Blue Chiffon |
| | S: Winter Blue    H: White |
| CERAMCOAT | ☐ Blue Mist |
| | S: Blue Danube    H: White |
| FOLK ART | ☐ * White + Light Blue 3:1 |
| JO SONJA | ☐ * White + Pthalo Blue 8:1 |
| LIQUITEX | ☐ * White + Phthalo Blue 8:1 |

**NOTES**

### TCS #BL-6-1-3

| ACCENT | ☐ * White + Pure Blue 4:1 |
| AMERICANA | ☐ * White + True Blue 4:1 |
| CERAMCOAT | ☐ Blue Danube |
| | S: Copen Blue    H: Blue Mist |
| FOLK ART | ☐ * Light Blue + Aqua Bright (T) |
| JO SONJA | ☐ * White + Cobalt Blue Hue 3:1 |
| LIQUITEX | ☐ * White + Phthalo Blue 4:1 |

**NOTES**

### TCS #BL-6-1-4

| ACCENT | ☐ * Pure Blue + Paradise Blue 10:1 |
| AMERICANA | ☐ * True Blue + Desert Turquoise 10:1 |
| CERAMCOAT | ☐ * Ultra Blue + Azure Blue 5:1 |
| FOLK ART | ☐ Cerulean Blue Hue (PP) |
| JO SONJA | ☐ * Ultramarine Blue + Aqua 8:1 |
| LIQUITEX | ☐ Cerulean Blue |

**NOTES**

### TCS #BL-6-1-5

| ACCENT | ☐ Clear Blue |
| | S: Ultramarine Blue    H: Paradise Blue |
| AMERICANA | ☐ * True Blue + White 1:1 |
| CERAMCOAT | ☐ Ocean Reef Blue |
| | S: Navy Blue    H: Blue Danube |
| FOLK ART | ☐ * Cerulean Blue Hue + Ultramarine Blue 3:1 |
| JO SONJA | ☐ * Ultramarine Blue + White 1:1 |
| LIQUITEX | ☐ * Swedish Blue + White 3:1 |

**NOTES**

### TCS #BL-6-1-6

| ACCENT | ☐ Ultramarine Blue Deep (ABC) |
| | S: Windsor Blue    H: Clear Blue |
| AMERICANA | ☐ * True Blue + Victorian Blue (T) |
| CERAMCOAT | ☐ Copen Blue |
| | S: Opaque Blue    H: Blue Danube |
| FOLK ART | ☐ Ultramarine |
| | S: Midnight    H: Light Blue |
| JO SONJA | ☐ * Cobalt Blue Hue + Ultramarine Blue 1:1 |
| LIQUITEX | ☐ Cerulean Blue Hue |

**NOTES**

### TCS #BL-6-1-8

| ACCENT | ☐ * Ultramarine Blue Deep + True Blue 1:1 |
| AMERICANA | ☐ * Ultra Blue Deep + Navy 3:1 |
| CERAMCOAT | ☐ * Pthalo Blue + Navy 3:1 |
| FOLK ART | ☐ Cobalt Blue (PP) |
| JO SONJA | ☐ Cobalt Blue Hue |
| LIQUITEX | ☐ Cobalt Blue |

**NOTES**

# BRAND          COLOR                                          COLOR

### TCS #BL-7-2-8

ACCENT
- ☐ Windsor Blue
  S: Payne's Grey (ABC)   H: Clear Blue

AMERICANA
- ☐ Midnite Blue
  S: Payne's Grey   H: Sapphire

CERAMCOAT
- ☐ Manganese Blue
  S: Black   H: Wedgewood Blue

FOLK ART
- ☐ * Thunder Blue + Ultramarine 1:1

JO SONJA
- ☐ * Sapphire + Storm Blue 1:1

LIQUITEX
- ☐ * Phthalo Blue + Cerulean Blue 2:1

**NOTES**

### TCS #BL-7-2-9

- ☐ * Windsor Blue + Deep Forest Green (T)

- ☐ Navy Blue
  S: Payne's Grey   H: Sapphire
- ☐ Prussian Blue
  S: Payne's Grey   H: Salem Blue

- ☐ * Cobalt Blue + Viridian 4:1

- ☐ * Pthalo Blue + Pthalo Green 4:1

- ☐ * Cobalt Blue + Phthalo Green 3:1

**NOTES**

### TCS #BL-7-4-7

ACCENT
- ☐ * Nevada Turquoise + Windsor Blue 2:1

AMERICANA
- ☐ * Blueberry + Neutral Grey 2:1

CERAMCOAT
- ☐ * Avalon Blue + Pthalo Blue 2:1

FOLK ART
- ☐ Blueberry Pie
  S: Licorice   H: Porcelain Blue

JO SONJA
- ☐ * Sapphire + Storm Blue 3:1

LIQUITEX
- ☐ * French Gray/Blue + Cerulean Blue 2:1

**NOTES**

### TCS #BL-7-4-8

- ☐ * Windsor Blue + White 6:1

- ☐ Wedgewood Blue
  S: Deep Midnight Blue   H: Sapphire
- ☐ Blueberry
  S: Midnight Blue   H: Ocean Reef Blue
- ☐ * Thunder Blue + White 6:1

- ☐ * Prussian Blue + White 4:1

- ☐ * Cobalt Blue + White 5:1

**NOTES**

### TCS #BL-7-4-9

ACCENT
- ☐ * Windsor Blue + Liberty Blue 2:1

AMERICANA
- ☐ Blueberry
  S: Deep Midnight Blue   H: Sapphire

CERAMCOAT
- ☐ * Navy Blue + Black (T)

FOLK ART
- ☐ Thunder Blue
  S: Licorice   H: Light Blue

JO SONJA
- ☐ * Sapphire + Storm Blue 1:1

LIQUITEX
- ☐ * Ultra Blue + Burnt Umber (T)

**NOTES**

### TCS: BG-1-3-2

- ☐ * Soft Blue + White 1:1

- ☐ * Salem Blue + Buttermilk 2:1

- ☐ Salem Blue
  S: Blue Haze   H: Blue Mist
- ☐ * Vacation Blue + Buttercream 1:1

- ☐ * Colony Blue + Warm White 1:1

- ☐ * Cerulean Blue + Parchment 1:1

**NOTES**

## BRAND COLOR COLOR

### TCS #BG-1-3-3

ACCENT    □ * Paradise Blue + Soft Blue 5:1

AMERICANA    □ Salem Blue
     S: Desert Turquoise    H: Sea Aqua

CERAMCOAT    □ Salem Blue (L)

FOLK ART    □ * White + Azure Blue 4:1

JO SONJA    □ * White + Colony Blue 4:1

LIQUITEX    □ * Permanent Light Blue + Baltic Green (T)

**NOTES**

### TCS #BG-1-3-4

ACCENT    □ Soft Blue    S: Larkspur Blue
     H: Soft Blue + White Wash 1:1

AMERICANA    □ * Salem Blue + Colonial Green (T)

CERAMCOAT    □ * Salem Blue + Blue Haze 1:1

FOLK ART    □ * Blue Bell + Summer Sky 1:1

JO SONJA    □ * Smoked Pearl + Sapphire 6:1

LIQUITEX    □ * Permanent Light Blue + Baltic Green 2:1

**NOTES**

### TCS #BG-1-3-7

ACCENT    □ Larkspur Blue    S: Windsor Blue
     H: Larkspur + White Wash 1:1

AMERICANA    □ * Victorian Blue + Salem Blue (T)

CERAMCOAT    □ * Avalon + Copen Blue 1:1

FOLK ART    □ * Azure Blue + Blue Ribbon (T)

JO SONJA    □ * Colony Blue + Sapphire 3:1

LIQUITEX    □ * Swedish Blue + White 2:1

**NOTES**

### TCS #BG-1-3-8

ACCENT    □ * Windsor Blue + White (T)

AMERICANA    □ Victorian Blue    S: Midnight Blue
     H: Victorian Blue + White 1:1

CERAMCOAT    □ * Manganese Blue + White 1:1

FOLK ART    □ Blue Ribbon
     S: Thunder Blue    H: Light Blue

JO SONJA    □ * Sapphire + French Blue (T)

LIQUITEX    □ Swedish Blue

**NOTES**

### TCS #BG-1-4-2

ACCENT    □ * Soft Blue + Off White 1:1

AMERICANA    □ * Salem Blue + Ice Blue 3:1

CERAMCOAT    □ Ocean Mist Blue
     S: Colonial Blue    H: Blue Mist

FOLK ART    □ * Teal Blue + Bluebonnet 4:1

JO SONJA    □ * Warm White + Storm Blue 15:1

LIQUITEX    □ * Soft White + Navy + Neutral Gray 10:1:1

**NOTES**

### TCS #BG-1-7-2

ACCENT    □ * Soft Blue + April Showers 1:1

AMERICANA    □ Blue Mist
     S: Colonial Green    H: Ice Blue

CERAMCOAT    □ Blue Wisp
     S: Blue Haze    H: Light Sage

FOLK ART    □ Teal Blue
     S: Bluebonnet    H: White

JO SONJA    □ * Smoked Pearl + Sapphire (T)

LIQUITEX    □ * Soft White + Baltic Blue 5:1

**NOTES**

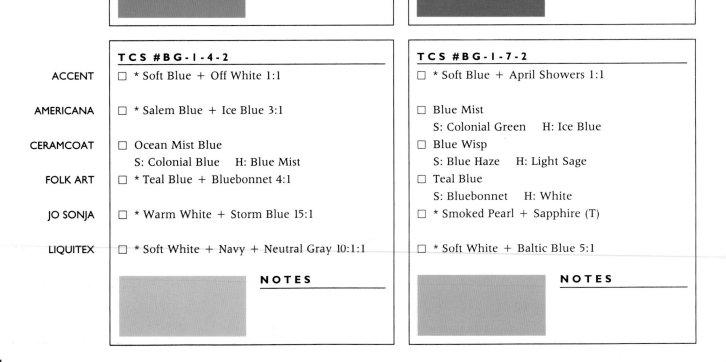

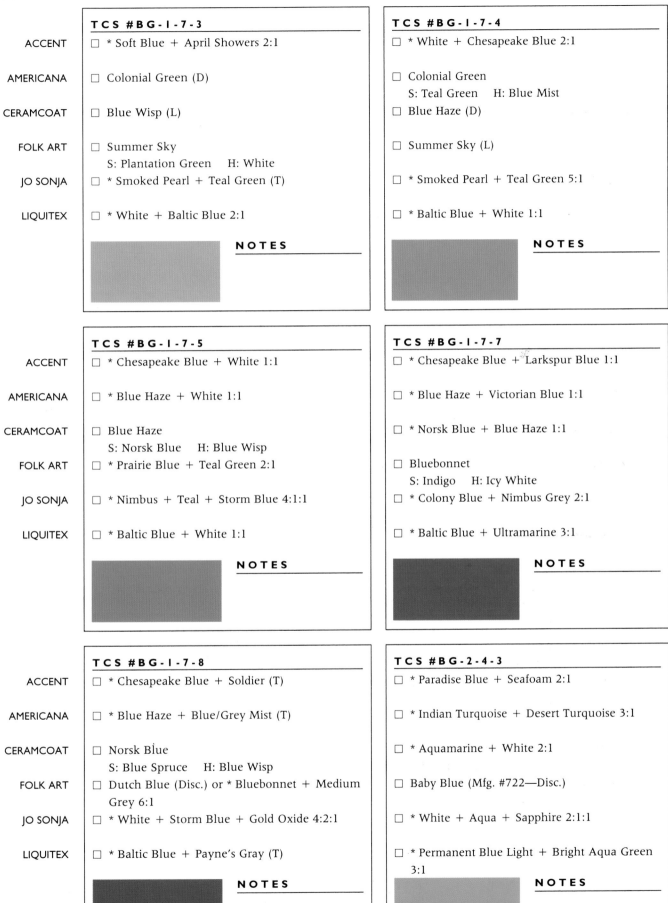

### TCS #BG-1-7-3

| ACCENT | ☐ * Soft Blue + April Showers 2:1 |
|---|---|
| AMERICANA | ☐ Colonial Green (D) |
| CERAMCOAT | ☐ Blue Wisp (L) |
| FOLK ART | ☐ Summer Sky<br>S: Plantation Green    H: White |
| JO SONJA | ☐ * Smoked Pearl + Teal Green (T) |
| LIQUITEX | ☐ * White + Baltic Blue 2:1 |

**NOTES**

### TCS #BG-1-7-4

| ACCENT | ☐ * White + Chesapeake Blue 2:1 |
|---|---|
| AMERICANA | ☐ Colonial Green<br>S: Teal Green    H: Blue Mist |
| CERAMCOAT | ☐ Blue Haze (D) |
| FOLK ART | ☐ Summer Sky (L) |
| JO SONJA | ☐ * Smoked Pearl + Teal Green 5:1 |
| LIQUITEX | ☐ * Baltic Blue + White 1:1 |

**NOTES**

### TCS #BG-1-7-5

| ACCENT | ☐ * Chesapeake Blue + White 1:1 |
|---|---|
| AMERICANA | ☐ * Blue Haze + White 1:1 |
| CERAMCOAT | ☐ Blue Haze<br>S: Norsk Blue    H: Blue Wisp |
| FOLK ART | ☐ * Prairie Blue + Teal Green 2:1 |
| JO SONJA | ☐ * Nimbus + Teal + Storm Blue 4:1:1 |
| LIQUITEX | ☐ * Baltic Blue + White 1:1 |

**NOTES**

### TCS #BG-1-7-7

| ACCENT | ☐ * Chesapeake Blue + Larkspur Blue 1:1 |
|---|---|
| AMERICANA | ☐ * Blue Haze + Victorian Blue 1:1 |
| CERAMCOAT | ☐ * Norsk Blue + Blue Haze 1:1 |
| FOLK ART | ☐ Bluebonnet<br>S: Indigo    H: Icy White |
| JO SONJA | ☐ * Colony Blue + Nimbus Grey 2:1 |
| LIQUITEX | ☐ * Baltic Blue + Ultramarine 3:1 |

**NOTES**

### TCS #BG-1-7-8

| ACCENT | ☐ * Chesapeake Blue + Soldier (T) |
|---|---|
| AMERICANA | ☐ * Blue Haze + Blue/Grey Mist (T) |
| CERAMCOAT | ☐ Norsk Blue<br>S: Blue Spruce    H: Blue Wisp |
| FOLK ART | ☐ Dutch Blue (Disc.) or * Bluebonnet + Medium Grey 6:1 |
| JO SONJA | ☐ * White + Storm Blue + Gold Oxide 4:2:1 |
| LIQUITEX | ☐ * Baltic Blue + Payne's Gray (T) |

**NOTES**

### TCS #BG-2-4-3

| ACCENT | ☐ * Paradise Blue + Seafoam 2:1 |
|---|---|
| AMERICANA | ☐ * Indian Turquoise + Desert Turquoise 3:1 |
| CERAMCOAT | ☐ * Aquamarine + White 2:1 |
| FOLK ART | ☐ Baby Blue (Mfg. #722—Disc.) |
| JO SONJA | ☐ * White + Aqua + Sapphire 2:1:1 |
| LIQUITEX | ☐ * Permanent Blue Light + Bright Aqua Green 3:1 |

**NOTES**

COLOR  COLOR

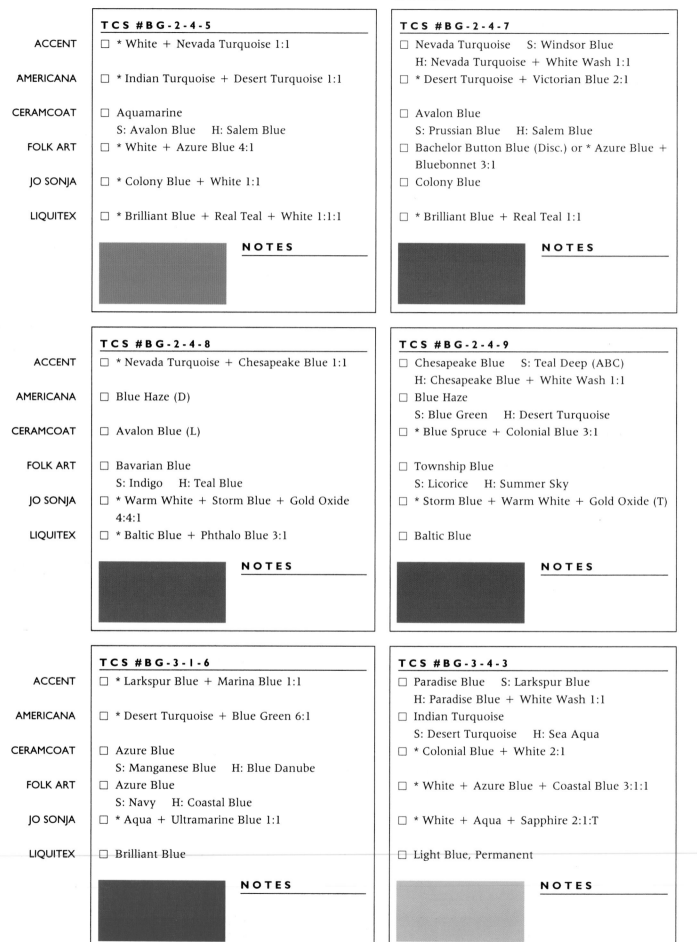

### TCS #BG-2-4-5

| | |
|---|---|
| ACCENT | □ * White + Nevada Turquoise 1:1 |
| AMERICANA | □ * Indian Turquoise + Desert Turquoise 1:1 |
| CERAMCOAT | □ Aquamarine<br>S: Avalon Blue   H: Salem Blue |
| FOLK ART | □ * White + Azure Blue 4:1 |
| JO SONJA | □ * Colony Blue + White 1:1 |
| LIQUITEX | □ * Brilliant Blue + Real Teal + White 1:1:1 |

NOTES

### TCS #BG-2-4-7

| | |
|---|---|
| ACCENT | □ Nevada Turquoise   S: Windsor Blue<br>H: Nevada Turquoise + White Wash 1:1 |
| AMERICANA | □ * Desert Turquoise + Victorian Blue 2:1 |
| CERAMCOAT | □ Avalon Blue<br>S: Prussian Blue   H: Salem Blue |
| FOLK ART | □ Bachelor Button Blue (Disc.) or * Azure Blue +<br>Bluebonnet 3:1 |
| JO SONJA | □ Colony Blue |
| LIQUITEX | □ * Brilliant Blue + Real Teal 1:1 |

NOTES

### TCS #BG-2-4-8

| | |
|---|---|
| ACCENT | □ * Nevada Turquoise + Chesapeake Blue 1:1 |
| AMERICANA | □ Blue Haze (D) |
| CERAMCOAT | □ Avalon Blue (L) |
| FOLK ART | □ Bavarian Blue<br>S: Indigo   H: Teal Blue |
| JO SONJA | □ * Warm White + Storm Blue + Gold Oxide<br>4:4:1 |
| LIQUITEX | □ * Baltic Blue + Phthalo Blue 3:1 |

NOTES

### TCS #BG-2-4-9

| | |
|---|---|
| ACCENT | □ Chesapeake Blue   S: Teal Deep (ABC)<br>H: Chesapeake Blue + White Wash 1:1 |
| AMERICANA | □ Blue Haze<br>S: Blue Green   H: Desert Turquoise |
| CERAMCOAT | □ * Blue Spruce + Colonial Blue 3:1 |
| FOLK ART | □ Township Blue<br>S: Licorice   H: Summer Sky |
| JO SONJA | □ * Storm Blue + Warm White + Gold Oxide (T) |
| LIQUITEX | □ Baltic Blue |

NOTES

### TCS #BG-3-1-6

| | |
|---|---|
| ACCENT | □ * Larkspur Blue + Marina Blue 1:1 |
| AMERICANA | □ * Desert Turquoise + Blue Green 6:1 |
| CERAMCOAT | □ Azure Blue<br>S: Manganese Blue   H: Blue Danube |
| FOLK ART | □ Azure Blue<br>S: Navy   H: Coastal Blue |
| JO SONJA | □ * Aqua + Ultramarine Blue 1:1 |
| LIQUITEX | □ Brilliant Blue |

NOTES

### TCS #BG-3-4-3

| | |
|---|---|
| ACCENT | □ Paradise Blue   S: Larkspur Blue<br>H: Paradise Blue + White Wash 1:1 |
| AMERICANA | □ Indian Turquoise<br>S: Desert Turquoise   H: Sea Aqua |
| CERAMCOAT | □ * Colonial Blue + White 2:1 |
| FOLK ART | □ * White + Azure Blue + Coastal Blue 3:1:1 |
| JO SONJA | □ * White + Aqua + Sapphire 2:1:T |
| LIQUITEX | □ Light Blue, Permanent |

NOTES

## BRAND   COLOR                                COLOR

### TCS #BG-3-4-5

ACCENT
☐ * Paradise Blue + Larkspur 3:1

AMERICANA
☐ * Indian Turquoise + Victorian Blue (T)

CERAMCOAT
☐ * Blue Heaven + Colonial Blue 1:1

FOLK ART
☐ Coastal Blue
   S: Thunder Blue    H: White

JO SONJA
☐ * White + Aqua + Sapphire 2:1:1

LIQUITEX
☐ Permanent Light Blue (L)

**NOTES**

### TCS #BG-4-1-2

ACCENT
☐ * Light Seafoam Green + Marina Blue 4:1

AMERICANA
☐ * Sea Aqua + White + Bluegrass 1:1:T

CERAMCOAT
☐ Tropic Bay Blue
   S: Emerald Green    H: Tropic Bay + White 1:1
☐ * Aqua Bright + White 1:1

JO SONJA
☐ * White + Aqua 4:1

LIQUITEX
☐ * Bright Aqua Green + White 1:1

**NOTES**

### TCS #BG-4-1-3

ACCENT
☐ * Light Seafoam Green + Marina Blue 2:1

AMERICANA
☐ * Sea Aqua + Bluegrass 5:1

CERAMCOAT
☐ * Tropic Bay Blue + Turquoise 1:1

FOLK ART
☐ Patina
   S: Turquoise    H: White

JO SONJA
☐ * White + Aqua + Yellow Light 3:2:1

LIQUITEX
☐ * Bright Aqua + White 2:1

**NOTES**

### TCS #BG-4-1-4

ACCENT
☐ * Seafoam Green + Marina Blue 1:1

AMERICANA
☐ * Sea Aqua + Bluegrass 3:1

CERAMCOAT
☐ Turquoise
   S: Emerald Green    H: Turquoise + White 1:1
☐ Aqua Bright
   S: Emerald Isle    H: White

JO SONJA
☐ * Aqua + Yellow Lt. + White 1:1:1

☐ Bright Aqua Green

**NOTES**

### TCS #BG-4-1-5

ACCENT
☐ * Marina Blue + Pthalo Green 6:1

AMERICANA
☐ * Desert Turquoise + Bluegrass Green 1:1

CERAMCOAT
☐ Laguna Blue
   S: Pthalo Green    H: Tropic Bay Blue

FOLK ART
☐ * Seafoam + White 1:1

JO SONJA
☐ Aqua

LIQUITEX
☐ * Real Teal + Bright Aqua Green 1:1

**NOTES**

### TCS #BG-4-1-7

ACCENT
☐ * Pthalo Green + Marina Blue 1:1

AMERICANA
☐ * Blue Green + Sea Aqua 3:1

CERAMCOAT
☐ * Hunter Green + Emerald Green 2:1

FOLK ART
☐ Teal
   S: Wintergreen    H: Aqua Bright
☐ * Pthalo Green + Aqua 2:1

LIQUITEX
☐ * Turquoise Green + Phthalo Green 3:1

**NOTES**

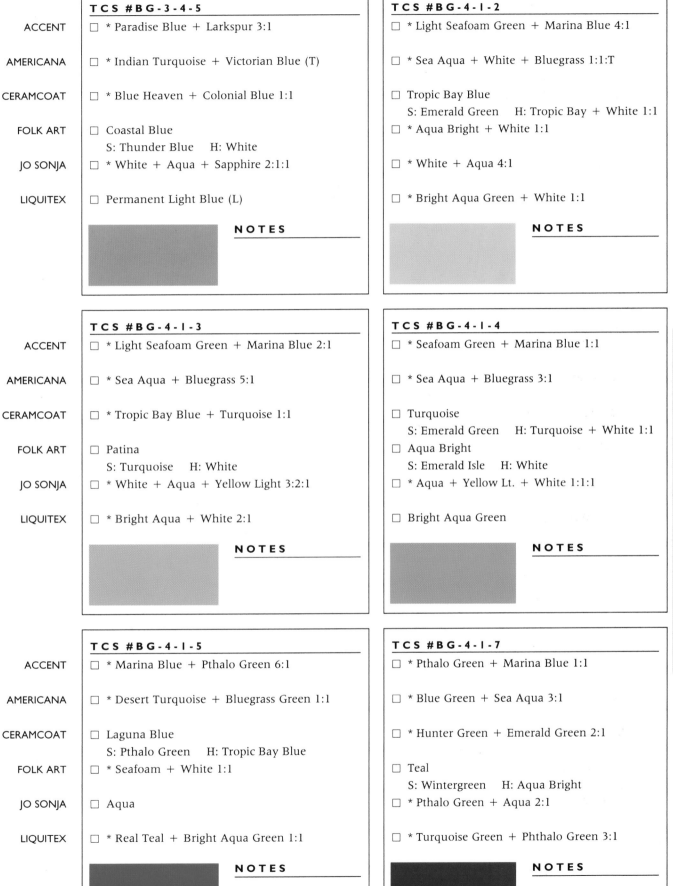

57

# BRAND          COLOR                    COLOR

## TCS #BG-4-1-8

| ACCENT | ☐ * Pthalo Green + Marina Blue 2:1 |
|---|---|
| AMERICANA | ☐ Blue Green |
|  | S: Payne's Grey   H: Bluegrass |
| CERAMCOAT | ☐ * Hunter Green + Emerald Green 1:1 |
| FOLK ART | ☐ Teal (L) |
| JO SONJA | ☐ * Pthalo Green + Aqua 3:1 |
| LIQUITEX | ☐ Real Teal |

NOTES

## TCS #BG-4-1-9

| ACCENT | ☐ * Pure Blue + Pthalo Green 2:1 |
|---|---|
| AMERICANA | ☐ * Viridian Green + Ultra Blue Deep 1:1 |
| CERAMCOAT | ☐ * Emerald Green + Pthalo Blue 2:1 |
| FOLK ART | ☐ * Turquoise + Ultramarine 1:1 |
| JO SONJA | ☐ * Pthalo Green + Ultramarine Blue 1:1 |
| LIQUITEX | ☐ Turquoise Deep |

NOTES

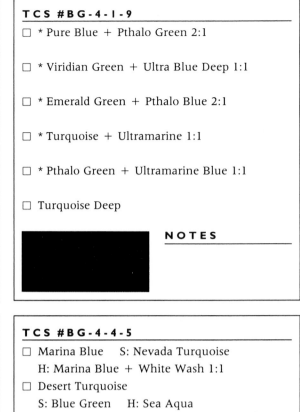

## TCS #BG-4-4-3

| ACCENT | ☐ * Marina Blue + White 1:1 |
|---|---|
| AMERICANA | ☐ * Desert Turquoise + White 1:1 |
| CERAMCOAT | ☐ Caribbean Blue |
|  | S: Aquamarine   H: White |
| FOLK ART | ☐ * Coastal Blue + Aqua Bright 1:1 |
| JO SONJA | ☐ * Aqua + Colony Blue + White 3:1:1 |
| LIQUITEX | ☐ * Perm. Blue Light + Bright Aqua Green 4:1 |

NOTES

## TCS #BG-4-4-5

| ACCENT | ☐ Marina Blue   S: Nevada Turquoise |
|---|---|
|  | H: Marina Blue + White Wash 1:1 |
| AMERICANA | ☐ Desert Turquoise |
|  | S: Blue Green   H: Sea Aqua |
| CERAMCOAT | ☐ Colonial Blue |
|  | S: Avalon Blue   H: Caribbean Blue |
| FOLK ART | ☐ * Azure Blue + Aqua Bright 2:1 |
| JO SONJA | ☐ * Aqua + Colony Blue 3:1 |
| LIQUITEX | ☐ * Brilliant Blue + Phthalo Green 3:1 |

NOTES

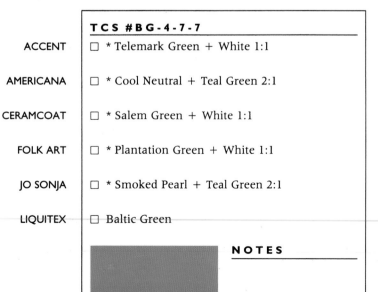

## TCS #BG-4-7-7

| ACCENT | ☐ * Telemark Green + White 1:1 |
|---|---|
| AMERICANA | ☐ * Cool Neutral + Teal Green 2:1 |
| CERAMCOAT | ☐ * Salem Green + White 1:1 |
| FOLK ART | ☐ * Plantation Green + White 1:1 |
| JO SONJA | ☐ * Smoked Pearl + Teal Green 2:1 |
| LIQUITEX | ☐ Baltic Green |

NOTES

## TCS #BG-4-7-8

| ACCENT | ☐ Telemark Green (D) |
|---|---|
| AMERICANA | ☐ * Teal Green + Cool Neutral 1:1 |
| CERAMCOAT | ☐ Salem Green |
|  | S: Woodland Night Green   H: Cactus Green |
| FOLK ART | ☐ Plantation Green |
|  | S: Licorice   H: Robin's Egg |
| JO SONJA | ☐ * Teal Green + Smoked Pearl 1:1 |
| LIQUITEX | ☐ * Baltic Green + Phthalo Green (T) |

NOTES

| BRAND | COLOR | COLOR |
|---|---|---|

**TCS #BG-4-7-9**

| | |
|---|---|
| ACCENT | ☐ Telemark Green    S: Deep Forest Green |
| | H: Telemark Green + Village Green 1:1 |
| AMERICANA | ☐ * Deep Teal + Teal Green 1:1 |
| CERAMCOAT | ☐ * Woodland Night Green + Blue Spruce 1:1 |
| FOLK ART | ☐ * Bavarian Blue + Wintergreen 1:1 |
| JO SONJA | ☐ * Teal Green + Colony Blue 1:1 |
| LIQUITEX | ☐ * Viridian Hue + Turquoise Deep 1:1 |

**NOTES**

**TCS #BG-5-1-6**

| | |
|---|---|
| ☐ * Marina Blue + Avon on the Green 3:1 |
| ☐ Bluegrass Green |
| S: Viridian Green    H: Sea Aqua |
| ☐ Emerald Green |
| S: Pthalo Green    H: Tropic Bay Blue |
| ☐ Turquoise |
| S: Wintergreen    H: White |
| ☐ * Aqua + Pthalo Green 4:1 |
| ☐ Turquoise Green |

**NOTES**

**TCS #BG-5-1-8**

| | |
|---|---|
| ACCENT | ☐ Teal Green |
| | S: Telemark Green    H: Seafoam Green |
| AMERICANA | ☐ * Bluegrass Green + Viridian Green 1:1 |
| CERAMCOAT | ☐ Mallard Green |
| | S: Black Green    H: Jade Green |
| FOLK ART | ☐ * Turquoise + Teal 1:1 |
| JO SONJA | ☐ * Aqua + Pthalo Green 1:1 |
| LIQUITEX | ☐ * Turquoise Green + Real Teal 1:1 |

**NOTES**

**TCS #BG-5-3-7**

| | |
|---|---|
| ☐ * Nevada Turquoise + Avon on the Green 1:1 |
| ☐ Teal Green |
| S: Blue Green    H: Desert Turquoise |
| ☐ * Avalon + Blue Spruce 2:1 |
| ☐ Seafoam |
| S: Wintergreen    H: Aqua Bright |
| ☐ * Nimbus Gray + Teal Green 2:1 |
| ☐ * Real Teal + Neutral Gray Value 5 3:1 |

**NOTES**

**TCS #BG-5-3-8**

| | |
|---|---|
| ACCENT | ☐ * Chesapeake Blue + Nevada Turquoise 1:1 |
| AMERICANA | ☐ Antique Teal |
| | S: Black Green    H: Teal Green |
| CERAMCOAT | ☐ Blue Spruce (D) |
| FOLK ART | ☐ * Seafoam + Wintergreen 1:1 |
| JO SONJA | ☐ * Colony Blue + Teal 2:1 |
| LIQUITEX | ☐ * Real Teal + Baltic Blue 1:1 |

**NOTES**

**TCS #BG-5-3-9**

| | |
|---|---|
| ☐ * Chesapeake Blue + Nevada Turquoise 2:1 |
| ☐ Antique Teal (L) |
| ☐ Blue Spruce |
| S: Black Green    H: Rainforest |
| ☐ * Wintergreen + Prussian Blue 4:1 |
| ☐ * Colony Blue + Teal 1:1 |
| ☐ * Baltic Blue + Turquoise Deep 3:1 |

**NOTES**

## BRAND COLOR COLOR

### TCS #BG-5-7-6

| | |
|---|---|
| ACCENT | ☐ * Chesapeake Blue + White 1:1 |
| AMERICANA | ☐ * Teal Green + White 1:1 |
| CERAMCOAT | ☐ * Blue Spruce + White 1:1 |
| FOLK ART | ☐ Teal Green<br>S: Wrought Iron    H: White |
| JO SONJA | ☐ * Teal Green + White 1:1 |
| LIQUITEX | ☐ * Baltic Blue + Baltic Green 1:1 |

NOTES

### TCS #BG-7-1-2

| | |
|---|---|
| ACCENT | ☐ Light Seafoam Green    S: Seafoam Green    H:<br>Light Seafoam Green + White Wash 1:1 |
| AMERICANA | ☐ * Sea Aqua + White 1:1 |
| CERAMCOAT | ☐ * Turquoise + Ivory 1:1 |
| FOLK ART | ☐ * Aqua Bright + White 1:1 |
| JO SONJA | ☐ * Aqua + Yellow Light 1:1 |
| LIQUITEX | ☐ * Bright Aqua Green + White 1:1 |

NOTES

### TCS #BG-7-1-3

| | |
|---|---|
| ACCENT | ☐ Seafoam Green<br>S: Avon on the Green    H: Light Seafoam Green |
| AMERICANA | ☐ Sea Aqua<br>S: Bluegrass Green    H: Sea Aqua + White 1:1 |
| CERAMCOAT | ☐ * Turquoise + Ivory 2:1 |
| FOLK ART | ☐ * White + Teal 4:1 |
| JO SONJA | ☐ * White + Aqua + Yellow Light 2:1:1 |
| LIQUITEX | ☐ * White + Turquoise Green 1:1 |

NOTES

### TCS #BG-7-1-5

| | |
|---|---|
| ACCENT | ☐ * White + Pthalo Green 4:1 |
| AMERICANA | ☐ * White + Bluegrass Green 2:1 |
| CERAMCOAT | ☐ Light Jade Green<br>S: Emerald Green    H: Pale Mint Green |
| FOLK ART | ☐ * White + Pthalo Green 3:1 |
| JO SONJA | ☐ * White + Pthalo Green 4:1 |
| LIQUITEX | ☐ * White + Turquoise Green 2:1 |

NOTES

### TCS #BG-7-1-6

| | |
|---|---|
| ACCENT | ☐ * White + Pthalo Green 2:1 |
| AMERICANA | ☐ * Bluegrass Green + White 1:1 |
| CERAMCOAT | ☐ Jade Green<br>S: Pthalo Green    H: Jade Green + White 1:1 |
| FOLK ART | ☐ * White + Phthalo Green 1:1 |
| JO SONJA | ☐ * White + Pthalo Green 1:1 |
| LIQUITEX | ☐ * Turquoise Green + White 1:1 |

NOTES

### TCS #BG-7-4-5

| | |
|---|---|
| ACCENT | ☐ * Village Green + Larkspur 4:1 |
| AMERICANA | ☐ * Colonial Green + Sea Aqua 1:1 |
| CERAMCOAT | ☐ Heritage Green<br>S: Woodland Night Green    H: Cactus Green |
| FOLK ART | ☐ * Robin's Egg + Seafoam 2:1 |
| JO SONJA | ☐ * Aqua + Jade 4:1 |
| LIQUITEX | ☐ * Turquoise Green + Chrome Green Ox. 3:1 |

NOTES

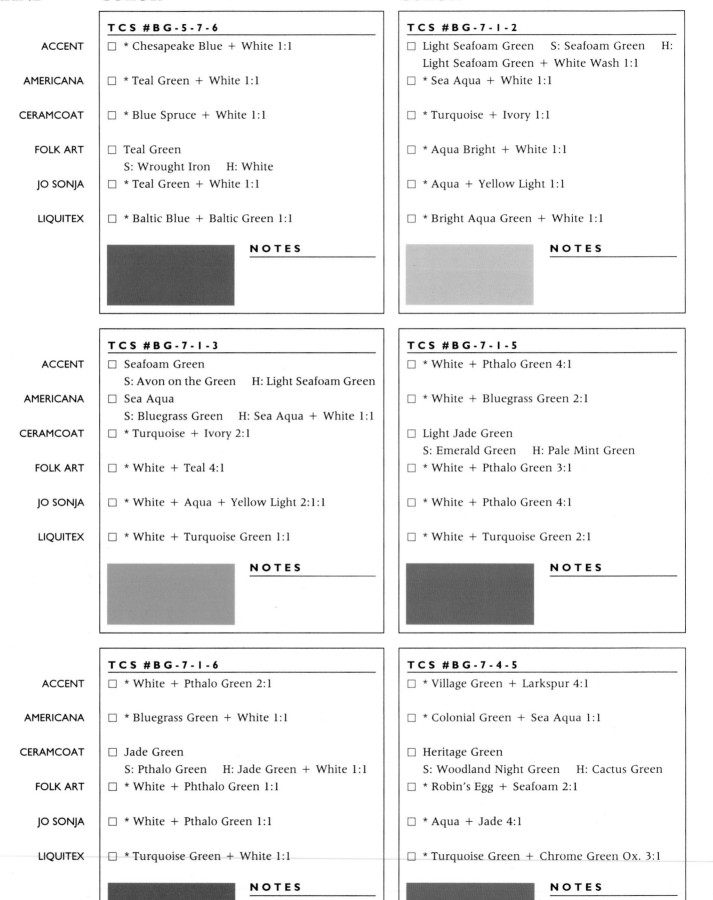

## TCS # B G - 8 - 2 - 8

ACCENT
☐ Avon on the Green    S: Pthalo Green
H: Avon on the Green + White Wash 1:1

AMERICANA
☐ * Viridian + Deep Teal (T)

CERAMCOAT
☐ * Pthalo Green + Christmas Green (T)

FOLK ART
☐ Viridian (PP)

JO SONJA
☐ * Pthalo Green + Aqua (T)

LIQUITEX
☐ * Phthalo Green + Emerald 1:1

**NOTES**

## TCS # B G - 8 - 2 - 9

☐ * Prairie Green + Avon on the Green 1:1

☐ * Deep Teal + Viridian Green 1:1

☐ * Woodland Night Green + Hunter Green 1:1

☐ Emerald Isle
S: Licorice    H: Robin's Egg
☐ * Pthalo Green + Teal Green 4:1

☐ * Phthalo Green + Perm. Hooker's Green 3:1

**NOTES**

## TCS # B G - 8 - 6 - 1

ACCENT
☐ * Lt. Village Green + White + Seafoam 6:2:1

AMERICANA
☐ * Mint Julip + Jade (T)

CERAMCOAT
☐ * Cactus Green + White 2:1

FOLK ART
☐ Mint Green
S: Poetry Green    H: White

JO SONJA
☐ * White + Jade 5:1

LIQUITEX
☐ * White + Baltic Green 6:1

**NOTES**

## TCS # B G - 8 - 6 - 2

☐ * Light Village Green + Seafoam 6:1

☐ * Mint Julip + Jade 1:1

☐ Cactus Green
S: Salem Green    H: Pale Mint Green
☐ Robin's Egg
S: Plantation Green    H: Tapioca
☐ * White + Jade 2:1

☐ * Baltic Green + White 1:1

**NOTES**

## TCS # B G - 8 - 6 - 4

ACCENT
☐ * White + Telemark Green 2:1

AMERICANA
☐ * Teal Green + Colonial Green + White 1:1:1

CERAMCOAT
☐ Rainforest Green
S: Blue Spruce    H: Cactus Green

FOLK ART
☐ Bluegrass
S: Wrought Iron    H: Summer Sky

JO SONJA
☐ * Smoked Pearl + Teal Green 10:1

LIQUITEX
☐ * Baltic Blue + White 1:1

**NOTES**

## TCS # B G - 8 - 8 - 1

☐ * Sage + White 1:1

☐ * Silver Sage Green + White 1:1

☐ Light Sage
S: Silver Pine    H: White
☐ * Gray Flannel + Robin's Egg 2:1

☐ * White + Smoked Pearl + Jade 2:2:1

☐ * White + Baltic Green + Neut. Gray 6:4:1

**NOTES**

## TCS #BG-8-8-3

| ACCENT | ☐ Sage |
| | S: Village Green   H: April Showers |
| AMERICANA | ☐ Silver Sage Green |
| | S: Green Mist   H: Dove Grey |
| CERAMCOAT | ☐ * Silver Pine |
| | S: Rainforest Green   H: Light Sage |
| FOLK ART | ☐ * Robin's Egg + Gray Flannel 2:1 |
| JO SONJA | ☐ * White + Smoked Pearl + Jade 1:1:1 |
| LIQUITEX | ☐ * Baltic Green + White + Neutral Gray 6:6:1 |

NOTES

## TCS #BG-9-1-8

| ACCENT | ☐ Pthalo Green (ABC) |
| | S: Deep Forest Green   H: True Green |
| AMERICANA | ☐ Viridian Green |
| | S: Payne's Grey   H: Bluegrass Green |
| CERAMCOAT | ☐ Phthalo Green |
| | S: Black Green   H: Light Jade Green |
| FOLK ART | ☐ Pthalo Green (PP) |
| JO SONJA | ☐ Pthalo Green |
| LIQUITEX | ☐ Phthalo Green |

NOTES

## TCS #BG-9-6-8

| ACCENT | ☐ Prairie Green (D) |
| AMERICANA | ☐ Deep Teal (D) |
| CERAMCOAT | ☐ Alpine Green |
| | S: Deep River Green   H: Cactus Green |
| FOLK ART | ☐ Tartan Green |
| | S: Wrought Iron   H: Buttercream |
| JO SONJA | ☐ * Jade + Ultra Blue 4:1 |
| LIQUITEX | ☐ * Phthalo Green + Sandalwood 1:1 |

NOTES

## TCS #BG-9-6-9

| ACCENT | ☐ Prairie Green |
| | S: Teal Deep   H: True Green |
| AMERICANA | ☐ Deep Teal |
| | S: Viridian Green   H: Bluegrass Green |
| CERAMCOAT | ☐ Woodland Night Green |
| | S: Black Green   H: Jade Green |
| FOLK ART | ☐ Wintergreen |
| | S: Licorice   H: Summer Sky |
| JO SONJA | ☐ * Teal Green + White (T) |
| LIQUITEX | ☐ * Permanent Hooker's Green + Phthalo Green 1:1 |

NOTES

## TCS #BG-9-7-6

| ACCENT | ☐ * Prairie Green + Warm Neutral 3:1 |
| AMERICANA | ☐ * Deep Teal + Olive Green 2:1 |
| CERAMCOAT | ☐ * Woodland Night Green + Green Sea 1:1 |
| FOLK ART | ☐ Aspen Green |
| | S: Wrought Iron   H: Tapioca |
| JO SONJA | ☐ * Moss Green + Teal 2:1 |
| LIQUITEX | ☐ * Viridian Hue + Baltic Green 1:1 |

NOTES

## TCS #BG-9-7-9

| ACCENT | ☐ Teal Deep (ABC) |
| | S: Deep Forest Green   H: True Green |
| AMERICANA | ☐ * Hauser Green Dark + Deep Teal 1:1 |
| CERAMCOAT | ☐ * Blue Spruce + Pthalo Green 1:1 |
| FOLK ART | ☐ * Emerald + Navy Blue 3:1 |
| JO SONJA | ☐ Teal Green |
| LIQUITEX | ☐ * Permanent Hooker's Green + Cobalt Blue 1:1 |

NOTES

**BRAND**  **COLOR**                    **COLOR**

| | |
|---|---|

### TCS #GR-1-4-1

ACCENT     ☐ * White + Light Village Green 5:1

AMERICANA     ☐ * White + Mint Julip 6:1

CERAMCOAT     ☐ Pale Mint Green
         S: Village Green    H: White

FOLK ART     ☐ * White + Bayberry 6:1

JO SONJA     ☐ * White + Brilliant Green 10:1

LIQUITEX     ☐ * White + Christmas Green 10:1

**NOTES**

### TCS #GR-3-2-4

ACCENT     ☐ * True Green + Pthalo Green 4:1

AMERICANA     ☐ Kelly Green
         S: Dark Pine    H: Bright Green
    ☐ Spring Green
         S: Hunter Green    H: Pale Mint Green
    ☐ Kelly Green
         S: Wrought Iron    H: White
    ☐ * Brilliant Green + Aqua 1:1

    ☐ * Emerald Green + Permanent Green Light 1:1

**NOTES**

### TCS #GR-3-3-3

ACCENT     ☐ * Light Seafoam Green + Light Village Green 1:1

AMERICANA     ☐ Mint Julip Green    S: Green Mist
         H: Mint Julip Green + White 1:1

CERAMCOAT     ☐ * White + Christmas Green 6:1

FOLK ART     ☐ * White + Shamrock 6:1

JO SONJA     ☐ * White + Jade 4:1

LIQUITEX     ☐ * White + Chrome Oxide Green 6:1

**NOTES**

### TCS #GR-3-3-5

ACCENT     ☐ * Pthalo Green + True Green 2:1

AMERICANA     ☐ Holly Green
         S: Hauser Dark Green    H: Bright Green
    ☐ * Green Isle + Pthalo Green 2:1

    ☐ * Evergreen + Viridian 1:1

    ☐ * Brilliant Green + Pthalo Green 2:1

    ☐ Emerald Green

**NOTES**

### TCS #GR-3-3-6

ACCENT     ☐ * Green Olive + Prairie Green 1:1

AMERICANA     ☐ Dark Pine
         S: Black Forest Green    H: Bluegrass Green

CERAMCOAT     ☐ * Christmas Green + Pthalo Green 1:1

FOLK ART     ☐ * Shamrock + Tartan Green 1:1

JO SONJA     ☐ * Teal Green + Moss Green 1:1

LIQUITEX     ☐ * Emerald Green + Chrome Oxide Green 1:1

**NOTES**

### TCS #GR-3-5-5

ACCENT     ☐ * Deep Forest Green + White 1:1

AMERICANA     ☐ * Pine Green + White 2:1

CERAMCOAT     ☐ * Hunter Green + White 2:1

FOLK ART     ☐ Leaf Green
         S: Green Forest    H: Spring White

JO SONJA     ☐ * White + Brill. Green + Pthalo Green 2:1:1

LIQUITEX     ☐ * Viridian Hue + Christmas Green 1:1

**NOTES**

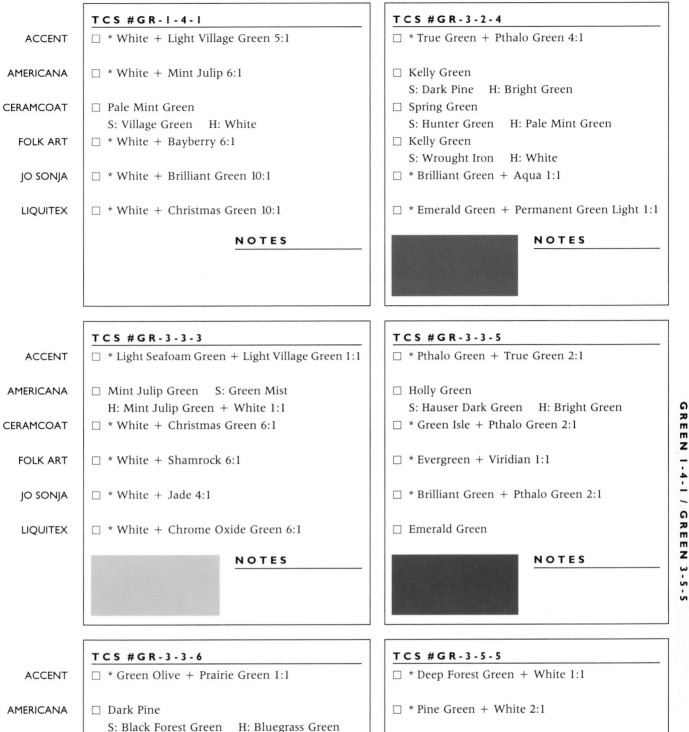

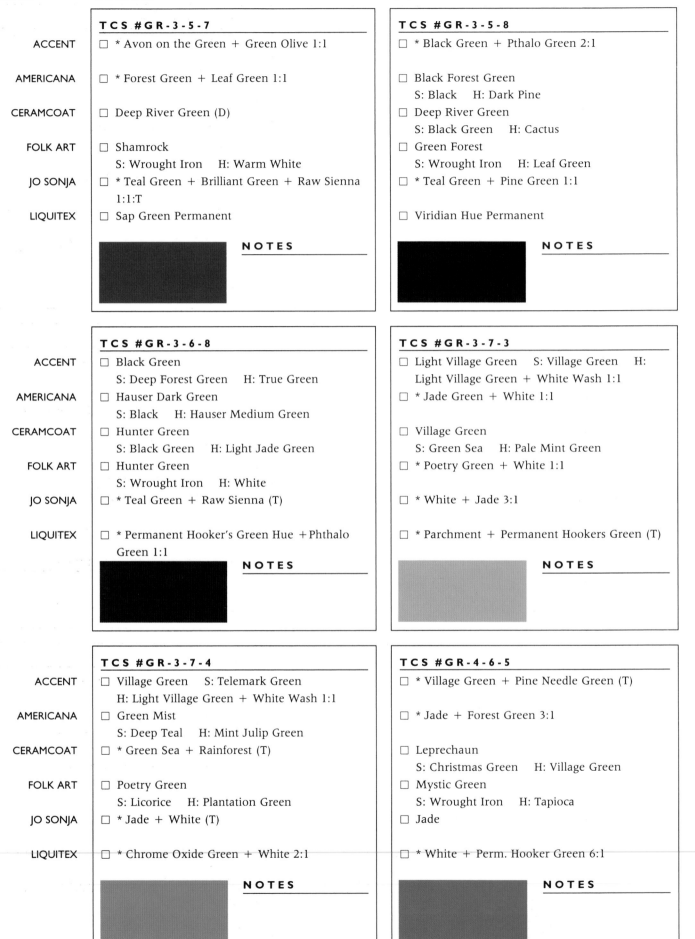

**T C S # G R - 3 - 5 - 7**

ACCENT ☐ * Avon on the Green + Green Olive 1:1

AMERICANA ☐ * Forest Green + Leaf Green 1:1

CERAMCOAT ☐ Deep River Green (D)

FOLK ART ☐ Shamrock
S: Wrought Iron    H: Warm White

JO SONJA ☐ * Teal Green + Brilliant Green + Raw Sienna
1:1:T

LIQUITEX ☐ Sap Green Permanent

NOTES

---

**T C S # G R - 3 - 5 - 8**

☐ * Black Green + Pthalo Green 2:1

☐ Black Forest Green
S: Black    H: Dark Pine
☐ Deep River Green
S: Black Green    H: Cactus
☐ Green Forest
S: Wrought Iron    H: Leaf Green
☐ * Teal Green + Pine Green 1:1

☐ Viridian Hue Permanent

NOTES

---

**T C S # G R - 3 - 6 - 8**

ACCENT ☐ Black Green
S: Deep Forest Green    H: True Green

AMERICANA ☐ Hauser Dark Green
S: Black    H: Hauser Medium Green

CERAMCOAT ☐ Hunter Green
S: Black Green    H: Light Jade Green

FOLK ART ☐ Hunter Green
S: Wrought Iron    H: White

JO SONJA ☐ * Teal Green + Raw Sienna (T)

LIQUITEX ☐ * Permanent Hooker's Green Hue + Phthalo
Green 1:1

NOTES

---

**T C S # G R - 3 - 7 - 3**

☐ Light Village Green    S: Village Green    H:
Light Village Green + White Wash 1:1
☐ * Jade Green + White 1:1

☐ Village Green
S: Green Sea    H: Pale Mint Green
☐ * Poetry Green + White 1:1

☐ * White + Jade 3:1

☐ * Parchment + Permanent Hookers Green (T)

NOTES

---

**T C S # G R - 3 - 7 - 4**

ACCENT ☐ Village Green    S: Telemark Green
H: Light Village Green + White Wash 1:1

AMERICANA ☐ Green Mist
S: Deep Teal    H: Mint Julip Green

CERAMCOAT ☐ * Green Sea + Rainforest (T)

FOLK ART ☐ Poetry Green
S: Licorice    H: Plantation Green

JO SONJA ☐ * Jade + White (T)

LIQUITEX ☐ * Chrome Oxide Green + White 2:1

NOTES

---

**T C S # G R - 4 - 6 - 5**

☐ * Village Green + Pine Needle Green (T)

☐ * Jade + Forest Green 3:1

☐ Leprechaun
S: Christmas Green    H: Village Green
☐ Mystic Green
S: Wrought Iron    H: Tapioca
☐ Jade

☐ * White + Perm. Hooker Green 6:1

NOTES

| BRAND | COLOR | COLOR |
|---|---|---|

**TCS #GR-5-1-1**

| ACCENT | ☐ * White + Holiday Green (T) |
| AMERICANA | ☐ * White + Holly Green (T) |
| CERAMCOAT | ☐ * White + Green Isle (T) |
| FOLK ART | ☐ Spring White<br>S: Bayberry    H: White |
| JO SONJA | ☐ * White + Brilliant Green (T) |
| LIQUITEX | ☐ * White + Christmas Green (T) |

**NOTES**

**TCS #GR-5-1-5**

| ACCENT | ☐ * Holiday Green + Avon on the Green (T) |
| AMERICANA | ☐ * Mistletoe + Leaf Green 1:1 |
| CERAMCOAT | ☐ Green Isle<br>S: Hunter Green   H: Kelly Green |
| FOLK ART | ☐ * Shamrock + Fresh Foliage 4:1 |
| JO SONJA | ☐ * Brilliant Green + Teal Green 3:1 |
| LIQUITEX | ☐ * Chrome Green Oxide + Christmas Green 1:1 |

**NOTES**

**TCS #GR-5-3-8**

| ACCENT | ☐ * Teal Deep + Tumbleweed 2:1 |
| AMERICANA | ☐ Midnite Green<br>S: Black Green   H: Forest Green |
| CERAMCOAT | ☐ * Deep River Green + Christmas Green 1:1 |
| FOLK ART | ☐ * Thicket + Shamrock 1:1 |
| JO SONJA | ☐ * Teal Green + Raw Sienna 2:1 |
| LIQUITEX | ☐ * Hooker's Green Permanent + Chrome Green Ox. 2:1 |

**NOTES**

**TCS #GR-5-3-9**

| ACCENT | ☐ * Deep Forest Green + Black 3:1 |
| AMERICANA | ☐ Black Green<br>S: Lamp (Ebony) Black   H: Forest Green |
| CERAMCOAT | ☐ Black Green<br>S: None    H: Blue Haze |
| FOLK ART | ☐ Wrought Iron<br>S: Licorice    H: Bayberry |
| JO SONJA | ☐ * Teal Green + Black 3:1 |
| LIQUITEX | ☐ * Chrome Green Oxide + Black 3:1 |

**NOTES**

**TCS #GR-5-4-6**

| ACCENT | ☐ * Village Green + Pine Needle Green (T) |
| AMERICANA | ☐ * Jade Green + Kelly Green 4:1 |
| CERAMCOAT | ☐ Green Sea<br>S: Chrome Green Light   H: Village Green |
| FOLK ART | ☐ Spring Green<br>S: Aspen Green   H: Spring White |
| JO SONJA | ☐ * Jade + Moss Green 6:1 |
| LIQUITEX | ☐ * White + Chrome Oxide Green 2:1 |

**NOTES**

**TCS #GR-5-4-7**

| ACCENT | ☐ * True Green + Pthalo Green 2:1 |
| AMERICANA | ☐ Leaf Green<br>S: Hauser Dark Green   H: Mistletoe |
| CERAMCOAT | ☐ Christmas Green<br>S: Hunter Green   H: Kelly Green |
| FOLK ART | ☐ * Shamrock + Evergreen 1:1 |
| JO SONJA | ☐ * Brilliant Green + Teal 6:1 |
| LIQUITEX | ☐ * Emerald Green + Yellow Light Hansa 1:1 |

**NOTES**

# BRAND  COLOR  COLOR

## TCS #GR-5-6-4

| ACCENT | ☐ * Light Village Green + Pine Needle Green 5:1 |
|---|---|
| AMERICANA | ☐ Jade Green |
| | S: Light Avocado    H: Jade Green + White 1:1 |
| CERAMCOAT | ☐ Wedgewood Green    S: Forest Green    H: Wedgewood Green + White 1:1 |
| FOLK ART | ☐ Bayberry |
| | S: Thicket    H: White |
| JO SONJA | ☐ * Nimbus Grey + Jade 1:1 |
| LIQUITEX | ☐ * Unbleached Titanium + Perm. Hooker's Green 4:1 |

**NOTES**

## TCS #GR-6-2-5

| ACCENT | ☐ Holiday Green    S: Pthalo Green |
|---|---|
| | H: Holiday Green + White Wash 1:1 |
| AMERICANA | ☐ * Holly Green + Bright Green 1:1 |
| CERAMCOAT | ☐ * Jubilee Green + Green Isle 1:1 |
| FOLK ART | ☐ * Evergreen + Fresh Foliage 4:1 |
| JO SONJA | ☐ * Brilliant Green + Pthalo Green (T) |
| LIQUITEX | ☐ * Christmas Green + Phthalo Green (T) |

**NOTES**

## TCS #GR-6-4-5

| ACCENT | ☐ * Holiday Green + Green Olive (T) |
|---|---|
| AMERICANA | ☐ Mistletoe |
| | S: Forest Green    H: Bright Green |
| CERAMCOAT | ☐ Kelly Green |
| | S: Christmas Green    H: Apple Green |
| FOLK ART | ☐ Evergreen |
| | S: Southern Pine    H: White |
| JO SONJA | ☐ * Brilliant Green + Green Oxide 1:1 |
| LIQUITEX | ☐ * Permanent Green Light + Chrome Green Oxide 1:1 |

**NOTES**

## TCS #GR-6-6-6

| ACCENT | ☐ Forest Green |
|---|---|
| | S: Black Green    H: Light Yellow Green |
| AMERICANA | ☐ Forest Green |
| | S: Hauser Dark Green    H: Mistletoe |
| CERAMCOAT | ☐ * Chrome Green Light + Forest Green 1:1 |
| FOLK ART | ☐ Green Meadow |
| | S: Licorice    H: Basil Green |
| JO SONJA | ☐ * Green Oxide + Pine Green 6:1 |
| LIQUITEX | ☐ * Chromium Oxide Green + Hooker's Green 6:1 |

**NOTES**

## TCS #GR-7-2-5

| ACCENT | ☐ True Green |
|---|---|
| | S: Avon on the Green    H: New Leaf |
| AMERICANA | ☐ * Bright Green + Kelly 1:1 |
| CERAMCOAT | ☐ Jubilee Green |
| | S: Christmas Green    H: Apple Green |
| FOLK ART | ☐ * Evergreen + Fresh Foliage 1:1 |
| JO SONJA | ☐ Brilliant Green |
| LIQUITEX | ☐ Green Light, Permanent |

**NOTES**

## TCS #GR-7-3-5

| ACCENT | ☐ * Holiday Green + New Leaf 3:1 |
|---|---|
| AMERICANA | ☐ * Mistletoe + Green Olive 4:1 |
| CERAMCOAT | ☐ * Kelly Green + Leaf Green 2:1 |
| FOLK ART | ☐ Grass Green |
| | S: Shamrock    H: Warm White |
| JO SONJA | ☐ * Green Oxide + Moss Green 3:1 |
| LIQUITEX | ☐ * Chrome Oxide Green + Cadmium Yellow Med. 4:1 |

**NOTES**

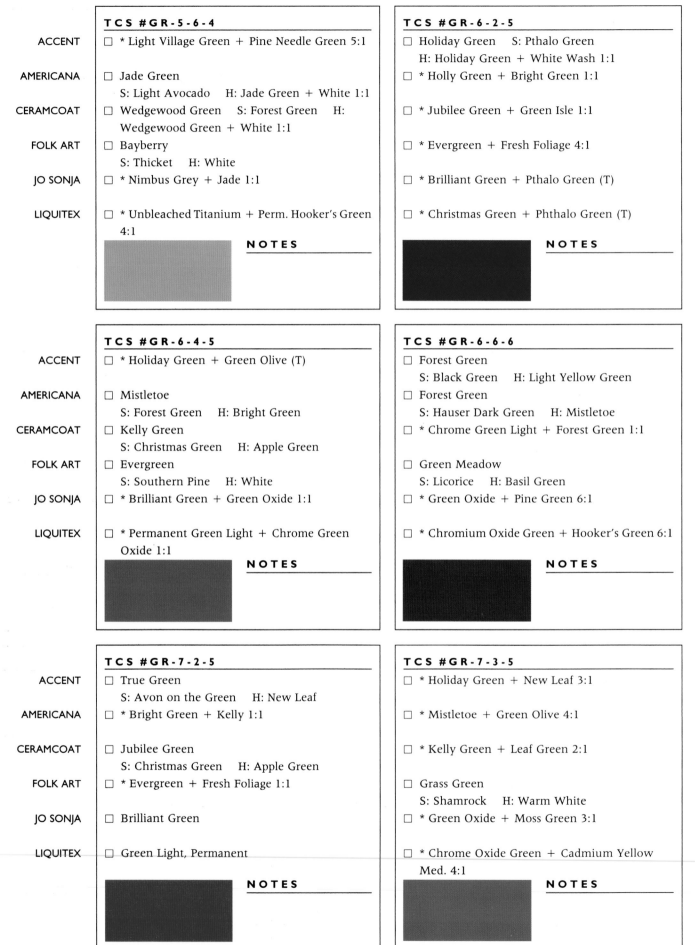

| BRAND | COLOR | COLOR |
|-------|-------|-------|

## TCS #GR-7-4-5

| ACCENT | ☐ * Olive Green + New Leaf 2:1 |
|--------|--------------------------------|
| AMERICANA | ☐ Hauser Medium Green<br>S: Hauser Dark Green    H: Hauser Light Green |
| CERAMCOAT | ☐ * Chrome Green Light + Seminole 1:1 |
| FOLK ART | ☐ Sap Green (PP) |
| JO SONJA | ☐ * Green Oxide + Moss Green 4:1 |
| LIQUITEX | ☐ * Chrome Oxide Green + Yellow Oxide 5:1 |

**NOTES**

## TCS #GR-7-8-1

| ACCENT | ☐ * Off White + Light Village Green 9:1 |
|--------|------------------------------------------|
| AMERICANA | ☐ * Desert Sand + Jade Green 8:1 |
| CERAMCOAT | ☐ * Sandstone + Village Green 7:1 |
| FOLK ART | ☐ * Vanilla Cream + Bayberry 8:1 |
| JO SONJA | ☐ * Smoked Pearl + Jade 10:1 |
| LIQUITEX | ☐ Parchment |

**NOTES**

## TCS #GR-7-8-4

| ACCENT | ☐ Mushroom<br>S: Forest Green    H: Off White |
|--------|------------------------------------------------|
| AMERICANA | ☐ Shale Green<br>S: Light Avocado    H: Cool Neutral Toning |
| CERAMCOAT | ☐ * Stonewedge + Lichen Grey 2:1 |
| FOLK ART | ☐ * Basil Green + Barn Wood 5:1 |
| JO SONJA | ☐ * Smoked Pearl + Nimbus Grey 2:1 |
| LIQUITEX | ☐ * Parchment + Olive 4:1 |

**NOTES**

## TCS #GR-7-9-2

| ACCENT | ☐ Celery<br>S: Apple Green    H: Off White |
|--------|---------------------------------------------|
| AMERICANA | ☐ * Desert Sand + Jade 3:1 |
| CERAMCOAT | ☐ * Stonewedge + White 1:1 |
| FOLK ART | ☐ * Basil Green + White 1:1 |
| JO SONJA | ☐ * White + Nimbus Grey + Pine Green 4:2:1 |
| LIQUITEX | ☐ * Parchment + Olive 3:1 |

**NOTES**

## TCS #GR-7-9-4

| ACCENT | ☐ * Antique White + Light Village Green 1:1 |
|--------|----------------------------------------------|
| AMERICANA | ☐ * Jade + Desert Sand 1:1 |
| CERAMCOAT | ☐ Stonewedge Green S: English Yew Green<br>H: Stonewedge + White 1:1 |
| FOLK ART | ☐ Basil Green<br>S: Southern Pine    H: Warm White |
| JO SONJA | ☐ * Nimbus Grey + Pine Green 4:1 |
| LIQUITEX | ☐ * Parchment + Olive 1:1 |

**NOTES**

## TCS #GR-8-2-4

| ACCENT | ☐ * True Green + White (T) |
|--------|-----------------------------|
| AMERICANA | ☐ Bright Green<br>S: Forest Green    H: Bright Green + White 1:1 |
| CERAMCOAT | ☐ Lime Green<br>S: Kelly Green    H: Lima Green |
| FOLK ART | ☐ Green<br>S: Shamrock    H: White |
| JO SONJA | ☐ * Brilliant Green + White 5:1 |
| LIQUITEX | ☐ Christmas Green |

**NOTES**

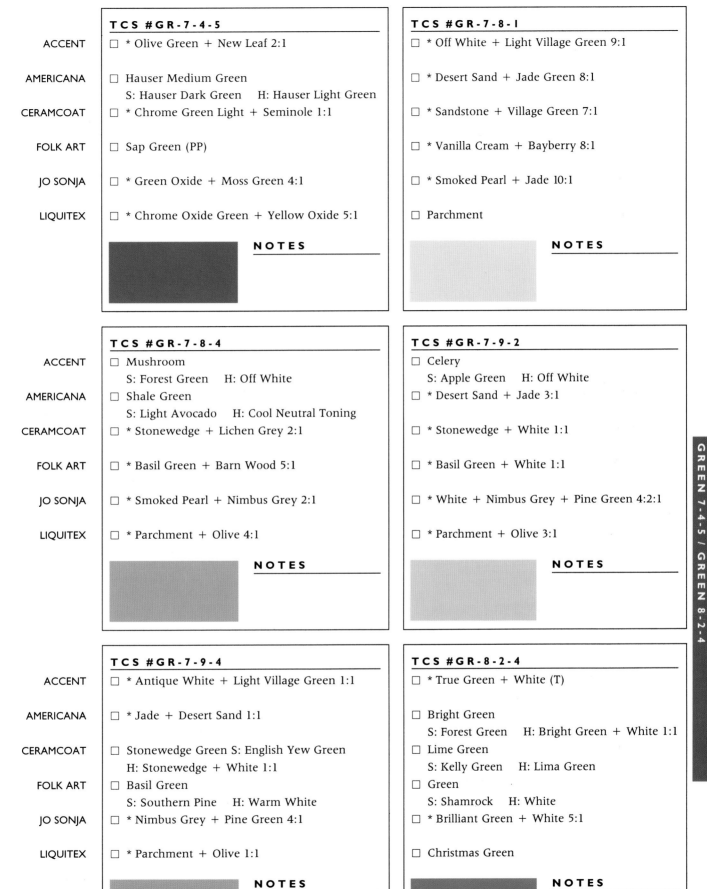

GREEN 7-4-5 / GREEN 8-2-4

COLOR                    COLOR

### TCS #GR-8-3-9

| ACCENT | ☐ Deep Forest Green |
| | S: Soft Black    H: True Green |
| AMERICANA | ☐ * Black Forest Green + Evergreen 1:1 |
| CERAMCOAT | ☐ * Deep River Green + Black Green 1:1 |
| FOLK ART | ☐ * Teal + Hunter Green 3:1 |
| JO SONJA | ☐ * Teal Green + Pine Green 2:1 |
| LIQUITEX | ☐ Hooker's Green Hue, Permanent |

NOTES

### TCS #GR-8-6-5

| ACCENT | ☐ Green Olive (D) |
| AMERICANA | ☐ * Avocado + Evergreen 1:1 |
| CERAMCOAT | ☐ Chrome Green Light |
| | S: Dark Forest    H: Green Sea |
| FOLK ART | ☐ * Old Ivy + Clover 1:1 |
| JO SONJA | ☐ Green Oxide |
| LIQUITEX | ☐ Chrome Oxide Green (D) |

NOTES

### TCS #GR-8-6-6

| ACCENT | ☐ Green Olive |
| | S: Forest Green    H: Light Yellow Green |
| AMERICANA | ☐ * Avocado + Evergreen 2:1 |
| CERAMCOAT | ☐ Forest Green |
| | S: Dark Forest    H: Leprechaun |
| FOLK ART | ☐ Old Ivy |
| | S: Wrought Iron    H: Bayberry |
| JO SONJA | ☐ * Green Oxide + Pine Green (T) |
| LIQUITEX | ☐ Chrome Oxide Green |

NOTES

### TCS #GR-8-6-8

| ACCENT | ☐ * Deep Forest Green + Pine Needle Green 1:1 |
| AMERICANA | ☐ * Evergreen + Midnite Green 1:1 |
| CERAMCOAT | ☐ Pine Green |
| | S: Black Green    H: Jubilee Green |
| FOLK ART | ☐ * Thicket + Old Ivy 2:1 |
| JO SONJA | ☐ * Pine Green + Green Oxide + Payne's Grey 2:1:1 |
| LIQUITEX | ☐ * Chrome Oxide Green + Ivory Black 6:1 |

NOTES

### TCS #YG-3-2-6

| ACCENT | ☐ * Light Yellow Green + Green Olive 3:1 |
| AMERICANA | ☐ * Avocado + Yellow Green 1:1 |
| CERAMCOAT | ☐ Vibrant Green |
| | S: Dark Jungle    H: Leaf Green |
| FOLK ART | ☐ * Clover + Old Ivy 2:1 |
| JO SONJA | ☐ * Green Oxide + Yellow Light 1:1 |
| LIQUITEX | ☐ * Permanent Green Light + Olive 1:1 |

NOTES

### TCS #YG-4-3-2

| ACCENT | ☐ Light Yellow Green |
| | S: Green Olive    H: New Leaf |
| AMERICANA | ☐ * Cadmium Yellow + Leaf Green 6:1 |
| CERAMCOAT | ☐ * Leaf Green + Lima Green 3:1 |
| FOLK ART | ☐ Fresh Foliage |
| | S: Thicket    H: Warm White |
| JO SONJA | ☐ * Yellow Light + Green Oxide 4:1 |
| LIQUITEX | ☐ * Chrome Green Oxide + Brilliant Yellow 1:1 |

NOTES

## TCS #YG-4-3-3

ACCENT ☐ Light Yellow Green (L)

AMERICANA ☐ Hauser Light Green
S: Hauser Medium Green    H: Olive Green

CERAMCOAT ☐ Leaf Green
S: Seminole Green    H: Lima Green

FOLK ART ☐ Fresh Foliage (L)

JO SONJA ☐ * Yellow Light + Green Oxide 2:1

LIQUITEX ☐ * Brilliant Yellow + Chrome Oxide Green 2:1

**NOTES**

## TCS #YG-4-3-6

ACCENT ☐ * Light Yellow Green + Pine Needle Green (T)

AMERICANA ☐ Avocado
S: Evergreen    H: Light Avocado

CERAMCOAT ☐ Seminole Green
S: Dark Forest    H: Leaf Green

FOLK ART ☐ Clover
S: Shamrock    H: Warm White

JO SONJA ☐ * Green Oxide + Brilliant Green 2:1

LIQUITEX ☐ * Chrome Oxide Green + Brilliant Yellow 5:1

**NOTES**

## TCS #YG-4-3-7

ACCENT ☐ * Pine Needle Green + White 3:1

AMERICANA ☐ Evergreen
S: Black    H: Avocado

CERAMCOAT ☐ Dark Jungle Green
S: Gamal Green    H: Leaf Green

FOLK ART ☐ Olive Green
S: Wrought Iron    H: Fresh Foliage

JO SONJA ☐ Pine Green (D)

LIQUITEX ☐ * Chrome Oxide Green + Brilliant Yellow 1:1

**NOTES**

## TCS #YG-4-3-8

ACCENT ☐ * Green Olive + Pine Needle Green 2:1

AMERICANA ☐ * Evergreen + Plantation Pine 1:1

CERAMCOAT ☐ Dark Forest Green
S: Black Green    H: Seminole

FOLK ART ☐ Thicket
S: Wrought Iron    H: Basil Green

JO SONJA ☐ Pine Green

LIQUITEX ☐ * Chrome Oxide Green + Black 1:1

**NOTES**

## TCS #YG-4-3-9

ACCENT ☐ Pine Needle Green
S: Deep Forest Green    H: Green Olive

AMERICANA ☐ Plantation Pine
S: Black Green    H: Avocado

CERAMCOAT ☐ Gamal Green
S: Black Green    H: Seminole

FOLK ART ☐ Southern Pine
S: Licorice    H: Basil Green

JO SONJA ☐ * Yellow Oxide + Pine Green + Black 8:2:1

LIQUITEX ☐ * Olive + Burnt Umber 3:1

**NOTES**

## TCS #YG-5-6-2

ACCENT ☐ * Light Yellow Green + Warm Neutral 2:1

AMERICANA ☐ Olive Green
S: Hauser Medium Green    H: Yellow Light

CERAMCOAT ☐ * Leaf Green + White 1:1

FOLK ART ☐ * Fresh Foliage + Green Olive (T)

JO SONJA ☐ * Moss Green + Brilliant Green 4:1

LIQUITEX ☐ * Brilliant Yellow + Hooker's Green 6:1

**NOTES**

COLOR                                           COLOR

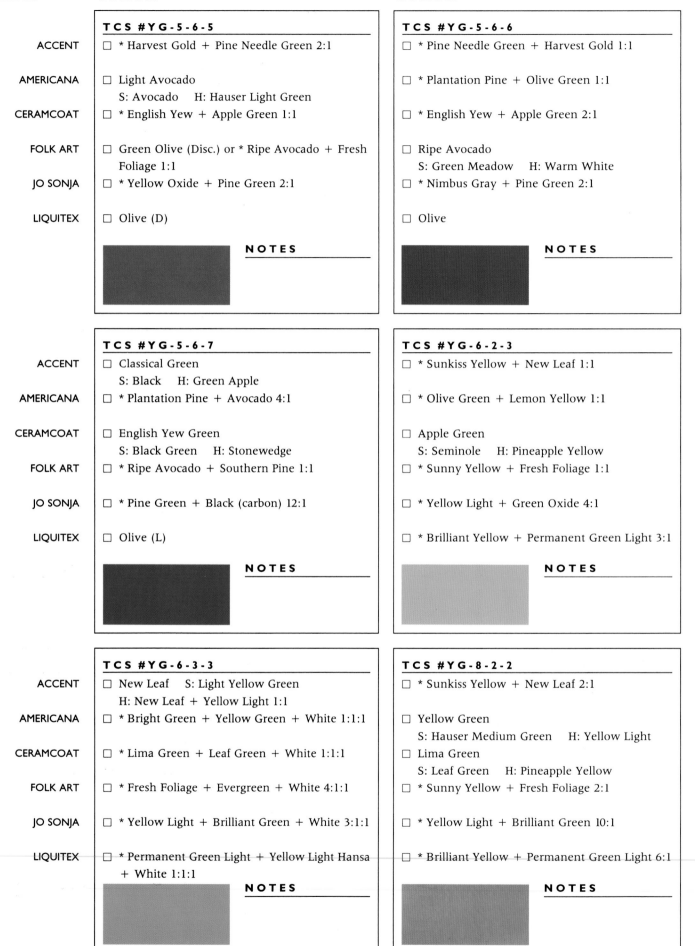

**T C S # Y G - 5 - 6 - 5**

ACCENT
☐ * Harvest Gold + Pine Needle Green 2:1

AMERICANA
☐ Light Avocado
   S: Avocado    H: Hauser Light Green

CERAMCOAT
☐ * English Yew + Apple Green 1:1

FOLK ART
☐ Green Olive (Disc.) or * Ripe Avocado + Fresh
   Foliage 1:1

JO SONJA
☐ * Yellow Oxide + Pine Green 2:1

LIQUITEX
☐ Olive (D)

**N O T E S**

---

**T C S # Y G - 5 - 6 - 6**

☐ * Pine Needle Green + Harvest Gold 1:1

☐ * Plantation Pine + Olive Green 1:1

☐ * English Yew + Apple Green 2:1

☐ Ripe Avocado
   S: Green Meadow    H: Warm White

☐ * Nimbus Gray + Pine Green 2:1

☐ Olive

**N O T E S**

---

**T C S # Y G - 5 - 6 - 7**

ACCENT
☐ Classical Green
   S: Black    H: Green Apple

AMERICANA
☐ * Plantation Pine + Avocado 4:1

CERAMCOAT
☐ English Yew Green
   S: Black Green    H: Stonewedge

FOLK ART
☐ * Ripe Avocado + Southern Pine 1:1

JO SONJA
☐ * Pine Green + Black (carbon) 12:1

LIQUITEX
☐ Olive (L)

**N O T E S**

---

**T C S # Y G - 6 - 2 - 3**

☐ * Sunkiss Yellow + New Leaf 1:1

☐ * Olive Green + Lemon Yellow 1:1

☐ Apple Green
   S: Seminole    H: Pineapple Yellow

☐ * Sunny Yellow + Fresh Foliage 1:1

☐ * Yellow Light + Green Oxide 4:1

☐ * Brilliant Yellow + Permanent Green Light 3:1

**N O T E S**

---

**T C S # Y G - 6 - 3 - 3**

ACCENT
☐ New Leaf    S: Light Yellow Green
   H: New Leaf + Yellow Light 1:1

AMERICANA
☐ * Bright Green + Yellow Green + White 1:1:1

CERAMCOAT
☐ * Lima Green + Leaf Green + White 1:1:1

FOLK ART
☐ * Fresh Foliage + Evergreen + White 4:1:1

JO SONJA
☐ * Yellow Light + Brilliant Green + White 3:1:1

LIQUITEX
☐ * Permanent Green Light + Yellow Light Hansa
   + White 1:1:1

**N O T E S**

---

**T C S # Y G - 8 - 2 - 2**

☐ * Sunkiss Yellow + New Leaf 2:1

☐ Yellow Green
   S: Hauser Medium Green    H: Yellow Light

☐ Lima Green
   S: Leaf Green    H: Pineapple Yellow

☐ * Sunny Yellow + Fresh Foliage 2:1

☐ * Yellow Light + Brilliant Green 10:1

☐ * Brilliant Yellow + Permanent Green Light 6:1

**N O T E S**

| BRAND | COLOR | COLOR |
|---|---|---|

**T C S # Y G - 8 - 8 - 3**

ACCENT □ * Wild Honey + Classical Green 2:1

AMERICANA □ Dried Basil Green
S: Antique Green    H: Cool Neutral

CERAMCOAT □ * Lichen Grey + Boston Fern 3:1

FOLK ART □ * Butter Pecan + Ripe Avocado 3:1

JO SONJA □ * Moss Green + Territorial Beige + Nimbus Grey 2:2:1

LIQUITEX □ * Unbleached Titanium + Olive + Bronze Yellow 2:2:1

**N O T E S**

**T C S # Y G - 8 - 8 - 4**

□ * White + Yellow Oxide + Pine Needle 4:1:1

□ * White + Antique Green 4:1

□ Olive Yellow
S: Avocado    H: Pineapple Yellow

□ * White + Ripe Avocado + English Mustard 4:1:1

□ * White + Yellow Oxide + Pine Green 4:2:1

□ * White + Olive + Bronze Yellow 4:2:1

**N O T E S**

**T C S # Y G - 8 - 8 - 7**

ACCENT □ * Golden Oxide + Pine Needle Green 3:1

AMERICANA □ Antique Green
S: Plantation Pine    H: Hauser Light Green

CERAMCOAT □ Boston Fern
S: Gamal Green    H: Antique Gold

FOLK ART □ * Ripe Avocado + English Mustard 1:1

JO SONJA □ * Yellow Oxide + Pine Green 2:1

LIQUITEX □ * Olive + Bronze Yellow 2:1

**N O T E S**

**T C S # Y G - 9 - 4 - 6**

□ * Golden Harvest + Classical Green 4:1

□ Antique Gold Deep
S: Antique Green    H: Olde Gold

□ * Cloudberry Tan + Timberline 4:1

□ * Ripe Avocado + Harvest Gold 2:1

□ * Moss Green + Yellow Oxide 1:1

□ * Yellow Oxide + Olive 4:1

**N O T E S**

**T C S # Y G - 9 - 6 - 2**

ACCENT □ * Antique White + Harvest Gold + Pine Needle Green 4:1:1

AMERICANA □ * Olive Green + Antique Gold 3:1

CERAMCOAT □ * Apple Green + Avocado 2:1

FOLK ART □ * Ripe Avocado + Harvest Gold 1:1

JO SONJA □ Moss Green

LIQUITEX □ * Olive + Yellow Oxide 2:1

**N O T E S**

**T C S # Y G - 9 - 8 - 7**

□ * Light Yellow Green + Burnt Umber 3:1

□ * Antique Green + Antique Gold 2:1

□ Avocado
S: Gamal Green    H: Antique Gold

□ * Ripe Avocado + Teddy Bear Tan 1:1

□ * Raw Sienna + Pine Green 1:1

□ * Olive + Bronze Yellow 1:1

**N O T E S**

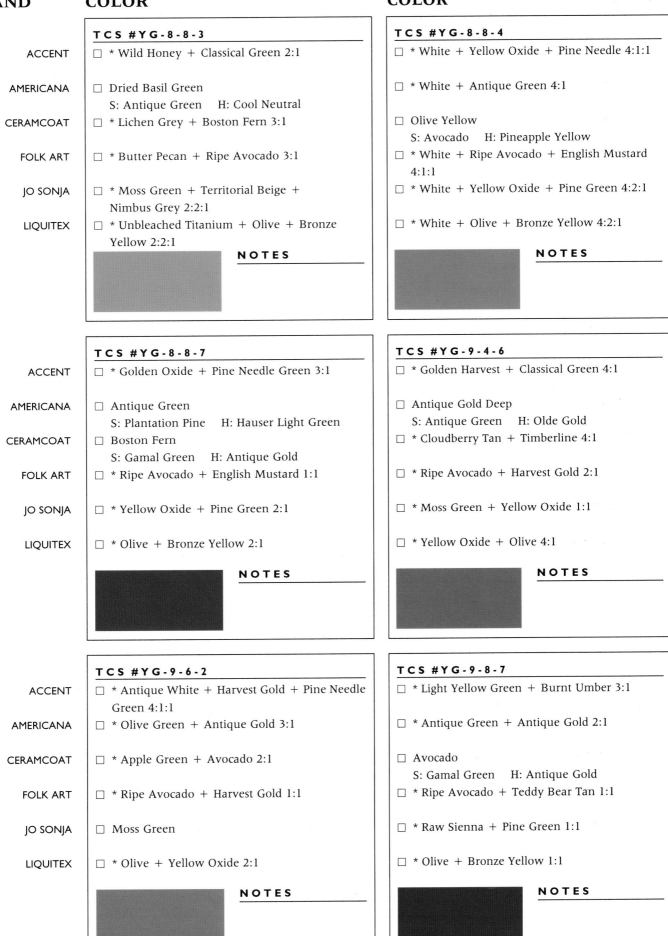

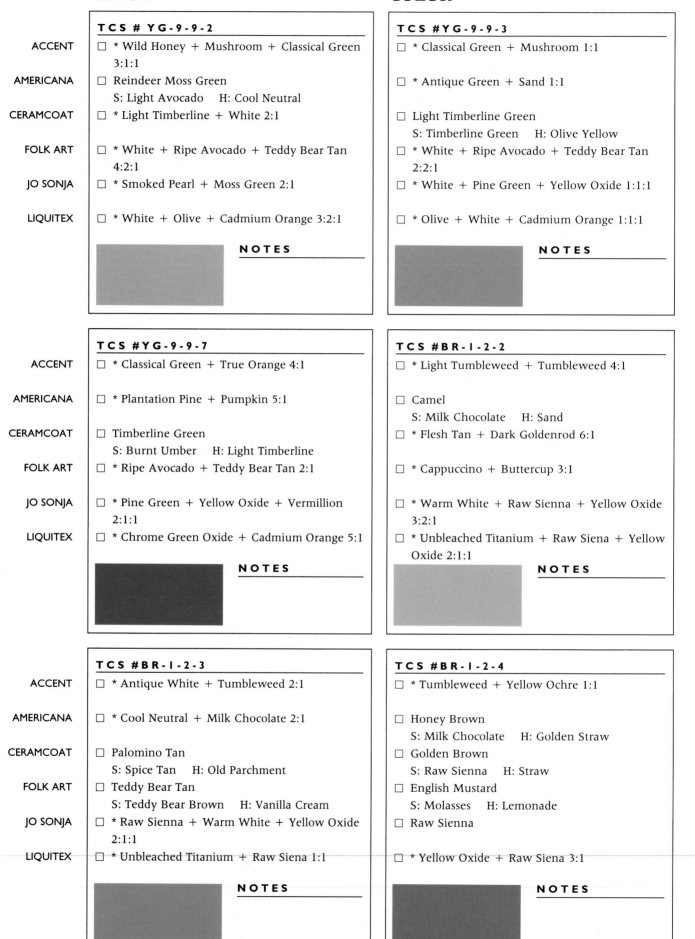

### TCS # YG-9-9-2

ACCENT — ☐ * Wild Honey + Mushroom + Classical Green 3:1:1

AMERICANA — ☐ Reindeer Moss Green
S: Light Avocado    H: Cool Neutral

CERAMCOAT — ☐ * Light Timberline + White 2:1

FOLK ART — ☐ * White + Ripe Avocado + Teddy Bear Tan 4:2:1

JO SONJA — ☐ * Smoked Pearl + Moss Green 2:1

LIQUITEX — ☐ * White + Olive + Cadmium Orange 3:2:1

**NOTES**

### TCS #YG-9-9-3

ACCENT — ☐ * Classical Green + Mushroom 1:1

AMERICANA — ☐ * Antique Green + Sand 1:1

CERAMCOAT — ☐ Light Timberline Green
S: Timberline Green    H: Olive Yellow

FOLK ART — ☐ * White + Ripe Avocado + Teddy Bear Tan 2:2:1

JO SONJA — ☐ * White + Pine Green + Yellow Oxide 1:1:1

LIQUITEX — ☐ * Olive + White + Cadmium Orange 1:1:1

**NOTES**

### TCS #YG-9-9-7

ACCENT — ☐ * Classical Green + True Orange 4:1

AMERICANA — ☐ * Plantation Pine + Pumpkin 5:1

CERAMCOAT — ☐ Timberline Green
S: Burnt Umber    H: Light Timberline

FOLK ART — ☐ * Ripe Avocado + Teddy Bear Tan 2:1

JO SONJA — ☐ * Pine Green + Yellow Oxide + Vermillion 2:1:1

LIQUITEX — ☐ * Chrome Green Oxide + Cadmium Orange 5:1

**NOTES**

### TCS #BR-1-2-2

ACCENT — ☐ * Light Tumbleweed + Tumbleweed 4:1

AMERICANA — ☐ Camel
S: Milk Chocolate    H: Sand

CERAMCOAT — ☐ * Flesh Tan + Dark Goldenrod 6:1

FOLK ART — ☐ * Cappuccino + Buttercup 3:1

JO SONJA — ☐ * Warm White + Raw Sienna + Yellow Oxide 3:2:1

LIQUITEX — ☐ * Unbleached Titanium + Raw Siena + Yellow Oxide 2:1:1

**NOTES**

### TCS #BR-1-2-3

ACCENT — ☐ * Antique White + Tumbleweed 2:1

AMERICANA — ☐ * Cool Neutral + Milk Chocolate 2:1

CERAMCOAT — ☐ Palomino Tan
S: Spice Tan    H: Old Parchment

FOLK ART — ☐ Teddy Bear Tan
S: Teddy Bear Brown    H: Vanilla Cream

JO SONJA — ☐ * Raw Sienna + Warm White + Yellow Oxide 2:1:1

LIQUITEX — ☐ * Unbleached Titanium + Raw Siena 1:1

**NOTES**

### TCS #BR-1-2-4

ACCENT — ☐ * Tumbleweed + Yellow Ochre 1:1

AMERICANA — ☐ Honey Brown
S: Milk Chocolate    H: Golden Straw

CERAMCOAT — ☐ Golden Brown
S: Raw Sienna    H: Straw

FOLK ART — ☐ English Mustard
S: Molasses    H: Lemonade

JO SONJA — ☐ Raw Sienna

LIQUITEX — ☐ * Yellow Oxide + Raw Sienna 3:1

**NOTES**

## TCS #BR-1-2-5

| | |
|---|---|
| ACCENT | ☐ Tumbleweed   S: Sedona Clay<br>H: Light Tumbleweed + Tumbleweed (T) |
| AMERICANA | ☐ Raw Sienna<br>S: Burnt Umber   H: Honey Brown |
| CERAMCOAT | ☐ Raw Sienna<br>S: Brown Iron Oxide   H: Antique Gold |
| FOLK ART | ☐ Raw Sienna (PP) |
| JO SONJA | ☐ * Raw Sienna + Gold Oxide (T) |
| LIQUITEX | ☐ Raw Siena |

**NOTES**

## TCS #BR-1-2-7

☐ * Golden Oxide + Wicker 1:1

☐ Terra Cotta<br>S: Burnt Sienna   H: Pumpkin

☐ * Raw Sienna + Toffee Brown 3:1

☐ Buckskin Brown<br>S: Dark Brown   H: Linen

☐ * Raw Sienna + Burnt Sienna 3:1

☐ * Raw Siena + Taupe 1:1

**NOTES**

## TCS #BR-2-2-2

| | |
|---|---|
| ACCENT | ☐ Light Tumbleweed   S: Tumbleweed<br>H: Light Tumbleweed + Adobe Wash 1:1 |
| AMERICANA | ☐ French Vanilla<br>S: Yellow Ochre   H: Buttermilk |
| CERAMCOAT | ☐ Flesh Tan<br>S: Spice Tan   H: Light Ivory |
| FOLK ART | ☐ French Vanilla<br>S: Teddy Bear Tan   H: White |
| JO SONJA | ☐ * Warm White + Yellow Oxide 8:1 |
| LIQUITEX | ☐ * Soft White + Raw Siena (T) |

**NOTES**

## TCS #BR-2-2-3

☐ * Blonde + Wicker 2:1

☐ * Sand + Yellow Ochre 1:1

☐ AC Flesh<br>S: Spice Tan   H: Antique White

☐ Almond Parfait<br>S: Brown Sugar   H: Georgia Peach

☐ * Opal + Provincial Beige 6:1

☐ Unbleached Titanium

**NOTES**

## TCS #BR-2-2-4

| | |
|---|---|
| ACCENT | ☐ * Mustard Seed + White + Burnt Umber 4:1:T |
| AMERICANA | ☐ * Antique Gold + Sable Brown 3:1 |
| CERAMCOAT | ☐ Spice Tan<br>S: Spice Brown   H: Flesh Tan |
| FOLK ART | ☐ Honeycomb<br>S: Coffee Bean   H: Linen |
| JO SONJA | ☐ * Raw Sienna + Yellow Oxide + Warm White 2:1:1 |
| LIQUITEX | ☐ * Bronze Yellow + Soft White + Raw Siena 2:1:T |

**NOTES**

## TCS #BR-2-2-5

☐ * Golden Oxide + Pennsylvania Clay (T)

☐ * Raw Sienna + Antique Gold 1:1

☐ Mocha Brown<br>S: Brown Iron Oxide   H: Maple Sugar Tan

☐ Caramel<br>S: Nutmeg   H: French Vanilla

☐ * Yellow Oxide + Burnt Sienna 4:1

☐ * Raw Siena + Turner's Yellow 1:1

**NOTES**

## TCS #BR-2-2-6

| | |
|---|---|
| ACCENT | ☐ * Burnt Sienna + White 1:1 |
| AMERICANA | ☐ Light Cinnamon<br>S: Burnt Umber  H: Sable Brown |
| CERAMCOAT | ☐ Autumn Brown<br>S: Brown Iron Oxide  H: Light Chocolate |
| FOLK ART | ☐ Brown Sugar<br>S: Dark Brown  H: Almond Parfait |
| JO SONJA | ☐ * Raw Sienna + Indian Red Oxide 4:1 |
| LIQUITEX | ☐ * Raw Siena + Titanium White 1:1 |

**NOTES**

## TCS #BR-2-2-7

| | |
|---|---|
| ACCENT | ☐ * Raw Sienna + Burnt Sienna 2:1 |
| AMERICANA | ☐ Milk Chocolate<br>S: Burnt Umber  H: Sable Brown |
| CERAMCOAT | ☐ Spice Brown<br>S: Burnt Umber  H: Light Chocolate |
| FOLK ART | ☐ Nutmeg<br>S: Chocolate Fudge  H: Country Twill |
| JO SONJA | ☐ * Raw Sienna + Indian Red Oxide 3:1 |
| LIQUITEX | ☐ * Raw Siena + Raw Umber 2:1 |

**NOTES**

## TCS #BR-2-2-8

| | |
|---|---|
| ACCENT | ☐ * Burnt Sienna + Raw Sienna 1:1 |
| AMERICANA | ☐ * Light Cinnamon + Dark Chocolate (T) |
| CERAMCOAT | ☐ Dark Brown<br>S: Dark Chocolate  H: Toffee Brown |
| FOLK ART | ☐ * Chocolate Fudge + Coffee Bean (T) |
| JO SONJA | ☐ * Raw Umber + Brown Earth 1:1 |
| LIQUITEX | ☐ * Raw Umber + Taupe (T) |

**NOTES**

## TCS #BR-2-3-3

| | |
|---|---|
| ACCENT | ☐ * White + Tumbleweed 1:1 |
| AMERICANA | ☐ * Yellow Ochre + Terra Cotta 1:1 |
| CERAMCOAT | ☐ * Maple Sugar Tan + Spice Tan 1:1 |
| FOLK ART | ☐ Cappuccino<br>S: Buckskin Brown  H: Buttercrunch |
| JO SONJA | ☐ * Opal + Raw Sienna 2:1 |
| LIQUITEX | ☐ * Unbleached Titanium + Raw Siena 2:1 |

**NOTES**

## TCS #BR-2-4-4

| | |
|---|---|
| ACCENT | ☐ Wild Honey<br>S: Raw Sienna  H: Antique White |
| AMERICANA | ☐ * Yellow Ochre + Burnt Umber (T) |
| CERAMCOAT | ☐ * Sandstone + Palomino Tan 2:1 |
| FOLK ART | ☐ Camel<br>S: Honeycomb  H: Vanilla Cream |
| JO SONJA | ☐ * Provincial Beige + Yellow Oxide 5:1 |
| LIQUITEX | ☐ * Unbleached Titanium + Bronze Yellow 3:1 |

**NOTES**

## TCS #BR-2-4-6

| | |
|---|---|
| ACCENT | ☐ * Golden Harvest + Burnt Umber 6:1 |
| AMERICANA | ☐ * Antique Gold + Antique Gold Deep 2:1 |
| CERAMCOAT | ☐ Cloudberry Tan<br>S: Boston Fern  H: Maple Sugar Tan |
| FOLK ART | ☐ * Teddy Bear Tan + Harvest Gold 3:1 |
| JO SONJA | ☐ * Yellow Light + Fawn 1:1 |
| LIQUITEX | ☐ * Bronze Yellow + White 2:1 |

**NOTES**

## BRAND    COLOR                    COLOR

### TCS #BR-2-5-8

ACCENT       ☐ * Golden Harvest + Burnt Umber 4:1

AMERICANA    ☐ * Antique Gold Deep + Antique Green 5:1

CERAMCOAT    ☐ * Cloudberry Tan + Raw Sienna 4:1

FOLK ART     ☐ * Teddy Bear Tan + English Mustard 1:1

JO SONJA     ☐ * Raw Sienna + Yellow Oxide + Warm White
                2:1:1

LIQUITEX     ☐ Bronze Yellow

**NOTES**

### TCS #BR-4-4-4

☐ * Wicker + Sweet Chocolate 2:1

☐ * Sable Brown + White (T)

☐ Territorial Beige
   S: Burnt Umber      H: Trail
☐ * Honeycomb + Coffee Bean (T)

☐ Provincial Beige

☐ * Taupe + Unbleached Titanium 1:1

**NOTES**

### TCS #BR-4-4-5

ACCENT       ☐ * Wicker + Sweet Chocolate 1:1

AMERICANA    ☐ Sable Brown
                S: Burnt Umber      H: Mink Tan
CERAMCOAT    ☐ * Spice Brown + White 2:1

FOLK ART     ☐ * Teddy Bear Tan + Teddy Bear Brown 1:1

JO SONJA     ☐ * Raw Sienna + Opal 3:1

LIQUITEX     ☐ * Raw Siena + Raw Umber + White 2:1:1

**NOTES**

### TCS #BR-5-1-5

☐ Burnt Sienna
   S: Sweet Chocolate      H: Tumbleweed
☐ * Light Cinnamon + Dark Chocolate 4:1

☐ Brown Iron Oxide
   S: Walnut      H: Toffee Brown
☐ Maple Syrup
   S: Chocolate Fudge      H: Clay Bisque
☐ Brown Earth

☐ * Burnt Umber + Burnt Siena 1:1

**NOTES**

### TCS #BR-5-1-6

ACCENT       ☐ Sweet Chocolate
                S: Burnt Umber (ABC)      H: Burnt Sienna
AMERICANA    ☐ * Light Cinnamon + Dark Chocolate 1:1

CERAMCOAT    ☐ Brown Velvet
                S: Walnut      H: Toffee Brown
FOLK ART     ☐ Dark Brown
                S: Chocolate Fudge      H: Brown Sugar
JO SONJA     ☐ * Raw Umber + Brown Earth 1:1

LIQUITEX     ☐ * Raw Umber + Burnt Umber 1:1

**NOTES**

### TCS #BR-5-2-7

☐ * Raw Sienna + Tumbleweed 2:1

☐ * Mink Tan + Sable Brown 1:1

☐ Toffee Brown
   S: Brown Iron Oxide      H: Light Chocolate
☐ * Buckskin Brown + Country Twill 4:1

☐ * Raw Sienna + Provincial Beige 4:1

☐ * Raw Siena + Sandalwood 4:1

**NOTES**

## TCS #BR-5-4-2

| | |
|---|---|
| ACCENT | ☐ * Blonde + Wicker 3:1 |
| AMERICANA | ☐ Toffee<br>S: Sable Brown   H: Buttermilk |
| CERAMCOAT | ☐ * White + Bambi 2:1 |
| FOLK ART | ☐ * Milkshake + Acorn Brown 3:1 |
| JO SONJA | ☐ * White + Fawn 2:1 |
| LIQUITEX | ☐ * Unbleached Titanium + Sandalwood 2:1 |

NOTES

## TCS #BR-5-4-3

| | |
|---|---|
| ACCENT | ☐ * Wicker + White 1:1 |
| AMERICANA | ☐ Cashmere Beige<br>S: Sable Brown   H: Toffee |
| CERAMCOAT | ☐ * Bambi + White 1:1 |
| FOLK ART | ☐ * Milkshake + Acorn Brown 2:1 |
| JO SONJA | ☐ * Fawn + White 1:1 |
| LIQUITEX | ☐ * Unbleached Titanium + Taupe (T) |

NOTES

## TCS #BR-5-4-4

| | |
|---|---|
| ACCENT | ☐ * Wicker + Raw Sienna (T) |
| AMERICANA | ☐ Mink Tan<br>S: Light Cinnamon   H: Cashmere Beige |
| CERAMCOAT | ☐ Bambi Brown<br>S: Brown Iron Oxide   H: Dunes Beige |
| FOLK ART | ☐ * Milkshake + Acorn Brown 1:1 |
| JO SONJA | ☐ Fawn |
| LIQUITEX | ☐ * Unbleached Titanium + Taupe 3:1 |

NOTES

## TCS #BR-6-1-5

| | |
|---|---|
| ACCENT | ☐ Sedona Clay (Wash) |
| AMERICANA | ☐ * Raw Sienna + Burnt Orange (Wash) |
| CERAMCOAT | ☐ * Burnt Sienna + Antique Gold 4:1 |
| FOLK ART | ☐ Trans. Oxide Red (PP) |
| JO SONJA | ☐ * Raw Sienna + Gold Oxide (Wash) |
| LIQUITEX | ☐ * Raw Siena + Red Oxide 6:1 |

NOTES

## TCS #BR-6-2-3

| | |
|---|---|
| ACCENT | ☐ * Sedona Clay + Burnt Sienna 3:1 |
| AMERICANA | ☐ * Light Cinnamon + Russet 3:1 |
| CERAMCOAT | ☐ * Burnt Sienna + Burgundy Rose (T) |
| FOLK ART | ☐ Earthenware<br>S: Dark Brown   H: Linen |
| JO SONJA | ☐ * Gold Oxide + Burnt Sienna 1:1 |
| LIQUITEX | ☐ Burnt Siena |

NOTES

## TCS #BR-6-2-5

| | |
|---|---|
| ACCENT | ☐ * Tumbleweed + Sedona Clay 3:1 |
| AMERICANA | ☐ * Terra Cotta + Burnt Orange 1:1 |
| CERAMCOAT | ☐ Burnt Sienna<br>S: Brown Iron Oxide   H: Georgia Clay |
| FOLK ART | ☐ Burnt Sienna (PP) |
| JO SONJA | ☐ * Gold Oxide + Burnt Sienna 3:1 |
| LIQUITEX | ☐ * Raw Siena + Burnt Siena 3:1 |

NOTES

## BRAND    COLOR    COLOR

| | TCS #BR-6-2-6 | TCS #BR-6-2-9 |
|---|---|---|

**ACCENT**
- ☐ Burnt Sienna (ABC)
  S: Sweet Chocolate    H: Sedona Clay

**AMERICANA**
- ☐ Burnt Sienna
  S: Antique Maroon    H: Georgia Clay

**CERAMCOAT**
- ☐ * Brown Iron Oxide + Red Iron Oxide 1:1

**FOLK ART**
- ☐ Molasses
  S: Chocolate Fudge    H: Clay Bisque

**JO SONJA**
- ☐ Burnt Sienna

**LIQUITEX**
- ☐ * Burnt Siena + Red Oxide 1:1

**NOTES**

---

TCS #BR-6-2-9

- ☐ * Fingerberry + Burnt Umber 2:1

- ☐ Russet
  S: Black Plum    H: Brandy Wine
- ☐ * Sonoma + Burnt Umber 1:1

- ☐ * Burnt Carmine + Burnt Umber 1:1

- ☐ * Indian Red Oxide + Brown Earth 1:1

- ☐ * Burgundy + Raw Umber 1:1

**NOTES**

---

| | TCS #BR-6-4-2 | TCS #BR-6-4-3 |
|---|---|---|

**ACCENT**
- ☐ * Apricot Stone + Antique White 1:1

**AMERICANA**
- ☐ Mocha (D)

**CERAMCOAT**
- ☐ Dunes Beige
  S: Dark Flesh    H: Santa's Flesh

**FOLK ART**
- ☐ * Almond Parfait + Acorn Brown 2:1

**JO SONJA**
- ☐ * Smoked Pearl + Gold Oxide + Raw Sienna 10:1:1

**LIQUITEX**
- ☐ * Sandalwood + Unbleached Titanium + Apricot 1:1:T

**NOTES**

---

TCS #BR-6-4-3

- ☐ * Peaches n' Cream + Victorian Mauve (T)

- ☐ Mocha
  S: Light Cinnamon    H: Mocha + White 1:1
- ☐ Light Chocolate (D)

- ☐ * Almond Parfait + Acorn Brown 1:1

- ☐ * Opal + Warm White + Gold Oxide 3:1:1

- ☐ * Sandalwood + Apricot 3:1

**NOTES**

---

| | TCS #BR-6-4-4 | TCS #BR-6-4-5 |
|---|---|---|

**ACCENT**
- ☐ * Peaches n' Cream + Wicker 2:1

**AMERICANA**
- ☐ * Mocha + Terra Cotta (T)

**CERAMCOAT**
- ☐ Light Chocolate
  S: Brown Iron Oxide    H: A.C. Flesh

**FOLK ART**
- ☐ Chocolate Parfait (Disc.) or * Acorn Brown + Almond Parfait 2:1

**JO SONJA**
- ☐ * Warm White + Gold Oxide + Raw Sienna 9:1:1

**LIQUITEX**
- ☐ * Unbleached Titanium + Taupe 4:1

**NOTES**

---

TCS #BR-6-4-5

- ☐ * Dark Flesh + Burnt Sienna 1:1

- ☐ * Shading Flesh + Terra Cotta 1:1

- ☐ * Toffee Brown + Burnt Sienna (T)

- ☐ Acorn Brown
  S: Coffee Bean    H: Almond Parfait
- ☐ * Fawn + Burnt Sienna 4:1

- ☐ * Sandalwood + Raw Siena 1:1

**NOTES**

BROWN 6-2-6 / BROWN 6-4-5

77

## TCS #BR-6-4-7

| BRAND | COLOR |
|---|---|
| ACCENT | ☐ * Sweet Chocolate + Wicker 3:1 |
| AMERICANA | ☐ * Light Cinnamon + Mink Tan 4:1 |
| CERAMCOAT | ☐ * Burnt Umber + Territorial Beige 1:1 |
| FOLK ART | ☐ Teddy Bear Brown<br>S: Chocolate Fudge    H: Vanilla Cream |
| JO SONJA | ☐ * Brown Earth + Provincial Beige 1:1 |
| LIQUITEX | ☐ * Taupe + Sandalwood (T) |

**NOTES**

## TCS #BR-7-4-3

| BRAND | COLOR |
|---|---|
| ACCENT | ☐ Wicker<br>S: Raw Sienna    H: Light Tumbleweed |
| AMERICANA | ☐ * Antique White + Mississippi Mud (T) |
| CERAMCOAT | ☐ Trail Tan<br>S: Territorial Beige    H: Putty |
| FOLK ART | ☐ Country Twill<br>S: Teddy Bear Brown    H: Linen |
| JO SONJA | ☐ * Smoked Pearl + Provincial Beige 1:1 |
| LIQUITEX | ☐ * Soft White + Taupe 3:1 |

**NOTES**

## TCS #BR-7-5-7

| BRAND | COLOR |
|---|---|
| ACCENT | ☐ Raw Sienna<br>S: Burnt Umber    H: Tumbleweed |
| AMERICANA | ☐ * Light Cinnamon + Burnt Umber 1:1 |
| CERAMCOAT | ☐ * Burnt Umber + Territorial Beige 1:1 |
| FOLK ART | ☐ Coffee Bean<br>S: Chocolate Fudge    H: Country Twill |
| JO SONJA | ☐ * Raw Umber + Brown Earth + Provincial Beige 6:6:1 |
| LIQUITEX | ☐ * Taupe + Sandalwood 3:1 |

**NOTES**

## TCS #BR-7-5-8

| BRAND | COLOR |
|---|---|
| ACCENT | ☐ * Raw Sienna + Burnt Umber 3:1 |
| AMERICANA | ☐ Asphaltum<br>S: Soft Black    H: Light Cinnamon |
| CERAMCOAT | ☐ Burnt Umber<br>S: Black    H: Light Chocolate |
| FOLK ART | ☐ Burnt Umber (PP) |
| JO SONJA | ☐ * Raw Umber + Brown Earth 1:1 |
| LIQUITEX | ☐ * Raw Umber + Raw Siena 3:1 |

**NOTES**

## TCS #BR-7-6-1

| BRAND | COLOR |
|---|---|
| ACCENT | ☐ * Adobe Wash + Cool Neutral 2:1 |
| AMERICANA | ☐ * White + Warm Neutral 2:1 |
| CERAMCOAT | ☐ * White + Wild Rice 2:1 |
| FOLK ART | ☐ Parchment<br>S: Milkshake    H: White |
| JO SONJA | ☐ * Warm White + Smoked Pearl + Opal 4:1:1 |
| LIQUITEX | ☐ * Soft White + Deep Portrait Pink (T) |

**NOTES**

## TCS #BR-7-6-3

| BRAND | COLOR |
|---|---|
| ACCENT | ☐ Cool Neutral (ABC)    S: Cool Neutral + Soft Grey (T)    H: Cool Neutral + Off White 1:1 |
| AMERICANA | ☐ Warm Neutral    S: Mississippi Mud<br>H: Warm Neutral + White 1:1 |
| CERAMCOAT | ☐ Wild Rice<br>S: Misty Mauve    H: Santa's Flesh |
| FOLK ART | ☐ Milkshake<br>S: Brown Sugar    H: White |
| JO SONJA | ☐ Opal |
| LIQUITEX | ☐ * Unbleached Titanium + Sandalwood 1:1 |

**NOTES**

| BRAND | COLOR | COLOR |
|---|---|---|

**TCS #BR-7-6-8**

ACCENT — ☐ Burnt Umber
S: Burnt Umber (ABC)    H: Raw Sienna

AMERICANA — ☐ Dark Chocolate
S: Soft Black    H: Milk Chocolate

CERAMCOAT — ☐ * Burnt Umber + Dark Chocolate 1:1

FOLK ART — ☐ * Burnt Umber + Raw Umber 1:1

JO SONJA — ☐ Burnt Umber (D)

LIQUITEX — ☐ Burnt Umber (D)

**NOTES**

**TCS #BR-7-6-9**

ACCENT — ☐ Burnt Umber (L)

AMERICANA — ☐ Burnt Umber
S: Asphaltum    H: Milk Chocolate

CERAMCOAT — ☐ Dark Burnt Umber
S: Black    H: Light Chocolate
☐ Chocolate Fudge
S: Licorice    H: Clay Bisque

JO SONJA — ☐ Burnt Umber

LIQUITEX — ☐ Burnt Umber

**NOTES**

**TCS #BR-8-5-7**

ACCENT — ☐ Classical Bronze
S: Black    H: Wicker

AMERICANA — ☐ Raw Umber
S: Soft Black    H: Mississippi Mud

CERAMCOAT — ☐ Walnut
S: Black    H: Trail Tan

FOLK ART — ☐ * Coffee Bean + White 3:1

JO SONJA — ☐ * Raw Umber + Provincial Beige 2:1

LIQUITEX — ☐ Taupe

**NOTES**

**TCS #BR-8-6-5**

ACCENT — ☐ * Raw Sienna + Wicker 1:1

AMERICANA — ☐ Mississippi Mud
S: Raw Umber    H: Sable Brown

CERAMCOAT — ☐ * Dark Chocolate + Trail 2:1

FOLK ART — ☐ * Coffee Bean + White 3:1

JO SONJA — ☐ * Raw Umber + Provincial Beige 2:1

LIQUITEX — ☐ * Taupe + Raw Umber 1:1

**NOTES**

**TCS #BR-8-6-8**

ACCENT — ☐ Raw Umber
S: Black    H: Sweet Chocolate

AMERICANA — ☐ Soft Black
S: Lamp (Ebony) Black    H: Burnt Umber

CERAMCOAT — ☐ Dark Chocolate
S: Black    H: Territorial Beige

FOLK ART — ☐ Raw Umber (PP)

JO SONJA — ☐ Raw Umber

LIQUITEX — ☐ Raw Umber

**NOTES**

**TCS #BR-8-6-9**

ACCENT — ☐ Burnt Umber (ABC)
S: Black    H: Sweet Chocolate

AMERICANA — ☐ Bittersweet Chocolate
S: Black    H: Driftwood

CERAMCOAT — ☐ * Brown Iron Oxide + Black 2:1

FOLK ART — ☐ * Raw Umber + Black 3:1

JO SONJA — ☐ * Brown Earth + Raw Umber + Black (Carbon) 4:1:1

LIQUITEX — ☐ * Burnt Umber + Black 1:1

**NOTES**

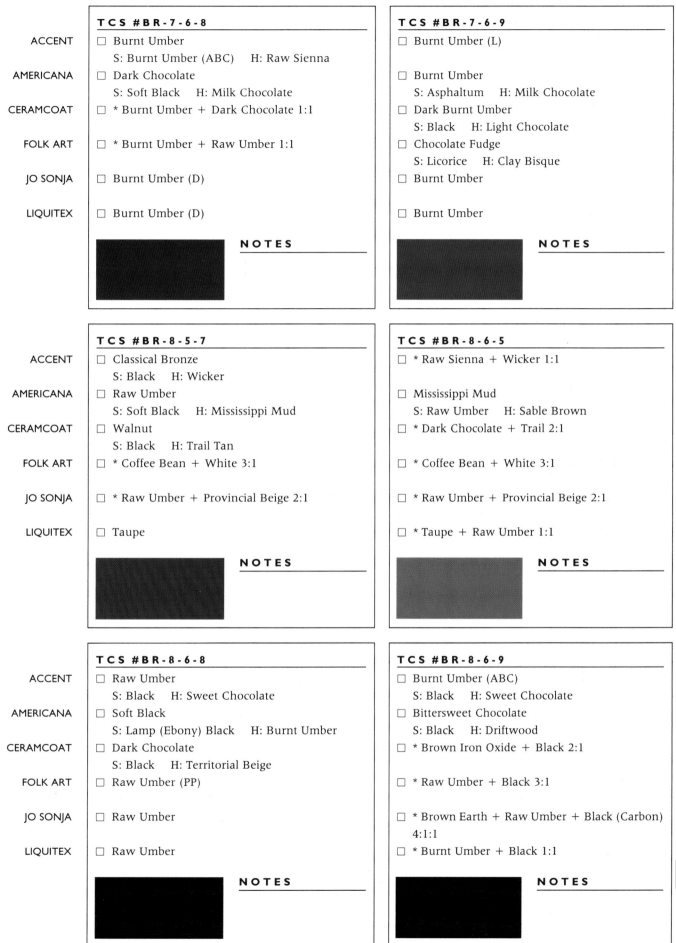

## BRAND        COLOR                          COLOR

|  | TCS #BK-1-7-8 |
| --- | --- |
| ACCENT | ☐ * Raw Umber + Soft Black 3:1 |
| AMERICANA | ☐ Charcoal Grey<br>    S: Soft Black    H: Neutral Grey |
| CERAMCOAT | ☐ * Dark Chocolate + Hippo Grey 5:1 |
| FOLK ART | ☐ Dark Gray<br>    S: Licorice    H: Barn Wood |
| JO SONJA | ☐ * Raw Umber + Black 12:1 |
| LIQUITEX | ☐ * Raw Umber + Ivory Black 8:1 |

**NOTES**

|  | TCS #BK-3-7-4 |
| --- | --- |
| ACCENT | ☐ * April Showers + Wicker 2:1 |
| AMERICANA | ☐ Driftwood<br>    S: Mississippi Mud    H: Cool Neutral (Toning) |
| CERAMCOAT | ☐ Lichen Grey<br>    S: Hammered Iron    H: Sandstone |
| FOLK ART | ☐ Barn Wood<br>    S: Medium Gray    H: Gray Mist |
| JO SONJA | ☐ * Smoked Pearl + Provincial Beige + Raw Umber 7:1:1 |
| LIQUITEX | ☐ * Unbleached Titanium + Neutral Gray 4:1 |

**NOTES**

|  | TCS #BK-3-7-5 |
| --- | --- |
| ACCENT | ☐ * Wicker + Soft Grey 1:1 |
| AMERICANA | ☐ Driftwood (L) |
| CERAMCOAT | ☐ Mudstone<br>    S: Hammered Iron    H: Sandstone |
| FOLK ART | ☐ Barn Wood (L) |
| JO SONJA | ☐ * Smoked Pearl + Provincial Beige + Raw Umber 5:1:1 |
| LIQUITEX | ☐ * Sandalwood + Neutral Gray 4:1 |

**NOTES**

|  | TCS #BK-3-7-8 |
| --- | --- |
| ACCENT | ☐ * Soft Grey + Warm Neutral 1:1 |
| AMERICANA | ☐ * Neutral Gray + Avocado (T) |
| CERAMCOAT | ☐ Hammered Iron<br>    S: Black Green    H: Lichen Grey |
| FOLK ART | ☐ Dapple Gray<br>    S: Dark Gray    H: Gray Flannel |
| JO SONJA | ☐ * Moss Green + Nimbus Grey 1:1 |
| LIQUITEX | ☐ * Olive + Neutral Gray 1:1 |

**NOTES**

|  | TCS #BK-4-5-5 |
| --- | --- |
| ACCENT | ☐ * Soft Gray + White 2:1 |
| AMERICANA | ☐ * Neutral Grey + Buttermilk 2:1 |
| CERAMCOAT | ☐ Cadet Grey<br>    S: Hippo Grey    H: Soft Grey |
| FOLK ART | ☐ * Light Gray + Dapple Gray 5:1 |
| JO SONJA | ☐ Nimbus Grey |
| LIQUITEX | ☐ * Neutral Gray + White 1:1 |

**NOTES**

|  | TCS #BK-5-1-2 |
| --- | --- |
| ACCENT | ☐ * White + Real Black 15:1 |
| AMERICANA | ☐ Dove Grey<br>    S: Slate Grey    H: White |
| CERAMCOAT | ☐ * White + Black 15:1 |
| FOLK ART | ☐ Light Gray<br>    S: Medium Gray    H: White |
| JO SONJA | ☐ * White + Carbon Black 15:1 |
| LIQUITEX | ☐ * White + Mars Black 15:1 |

**NOTES**

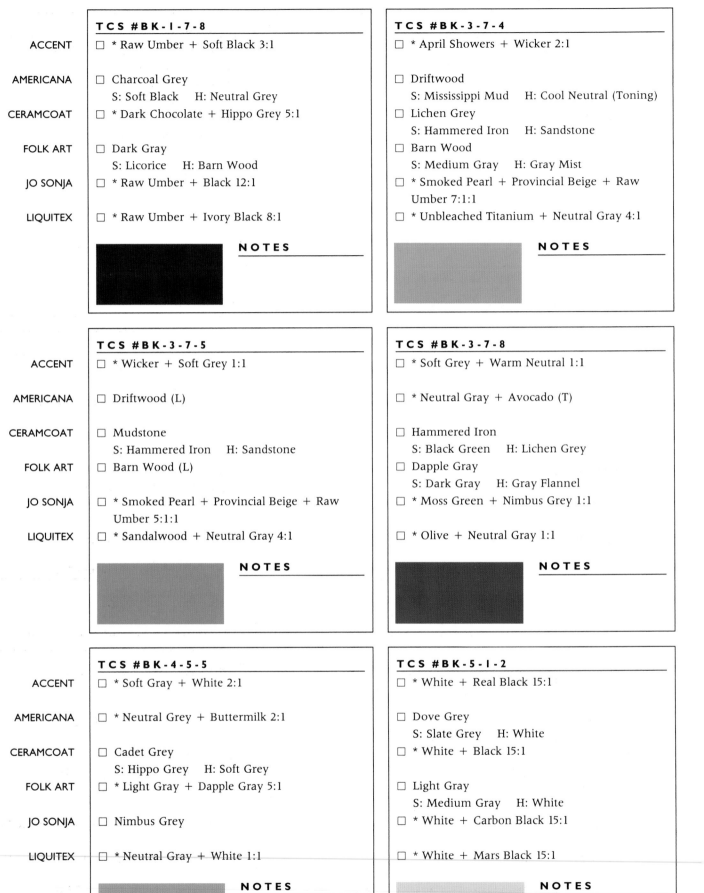

# BRAND

## COLOR

### TCS #BK-5-1-8

| BRAND | COLOR |
|---|---|
| ACCENT | ☐ Black (Soft)<br>S: None  H: Soldier Blue |
| AMERICANA | ☐ Black (Ebony/Lamp) (D)<br>S: None  H: Neutral Grey |
| CERAMCOAT | ☐ Black (D) |
| FOLK ART | ☐ Black (Ivory) (PP) |
| JO SONJA | ☐ Black (Carbon) (D) |
| LIQUITEX | ☐ Black (Ivory) |

**NOTES**

## COLOR

### TCS #BK-5-1-9

| | |
|---|---|
| ACCENT | ☐ Black (Real or Ebony (ABC) #2612)<br>S: None  H: Soldier Blue |
| AMERICANA | ☐ Black (Ebony/Lamp)<br>S: None  H: Neutral Grey |
| CERAMCOAT | ☐ Black<br>S: None  H: Bridgeport Gray |
| FOLK ART | ☐ Licorice<br>S: Midnight  H: Any lighter color |
| JO SONJA | ☐ Black (Carbon) |
| LIQUITEX | ☐ Black (Mars) |

**NOTES**

### TCS #BK-5-5-1

| | |
|---|---|
| ACCENT | ☐ * White + Soft Grey 10:1 |
| AMERICANA | ☐ * White + Neutral Grey Toning 12:1 |
| CERAMCOAT | ☐ * White + Cadet Grey 10:1 |
| FOLK ART | ☐ Gray Mist<br>S: Barn Wood  H: White |
| JO SONJA | ☐ * White + Nimbus Grey 12:1 |
| LIQUITEX | ☐ * White + Neutral Gray 12:1 |

**NOTES**

### TCS #BK-5-5-3

| | |
|---|---|
| ACCENT | ☐ * April Showers + Soft Gray 1:1 |
| AMERICANA | ☐ * Dove Grey + Neutral Grey Toning (T) |
| CERAMCOAT | ☐ Quaker Grey<br>S: Charcoal  H: White |
| FOLK ART | ☐ Gray Flannel<br>S: Medium Gray  H: White |
| JO SONJA | ☐ * Nimbus Grey + White 1:1 |
| LIQUITEX | ☐ * Neutral Gray + White 1:1 |

**NOTES**

### TCS #BK-5-5-5

| | |
|---|---|
| ACCENT | ☐ Soft Grey  S: Soft Grey + Black (T)<br>H: April Showers + Soft Grey 1:1 |
| AMERICANA | ☐ Neutral Grey<br>S: Graphite  H: Slate Grey |
| CERAMCOAT | ☐ Hippo Grey<br>S: Charcoal  H: Cadet Gray |
| FOLK ART | ☐ Medium Gray<br>S: Dark Gray  H: Light Gray |
| JO SONJA | ☐ * Black + White 1:1 |
| LIQUITEX | ☐ Neutral Gray |

**NOTES**

### TCS #BK-6-2-1

| | |
|---|---|
| ACCENT | ☐ * April Showers + White 2:1 |
| AMERICANA | ☐ * White + Dove Grey + Grey Sky 4:4:1 |
| CERAMCOAT | ☐ Soft Grey<br>S: Drizzle Grey  H: Magnolia White |
| FOLK ART | ☐ * Gray Mist + Dove Gray 4:1 |
| JO SONJA | ☐ * White + Nimbus Grey + Payne's Grey 16:1:1 |
| LIQUITEX | ☐ * White + Neutral Gray + Payne's Gray 16:1:1 |

**NOTES**

| | COLOR | COLOR |

---

**TCS #BK-6-2-2**

ACCENT · ☐ April Showers   S: April Showers + Black
(T)   H: White Wash + April Showers 1:1

AMERICANA · ☐ * Dove Grey + Grey Sky 4:1

CERAMCOAT · ☐ Drizzle Grey
S: Bridgeport Gray   H: White

FOLK ART · ☐ * Light Gray + Porcelain Blue 12:1

JO SONJA · ☐ * White + Nimbus Grey + Payne's Grey 12:1:1

LIQUITEX · ☐ * White + Neutral Gray + Payne's Gray 12:1:1

**NOTES**

---

**TCS #BK-6-2-8**

☐ * April Showers + Payne's Grey + Black 6:1:1

☐ * Slate Grey + Black 1:1

☐ Charcoal (D)

☐ Charcoal Grey
S: Licorice   H: Dark Gray

☐ * Nimbus Grey + White + Payne's Grey 10:1:1

☐ * Neutral Gray + Payne's Gray + White 10:1:1

**NOTES**

---

**TCS #BK-6-2-9**

ACCENT · ☐ * Black + Payne's Grey + White 5:1:T

AMERICANA · ☐ Graphite   S: Lamp (Ebony) Black
H: Neutral Grey Toning

CERAMCOAT · ☐ Charcoal
S: None   H: Bridgeport Grey

FOLK ART · ☐ * Charcoal Grey + Black 4:1

JO SONJA · ☐ * Black + Payne's Grey + White 4:4:1

LIQUITEX · ☐ * Black + Payne's Gray + White 4:4:1

**NOTES**

---

**TCS #BK-7-2-3**

☐ * April Showers + Soft Grey + Payne's Grey
6:1:1

☐ Slate Grey
S: Deep Midnight Blue   H: Grey Sky

☐ Bridgeport Grey
S: Charcoal   H: Drizzle Grey

☐ * Whipped Berry + Payne's Gray (T)

☐ * Nimbus Grey + French Blue 12:1

☐ * Neutral Gray + White + French Gray/Blue
1:1:T

**NOTES**

---

**TCS #BK-8-2-3**

ACCENT · ☐ * April Showers + Sapphire (T)

AMERICANA · ☐ Grey Sky
S: Slate Grey   H: White

CERAMCOAT · ☐ * Drizzle Grey + Blue Jay (T)

FOLK ART · ☐ Dove Gray
S: Charcoal   H: White

JO SONJA · ☐ * Nimbus Grey + White + Sapphire 1:1:T

LIQUITEX · ☐ * Neutral Gray + White + French Gray/Blue
1:1:T

**NOTES**

---

**TCS #WH-3-7-5**

☐ * Warm Neutral + Soft Grey 8:1

☐ Cool Neutral S: Mississippi Mud
H: Cool Neutral + White 1:1

☐ * Sandstone + Lichen Grey 5:1

☐ Porcelain White (Disc.) or * Clay Bisque + Barn
Wood (T)

☐ * Smoked Pearl + Nimbus Grey 12:1

☐ * Parchment + Neutral Gray 12:1

**NOTES**

**BRAND**  **COLOR**  **COLOR**

### TCS #WH-5-1-1

| ACCENT | ☐ White (Real or Titanium, ABC, #2617)<br>S: Highlight Hue of Predominant Color |
| AMERICANA | ☐ White (Snow or Titanium)<br>S: Grey Sky   H: None |
| CERAMCOAT | ☐ White   S: Highlight Hue of Predominant<br>Color   H: None |
| FOLK ART | ☐ White (Titanium) (PP) |
| JO SONJA | ☐ White (Titanium) |
| LIQUITEX | ☐ White (Titanium) |

**NOTES**

### TCS #WH-5-1-2

| ACCENT | ☐ Soft White   S: Highlight Hue of<br>Predominant Color   H: None |
| AMERICANA | ☐ White Wash<br>S: Grey Sky   H: None |
| CERAMCOAT | ☐ Magnolia White   S: Highlight Hue of<br>Predominant Color   H: None |
| FOLK ART | ☐ Wicker White<br>S: Any darker color   H: None |
| JO SONJA | ☐ Titanium White (L) |
| LIQUITEX | ☐ White (Titanium) (L) |

**NOTES**

### TCS #WH-6-3-1

| ACCENT | ☐ White Wash<br>S: Off White   H: Soft White |
| AMERICANA | ☐ * White Wash + Desert Sand 10:1 |
| CERAMCOAT | ☐ * White + Sandstone 20:1 |
| FOLK ART | ☐ * Titanium White + Tapioca (T) |
| JO SONJA | ☐ * Titanium White + Smoked Pearl (T) |
| LIQUITEX | ☐ * Titanium White + Parchment (T) |

**NOTES**

### TCS #WH-6-3-2

| ACCENT | ☐ Off White<br>S: Warm Neutral   H: White Wash |
| AMERICANA | ☐ * Eggshell + White 1:1 |
| CERAMCOAT | ☐ * White + Lichen Grey (T) |
| FOLK ART | ☐ Tapioca<br>S: Butter Pecan   H: White |
| JO SONJA | ☐ * White + Smoked Pearl 5:1 |
| LIQUITEX | ☐ * White + Parchment (T) |

**NOTES**

### TCS #WH-6-3-4

| ACCENT | ☐ * Off White + Mushroom 8:1 |
| AMERICANA | ☐ Eggshell<br>S: Shale Green   H: Light Buttermilk |
| CERAMCOAT | ☐ * White + Lichen Grey 6:1 |
| FOLK ART | ☐ * Tapioca + Barn Wood 2:1 |
| JO SONJA | ☐ * White + Smoked Pearl + Nimbus Grey 3:1:T |
| LIQUITEX | ☐ * Parchment + Neutral Gray (T) |

**NOTES**

### TCS #WH-6-4-1

| ACCENT | ☐ * White + Cool Neutral 18:1 |
| AMERICANA | ☐ * White + Warm Neutral 18:1 |
| CERAMCOAT | ☐ Oyster White<br>S: Santa's Flesh   H: White |
| FOLK ART | ☐ * White + Milkshake 15:1 |
| JO SONJA | ☐ * White + Opal 15:1 |
| LIQUITEX | ☐ * White + Sandalwood 20:1 |

**NOTES**

**COLOR**                                    **COLOR**

### TCS #WH-6-4-3

| | |
|---|---|
| ACCENT | ☐ * White + Warm Neutral 1:1 |
| AMERICANA | ☐ * Desert Sand + White 1:1 |
| CERAMCOAT | ☐ * Sandstone + White 1:1 |
| FOLK ART | ☐ Vanilla Cream<br>S: Country Twill    H: White |
| JO SONJA | ☐ * Smoked Pearl + White 1:1 |
| LIQUITEX | ☐ * White + Unbleached Titanium + Parchment 2:1:1 |

**NOTES**

### TCS #WH-6-4-5

| | |
|---|---|
| ACCENT | ☐ Warm Neutral (ABC)<br>S: Wicker   H: Off White |
| AMERICANA | ☐ Desert Sand (D) |
| CERAMCOAT | ☐ Sandstone (D) |
| FOLK ART | ☐ Clay Bisque (D) |
| JO SONJA | ☐ Smoked Pearl (D) |
| LIQUITEX | ☐ * Unbleached Titanium + Parchment 2:1 |

**NOTES**

### TCS #WH-6-4-6

| | |
|---|---|
| ACCENT | ☐ Linen<br>S: Wicker   H: Off White |
| AMERICANA | ☐ Desert Sand<br>S: Khaki Tan   H: Sand |
| CERAMCOAT | ☐ Sandstone<br>S: Lichen Grey   H: Antique White |
| FOLK ART | ☐ Clay Bisque<br>S: Coffee Bean   H: White |
| JO SONJA | ☐ Smoked Pearl |
| LIQUITEX | ☐ * Parchment + Unbleached Titanium 1:1 |

**NOTES**

### TCS #WH-6-4-9

| | |
|---|---|
| ACCENT | ☐ * Wicker + Antique White 1:1 |
| AMERICANA | ☐ Khaki Tan<br>S: Mississippi Mud   H: Desert Sand |
| CERAMCOAT | ☐ * Trail + Sandstone 1:1 |
| FOLK ART | ☐ Butter Pecan<br>S: Maple Syrup   H: White |
| JO SONJA | ☐ * Smoked Pearl + Prov. Beige + Raw Umber 5:1:1 |
| LIQUITEX | ☐ * Soft White + Raw Umber (T) |

**NOTES**

### TCS #WH-7-3-4

| | |
|---|---|
| ACCENT | ☐ * Off White + Wicker 3:1 |
| AMERICANA | ☐ Antique White<br>S: Mink Tan   H: Sand |
| CERAMCOAT | ☐ * Trail + White 1:1 |
| FOLK ART | ☐ Linen<br>S: Nutmeg   H: White |
| JO SONJA | ☐ * Smoked Pearl + Provincial Beige 1:1 |
| LIQUITEX | ☐ * Unbleached Titanium + Taupe (T) |

**NOTES**

### TCS #WH-8-2-1

| | |
|---|---|
| ACCENT | ☐ * White + Adobe Wash 2:1 |
| AMERICANA | ☐ * Light Buttermilk + White 1:1 |
| CERAMCOAT | ☐ * Light Ivory + White 1:1 |
| FOLK ART | ☐ Ivory White<br>S: Taffy   H: White |
| JO SONJA | ☐ * Warm White + White 1:1 |
| LIQUITEX | ☐ * Soft White + White 1:1 |

**NOTES**

## BRAND          COLOR                                    COLOR

| | |
|---|---|
| | **TCS #WH-8-2-2** |
| ACCENT | ☐ * Adobe Wash + White 1:1 |
| AMERICANA | ☐ Light Buttermilk<br>S: Desert Sand   H: White |
| CERAMCOAT | ☐ Light Ivory<br>S: Ivory   H: White |
| FOLK ART | ☐ Warm White<br>S: Clay Bisque   H: White |
| JO SONJA | ☐ Warm White |
| LIQUITEX | ☐ Soft White |

**NOTES**

| | |
|---|---|
| | **TCS #WH-8-2-3** |
| ☐ * Adobe Wash + White 2:1 |
| ☐ * Light Buttermilk + Buttermilk 1:1 |
| ☐ Butter Cream<br>S: Flesh Tan   H: White |
| ☐ * Warm White + Taffy 1:1 |
| ☐ * Warm White (L) |
| ☐ * Soft White (L) |

**NOTES**

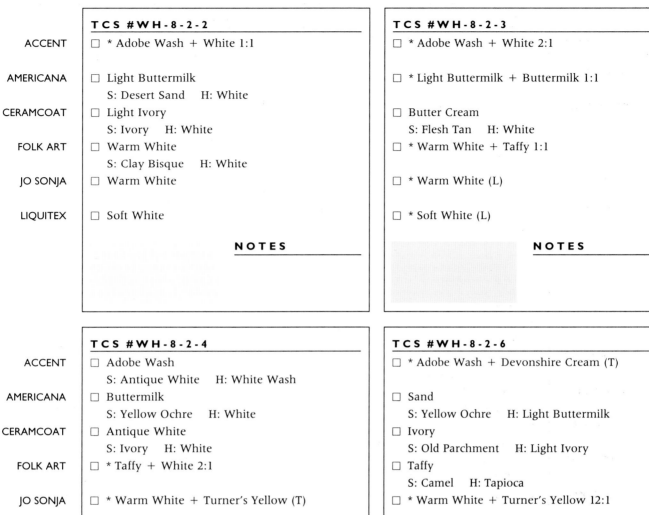

| | |
|---|---|
| | **TCS #WH-8-2-4** |
| ACCENT | ☐ Adobe Wash<br>S: Antique White   H: White Wash |
| AMERICANA | ☐ Buttermilk<br>S: Yellow Ochre   H: White |
| CERAMCOAT | ☐ Antique White<br>S: Ivory   H: White |
| FOLK ART | ☐ * Taffy + White 2:1 |
| JO SONJA | ☐ * Warm White + Turner's Yellow (T) |
| LIQUITEX | ☐ * Soft White + Turner's Yellow (T) |

**NOTES**

| | |
|---|---|
| | **TCS #WH-8-2-6** |
| ☐ * Adobe Wash + Devonshire Cream (T) |
| ☐ Sand<br>S: Yellow Ochre   H: Light Buttermilk |
| ☐ Ivory<br>S: Old Parchment   H: Light Ivory |
| ☐ Taffy<br>S: Camel   H: Tapioca |
| ☐ * Warm White + Turner's Yellow 12:1 |
| ☐ * Soft White + Turner's Yellow 12:1 |

**NOTES**

| | |
|---|---|
| | **TCS #WH-8-2-8** |
| ACCENT | ☐ Antique White   S: Highlight Hue of<br>Predominant Color   H: None |
| AMERICANA | ☐ * Antique White + Raw Sienna (T) |
| CERAMCOAT | ☐ * Sandstone + Trail (T) |
| FOLK ART | ☐ * Camel + White 1:1 |
| JO SONJA | ☐ * Smoked Pearl + Raw Sienna (T) |
| LIQUITEX | ☐ * Parchment + Unbleached Titanium 2:1 |

**NOTES**

# Alphabetic Index

Choose a color name from the alphabetic index. This index lists the color names in brand order. Select the brand of paint listed in your project. The index will list the TCS# and the page number.

## Accent® by Koh-I-Noor

| COLOR NAME | PG# | TCS# |
|---|---|---|
| Adobe Wash | 85 | WH-8-2-4 |
| Antique White | 85 | WH-8-2-8 |
| Apache Red | 30 | RE-4-3-8 |
| Apricot Stone | 24 | RO-2-3-3 |
| April Showers | 82 | BK-6-2-2 |
| Avon on the Green | 61 | BG-8-2-8 |
| Barn Red | 31 | RE-4-6-5 |
| Black (Real/Ebony) (ABC) | 81 | BK-5-1-9 |
| Black (Soft) | 81 | BK-5-1-8 |
| Black Green | 64 | GR-3-6-8 |
| Blonde | 20 | OR-4-2-1 |
| Blue Bonnet | 44 | BV-5-4-4 |
| Blue Smoke | 47 | BL-4-8-4 |
| Bordeaux | 38 | RV-1-2-8 |
| Burgundy (ABC) | 35 | RE-6-4-9 |
| Burgundy Deep | 39 | RV-2-2-8 |
| Burnt Sienna | 75 | BR-5-1-5 |
| Burnt Sienna (ABC) | 77 | BR-6-2-6 |
| Burnt Umber | 79 | BR-7-6-8 |
| Burnt Umber (ABC) | 79 | BR-8-6-9 |
| Butter Cream | 19 | YE-7-7-3 |
| Cactus Flower | 16 | YE-4-1-2 |
| Celery | 67 | GR-7-9-2 |
| Chesapeake Blue | 56 | BG-2-4-9 |
| Classical Bronze | 79 | BR-8-5-7 |
| Classical Gold | 16 | YE-2-4-5 |
| Classical Green | 70 | YG-5-6-7 |
| Clear Blue | 52 | BL-6-1-5 |
| Cool Neutral (ABC) | 78 | BR-7-6-3 |
| Coral Blush | 27 | RO-8-3-4 |
| Cottage Rose | 28 | RE-3-2-5 |
| Crimson (ABC) | 34 | RE-6-2-7 |
| Dark Flesh | 23 | OR-6-3-7 |
| Deep Forest Green | 68 | GR-8-3-9 |
| Devonshire Cream | 19 | YE-7-7-4 |
| Dijon Gold | 18 | YE-6-2-6 |
| Dioxazine Purple (ABC) | 43 | VI-5-1-9 |
| Eggplant | 42 | RV-9-2-9 |
| English Marmalade | 24 | RO-1-3-5 |
| Fingerberry Red | 33 | RE-5-6-9 |
| Forest Green | 66 | GR-6-6-6 |
| Fuschia | 38 | RV-1-2-6 |
| Golden Harvest | 18 | YE-6-4-5 |
| Golden Oxide | 19 | YO-2-1-3 |

| COLOR NAME | PG# | TCS# |
|---|---|---|
| Green Olive | 68 | GR-8-6-6 |
| Holiday Green | 66 | GR-6-2-5 |
| Holiday Red | 35 | RE-6-4-4 |
| Indian Sky | 46 | BL-3-3-2 |
| Jo Sonja Red | 33 | RE-6-1-5 |
| Larkspur Blue | 54 | BG-1-3-7 |
| Liberty Blue | 50 | BL-5-2-8 |
| Light Cactus Flower | 18 | YE-6-2-2 |
| Light Flesh | 22 | OR-6-3-2 |
| Light Peaches n' Cream | 23 | OR-6-3-3 |
| Light Roseberry | 37 | RE-6-7-4 |
| Light Seafoam Green | 60 | BG-7-1-2 |
| Light Stoneware Blue | 51 | BL-5-7-3 |
| Light Tumbleweed | 73 | BR-2-2-2 |
| Light Village Green | 64 | GR-3-7-3 |
| Light Yellow Green | 68 | YG-4-3-2 |
| Lilac | 40 | RV-5-8-4 |
| Linen | 84 | WH-6-4-6 |
| Marina Blue | 58 | BG-4-4-5 |
| Medium Flesh | 23 | OR-6-3-4 |
| Mellow Yellow | 17 | YE-5-2-3 |
| Midnight Blue | 49 | BL-5-1-9 |
| Monet Blue | 45 | BV-8-3-4 |
| Mushroom | 67 | GR-7-8-4 |
| Napthol Red Light (ABC) | 29 | RE-4-1-6 |
| Nevada Turquoise | 56 | BG-2-4-7 |
| New Leaf | 70 | YG-6-3-3 |
| Off White | 83 | WH-6-3-2 |
| Painted Desert | 34 | RE-6-2-3 |
| Paradise Blue | 56 | BG-3-4-3 |
| Payne's Grey (ABC) | 50 | BL-5-2-9 |
| Peaches n' Cream | 23 | OR-6-3-5 |
| Pennsylvania Clay | 26 | RO-5-4-7 |
| Pine Needle Green | 69 | YG-4-3-9 |
| Pink Blossom | 27 | RE-3-2-2 |
| Plum | 41 | RV-5-8-9 |
| Prairie Green | 62 | BG-9-6-9 |
| Pthalo Green (ABC) | 62 | BG-9-1-8 |
| Pueblo Red | 29 | RE-4-2-7 |
| Pure Blue | 48 | BL-5-1-6 |
| Pure Red | 33 | RE-6-1-6 |
| Pure Yellow | 16 | YE-4-1-5 |
| Purple Canyon | 41 | RV-9-2-8 |

| COLOR NAME | PG# | TCS# |
|---|---|---|
| Raw Sienna | 78 | BR-7-5-7 |
| Raw Umber | 79 | BR-8-6-8 |
| Razzle Red | 32 | RE-5-1-5 |
| Roseberry | 37 | RE-6-7-5 |
| Rose Blush | 30 | RE-4-3-5 |
| Royal Blue | 45 | BV-9-6-7 |
| Sage | 62 | BG-8-8-3 |
| Sapphire (ABC) | 47 | BL-4-5-6 |
| Seafoam Green | 60 | BG-7-1-3 |
| Sedona Clay | 26 | RO-5-4-5 |
| Soft Blue | 54 | BG-1-3-4 |
| Soft Grey | 81 | BK-5-5-5 |
| Soft White | 83 | WH-5-1-2 |
| Soldier Blue | 51 | BL-5-7-8 |
| Spring Pink | 30 | RE-4-3-3 |
| Stoneware Blue | 51 | BL-5-7-4 |
| Sunkiss Yellow | 17 | YE-5-1-6 |
| Sunsational Yellow | 18 | YE-6-2-4 |
| Sweet Chocolate | 75 | BR-5-1-6 |
| Teal Deep (ABC) | 62 | BG-9-7-9 |
| Teal Green | 59 | BG-5-1-8 |
| Telemark Green | 59 | BG-4-7-9 |
| True Green | 66 | GR-7-2-5 |
| True Orange | 20 | OR-4-1-5 |
| True Purple | 43 | VI-5-1-7 |
| Tumbleweed | 73 | BR-1-2-5 |
| Ultramarine Blue | 48 | BL-5-1-5 |
| Ultramar. Blue Dp. (ABC) | 52 | BL-6-1-6 |
| Vermillion (ABC) | 25 | RO-5-1-7 |
| Victorian Mauve | 24 | OR-6-7-4 |
| Village Green | 64 | GR-3-7-4 |
| Warm Neutral (ABC) | 84 | WH-6-4-5 |
| White (Titanium) (ABC) | 83 | WH-5-1-1 |
| White Wash | 83 | WH-6-3-1 |
| Wicker | 78 | BR-7-4-3 |
| Wild Heather | 42 | VI-5-1-4 |
| Wild Honey | 74 | BR-2-4-4 |
| Wild Hyacinth | 41 | RV-9-2-3 |
| Windsor Blue | 53 | BL-7-2-8 |
| Wineberry | 41 | RV-5-8-8 |
| Yellow Light (ABC) | 16 | YE-4-1-4 |
| Yellow Ochre (ABC) | 18 | YE-6-4-7 |

## A WORD ABOUT OUR MATCHES

A color match to exact or very close colors are listed whenever possible. When there is not an exact match, we offer a mixing recipe including ratios for attaining the color. Although pigments may vary between brands, and colors can change a bit in different dye lots, we make every effort to give you an exact match. Please read more about the process used to determine matching colors and their TCS numbers on page 13.

# Americana™ by DecoArt

| COLOR NAME | PG# | TCS# |
|---|---|---|
| Alizarin Crimson | 35 | RE-6-4-5 |
| Antique Gold | 18 | YE-6-4-5 |
| Antique Gold Deep | 71 | YG-9-4-6 |
| Antique Green | 71 | YG-8-8-7 |
| Antique Maroon | 33 | RE-5-5-8 |
| Antique Mauve | 36 | RE-6-5-7 |
| Antique Rose | 27 | RO-8-3-7 |
| Antique Teal | 59 | BG-5-3-8 |
| Antique White | 84 | WH-7-3-4 |
| Asphaltum | 78 | BR-7-5-8 |
| Avocado | 69 | YG-4-3-6 |
| Baby Blue | 49 | BL-5-2-2 |
| Baby Pink | 34 | RE-6-3-2 |
| Base Flesh | 24 | OR-6-7-2 |
| Berry Red | 33 | RE-6-1-6 |
| Bittersweet Chocolate | 79 | BR-8-6-9 |
| Black (Lamp or Ebony) | 81 | BK-5-1-9 |
| Black Forest Green | 64 | GR-3-5-8 |
| Black Green | 65 | GR-5-3-9 |
| Black Plum | 37 | RE-7-2-9 |
| Blue Chiffon | 52 | BL-6-1-2 |
| Blueberry | 53 | BL-7-4-9 |
| Bluegrass Green | 59 | BG-5-1-6 |
| Blue Green | 58 | BG-4-1-8 |
| Blue/Grey Mist | 48 | BL-4-9-5 |
| Blue Haze | 56 | BG-2-4-9 |
| Blue Mist | 54 | BG-1-7-2 |
| Blue Violet | 45 | BV-9-1-8 |
| Blush Flesh | 28 | RE-3-2-6 |
| Boysenberry Pink | 38 | RV-1-2-5 |
| Brandy Wine | 31 | RE-4-6-8 |
| Bright Green | 67 | GR-8-2-4 |
| Brilliant Red | 29 | RE-4-1-5 |
| Burgundy Wine | 35 | RE-6-4-8 |
| Burnt Orange | 26 | RO-5-4-5 |
| Burnt Sienna | 77 | BR-6-2-6 |
| Burnt Umber | 79 | BR-7-6-9 |
| Buttermilk | 85 | WH-8-2-4 |
| Cadmium Orange | 25 | RO-5-1-7 |
| Cadmium Red | 29 | RE-4-1-6 |
| Cadmium Yellow | 17 | YE-5-1-6 |
| Calico Red | 32 | RE-5-1-4 |
| Camel | 72 | BR-1-2-2 |
| Cashmere Beige | 76 | BR-5-4-3 |
| Charcoal Grey | 80 | BK-1-7-8 |
| Cherry Red | 32 | RE-5-1-6 |
| Colonial Green | 55 | BG-1-7-4 |
| Cool Neutral | 82 | WH-3-7-5 |
| Coral Rose | 27 | RO-8-3-4 |
| Country Blue | 45 | BV-8-3-4 |
| Country Red | 29 | RE-4-2-5 |
| Cranberry Wine | 36 | RE-6-5-8 |
| Crimson Tide | 29 | RE-4-2-7 |
| Dark Chocolate | 79 | BR-7-6-8 |
| Dark Pine | 63 | GR-3-3-6 |
| Deep Burgundy | 35 | RE-6-4-9 |
| Deep Midnight Blue | 50 | BL-5-2-8 |
| Deep Teal | 62 | BG-9-6-9 |
| Desert Sand | 84 | WH-6-4-6 |
| Desert Turquoise | 58 | BG-4-4-5 |
| Dioxazine Purple | 43 | VI-5-1-7 |
| Dove Grey | 80 | BK-5-1-2 |
| Dried Basil Green | 71 | YG-8-8-3 |
| Driftwood | 80 | BK-3-7-4 |
| Dusty Rose | 24 | OR-6-7-3 |
| Eggshell | 83 | WH-6-3-4 |
| Evergreen | 69 | YG-4-3-7 |
| Flesh Tone | 23 | OR-6-3-4 |
| Forest Green | 66 | GR-6-6-6 |
| French Grey/Blue | 51 | BL-5-7-4 |
| French Mauve | 37 | RE-6-7-4 |
| French Mocha | 33 | RE-5-8-5 |
| French Vanilla | 73 | BR-2-2-2 |
| Georgia Clay | 27 | RO-7-4-7 |
| Golden Straw | 18 | YE-5-5-5 |
| Gooseberry Pink | 31 | RE-4-4-5 |
| Graphite | 82 | BK-6-2-9 |
| Green Mist | 64 | GR-3-7-4 |
| Grey Sky | 82 | BK-8-2-3 |
| Hauser Dark Green | 64 | GR-3-6-8 |
| Hauser Light Green | 69 | YG-4-3-3 |
| Hauser Medium Green | 67 | GR-7-4-5 |
| Hi-Lite Flesh | 29 | RE-4-3-1 |
| Holly Green | 63 | GR-3-3-5 |
| Honey Brown | 72 | BR-1-2-4 |
| Ice Blue | 47 | BL-4-9-2 |
| Indian Turquoise | 56 | BG-3-4-3 |
| Jade Green | 66 | GR-5-6-4 |
| Kelly Green | 63 | GR-3-2-4 |
| Khaki Tan | 84 | WH-6-4-9 |
| Lavender | 43 | VI-5-1-5 |
| Leaf Green | 65 | GR-5-4-7 |
| Lemon Yellow | 16 | YE-4-1-4 |
| Light Avocado | 70 | YG-5-6-5 |
| Light Buttermilk | 85 | WH-8-2-2 |
| Light Cinnamon | 74 | BR-2-2-6 |
| Light French Blue | 47 | BL-4-8-4 |
| Lilac | 42 | VI-5-1-2 |
| Marigold | 18 | YE-6-2-6 |
| Mauve | 37 | RE-6-7-5 |
| Medium Flesh | 23 | OR-6-3-5 |
| Midnite Blue | 53 | BL-7-2-8 |
| Midnite Green | 65 | GR-5-3-8 |
| Milk Chocolate | 74 | BR-2-2-7 |
| Mink Tan | 76 | BR-5-4-4 |
| Mint Julip Green | 63 | GR-3-3-3 |
| Mississippi Mud | 79 | BR-8-6-5 |
| Mistletoe | 66 | GR-6-4-5 |
| Mocha | 77 | BR-6-4-3 |
| Moon Yellow | 19 | YE-7-7-3 |
| Napa Red | 38 | RV-1-2-8 |
| Napthol Red | 32 | RE-5-1-5 |
| Navy Blue | 53 | BL-7-2-9 |
| Neutral Grey | 81 | BK-5-5-5 |
| Olde Gold | 16 | YE-2-4-5 |
| Olive Green | 69 | YG-5-6-2 |
| Orchid | 40 | RV-5-2-3 |
| Oxblood | 26 | RO-5-4-7 |
| Pansy Lavender | 41 | RV-9-2-8 |
| Payne's Grey | 50 | BL-5-2-9 |
| Peaches 'n Cream | 25 | RO-3-3-3 |
| Pineapple | 16 | YE-4-1-2 |
| Pink Chiffon | 35 | RE-6-5-1 |
| Plantation Pine | 69 | YG-4-3-9 |
| Plum | 41 | RV-5-8-9 |
| Primary Blue | 48 | BL-5-1-5 |
| Primary Red | 34 | RE-6-2-6 |
| Primary Yellow | 17 | YE-5-1-7 |
| Prussian Blue | 49 | BL-5-2-7 |
| Pumpkin | 21 | OR-5-1-5 |
| Raspberry | 36 | RE-6-5-5 |
| Raw Sienna | 73 | BR-1-2-5 |
| Raw Umber | 79 | BR-8-5-7 |
| Red Iron Oxide | 31 | RE-4-6-5 |
| Red Violet | 39 | RV-2-2-8 |
| Reindeer Moss Green | 72 | YG-9-9-2 |
| Rookwood Red | 33 | RE-5-6-9 |
| Royal Fuchsia | 38 | RV-1-2-6 |
| Royal Purple | 42 | RV-9-2-9 |
| Russet | 77 | BR-6-2-9 |
| Sable Brown | 75 | BR-4-4-5 |
| Salem Blue | 54 | BG-1-3-3 |
| Sand | 85 | WH-8-2-6 |
| Santa Red | 34 | RE-6-2-7 |
| Sapphire | 46 | BL-4-2-6 |
| Sea Aqua | 60 | BG-7-1-3 |
| Shading Flesh | 23 | OR-6-3-8 |
| Shale Green | 67 | GR-7-8-4 |
| Silver Sage Green | 62 | BG-8-8-3 |
| Slate Grey | 82 | BK-7-2-3 |
| Soft Black | 79 | BR-8-6-8 |
| Spice Pink | 30 | RE-4-3-5 |
| Summer Lilac | 42 | RV-9-6-5 |
| Taffy Cream | 18 | YE-6-2-4 |
| Tangelo Orange | 25 | RO-5-1-6 |
| Tangerine | 19 | YO-5-1-4 |
| Taupe | 40 | RV-5-8-2 |
| Teal Green | 59 | BG-5-3-7 |
| Terra Cotta | 73 | BR-1-2-7 |
| Toffee | 76 | BR-5-4-2 |
| Tomato Red | 29 | RE-4-2-6 |
| True Blue | 48 | BL-5-1-6 |
| True Ochre | 18 | YE-6-4-7 |
| True Red | 33 | RE-6-1-5 |
| Ultra Blue Deep | 49 | BL-5-2-6 |
| Uniform Blue | 51 | BL-5-7-7 |
| Victorian Blue | 54 | BG-1-3-8 |
| Violet Haze | 43 | VI-9-6-6 |
| Viridian Green | 62 | BG-9-1-8 |
| Warm Neutral | 78 | BR-7-6-3 |
| Wedgewood Blue | 53 | BL-7-4-8 |
| White (Titanium or Snow) | 83 | WH-5-1-1 |

| Color Name | PG# | TCS# | Color Name | PG# | TCS# | Color Name | PG# | TCS# |
|---|---|---|---|---|---|---|---|---|
| White Wash | 83 | WH-5-1-2 | Caribbean Blue | 58 | BG-4-4-3 | Hydrangea Pink | 34 | RE-6-2-3 |
| Williamsburg Blue | 51 | BL-5-7-5 | Caucasian Flesh | 23 | OR-6-3-6 | Ice Storm Violet | 42 | RV-9-6-1 |
| Winter Blue | 50 | BL-5-5-3 | Cayenne | 22 | OR-5-9-8 | Indiana Rose | 26 | RO-5-3-2 |
| Yellow Green | 70 | YG-8-2-2 | Chambray Blue | 50 | BL-5-7-2 | Island Coral | 21 | OR-5-3-4 |
| Yellow Light | 17 | YE-5-1-5 | Charcoal | 82 | BK-6-2-9 | Ivory | 85 | WH-8-2-6 |
| Yellow Ochre | 19 | YE-7-7-6 | Christmas Green | 65 | GR-5-4-7 | Jade Green | 60 | BG-7-1-6 |

## Ceramcoat® by Delta

| COLOR NAME | PG# | TCS# | Color Name | PG# | TCS# | Color Name | PG# | TCS# |
|---|---|---|---|---|---|---|---|---|
| | | | Chrome Green Light | 68 | GR-8-6-5 | Jubilee Green | 66 | GR-7-2-5 |
| AC Flesh | 73 | BR-2-2-3 | Cinnamon | 21 | OR-4-7-9 | Kelly Green | 66 | GR-6-4-5 |
| Adobe Red | 27 | RO-8-3-7 | Cloudberry Tan | 74 | BR-2-4-6 | Laguna Blue | 57 | BG-4-1-5 |
| Adriatic Blue | 47 | BL-4-8-8 | Colonial Blue | 58 | BG-4-4-5 | Lavender | 43 | VI-5-8-5 |
| Alpine Green | 62 | BG-9-6-8 | Copen Blue | 52 | BL-6-1-6 | Lavender Lace | 45 | BV-7-8-3 |
| Antique Gold | 18 | YE-6-4-5 | Coral | 27 | RO-8-3-4 | Leaf Green | 69 | YG-4-3-3 |
| Antique Rose | 28 | RE-3-5-5 | Crimson | 35 | RE-6-4-4 | Leprechaun | 64 | GR-4-6-5 |
| Antique White | 85 | WH-8-2-4 | Crocus Yellow | 18 | YE-6-2-4 | Liberty Blue | 47 | BL-4-5-6 |
| Apple Green | 70 | YG-6-2-3 | Custard | 18 | YE-6-2-2 | Lichen Grey | 80 | BK-3-7-4 |
| Aquamarine | 56 | BG-2-4-5 | Dark Brown | 74 | BR-2-2-8 | Light Chocolate | 77 | BR-6-4-4 |
| Autumn Brown | 74 | BR-2-2-6 | Dark Burnt Umber | 79 | BR-7-6-9 | Light Ivory | 85 | WH-8-2-2 |
| Avalon Blue | 56 | BG-2-4-7 | Dark Chocolate | 79 | BR-8-6-8 | Light Jade Green | 60 | BG-7-1-5 |
| Avocado | 71 | YG-9-8-7 | Dark Flesh | 23 | OR-6-3-8 | Light Sage | 61 | BG-8-8-1 |
| Azure Blue | 56 | BG-3-1-6 | Dark Forest Green | 69 | YG-4-3-8 | Light Timberline Green | 72 | YG-9-9-3 |
| Bahama Purple | 44 | BV-5-2-4 | Dark Goldenrod | 20 | OR-4-7-4 | Lilac | 41 | RV-9-2-3 |
| Bambi Brown | 76 | BR-5-4-4 | Dark Jungle Green | 69 | YG-4-3-7 | Lilac Dust | 39 | RV-3-2-4 |
| Barn Red | 35 | RE-6-4-9 | Dark Night Blue | 48 | BL-4-9-9 | Lima Green | 70 | YG-8-2-2 |
| Berry Red | 37 | RE-7-2-5 | Deep Coral | 30 | RE-4-3-8 | Lime Green | 67 | GR-8-2-4 |
| Bittersweet Orange | 20 | OR-4-1-5 | Deep River Green | 64 | GR-3-5-8 | Lisa Pink | 34 | RE-6-2-4 |
| Black | 81 | BK-5-1-9 | Denim Blue | 47 | BL-4-5-5 | Luscious Lemon | 16 | YE-4-1-4 |
| Black Cherry | 35 | RE-6-4-8 | Desert Sun Orange | 22 | OR-5-9-6 | Magnolia White | 83 | WH-5-1-2 |
| Black Green | 65 | GR-5-3-9 | Dolphin Grey | 47 | BL-4-8-4 | Mallard Green | 59 | BG-5-1-8 |
| Blueberry | 53 | BL-7-4-8 | Dresden Flesh | 22 | OR-5-7-3 | Manganese Blue | 53 | BL-7-2-8 |
| Blue Danube | 52 | BL-6-1-3 | Drizzle Grey | 82 | BK-6-2-2 | Maple Sugar Tan | 19 | YE-7-7-4 |
| Blue Haze | 55 | BG-1-7-5 | Dunes Beige | 77 | BR-6-4-2 | Maroon | 35 | RE-6-4-7 |
| Blue Heaven | 49 | BL-5-2-2 | Dusty Mauve | 36 | RE-6-5-7 | Medium Flesh | 23 | OR-6-3-5 |
| Blue Jay | 49 | BL-5-2-4 | Dusty Plum | 40 | RV-5-8-4 | Mendocino Red | 38 | RV-1-2-8 |
| Blue Lagoon | 45 | BV-8-3-6 | Dusty Purple | 41 | RV-5-8-8 | Midnight Blue | 50 | BL-5-2-8 |
| Blue Mist | 52 | BL-6-1-2 | Egg Plant | 40 | RV-5-2-7 | Misty Mauve | 24 | OR-6-7-4 |
| Blue Spruce | 59 | BG-5-3-9 | Emerald Green | 59 | BG-5-1-6 | Mocha Brown | 73 | BR-2-2-5 |
| Blue Wisp | 54 | BG-1-7-2 | Empire Gold | 18 | YE-6-2-6 | Mudstone | 80 | BK-3-7-5 |
| Bonnie Blue | 50 | BL-5-5-5 | English Yew Green | 70 | YG-5-6-7 | Mulberry | 39 | RV-2-4-8 |
| Boston Fern | 71 | YG-8-8-7 | Fiesta Pink | 28 | RE-3-2-5 | Mustard | 16 | YE-2-4-5 |
| Bouquet Pink | 37 | RE-6-7-5 | Fire Red | 33 | RE-6-1-5 | Napa Wine | 41 | RV-5-9-8 |
| Bridgeport Grey | 82 | BK-7-2-3 | Fjord Blue | 48 | BL-4-9-8 | Napthol Crimson | 32 | RE-5-1-5 |
| Bright Red | 32 | RE-5-1-6 | Flesh Tan | 73 | BR-2-2-2 | Napthol Red Light | 34 | RE-6-2-6 |
| Bright Yellow | 17 | YE-5-1-5 | Fleshtone | 23 | OR-6-3-4 | Navy Blue | 49 | BL-5-2-6 |
| Brown Iron Oxide | 75 | BR-5-1-5 | Forest Green | 68 | GR-8-6-6 | Nectar Coral | 28 | RE-3-2-4 |
| Brown Velvet | 75 | BR-5-1-6 | Fuchsia | 38 | RV-1-2-5 | Nightfall Blue | 51 | BL-5-7-8 |
| Burgundy Rose | 31 | RE-4-6-8 | Gamal Green | 69 | YG-4-3-9 | Normandy Rose | 24 | OR-6-7-3 |
| Burnt Sienna | 76 | BR-6-2-5 | Georgia Clay | 26 | RO-5-4-4 | Norsk Blue | 55 | BG-1-7-8 |
| Burnt Umber | 78 | BR-7-5-8 | Golden Brown | 72 | BR-1-2-4 | Ocean Mist Blue | 54 | BG-1-4-2 |
| Butter Cream | 85 | WH-8-2-3 | G P Purple | 42 | VI-5-1-4 | Ocean Reef Blue | 52 | BL-6-1-5 |
| Butter Yellow | 17 | YE-5-4-5 | Grape | 40 | RV-3-2-7 | Old Parchment | 19 | YE-7-7-3 |
| Cactus Green | 61 | BG-8-6-2 | Green Isle | 65 | GR-5-1-5 | Olive Yellow | 71 | YG-8-8-4 |
| Cadet Grey | 80 | BK-4-5-5 | Green Sea | 65 | GR-5-4-6 | Opaque Blue | 49 | BL-5-2-5 |
| Calypso Orange | 20 | YO-6-1-3 | Gypsy Rose | 28 | RE-3-5-7 | Opaque Red | 32 | RE-5-1-4 |
| Candy Bar Brown | 33 | RE-5-5-8 | Hammered Iron | 80 | BK-3-7-8 | Opaque Yellow | 16 | YE-4-1-5 |
| Cape Cod Blue | 51 | BL-5-7-4 | Heritage Blue | 46 | BL-3-8-8 | Orange | 25 | RO-5-1-7 |
| Cardinal Red | 33 | RE-6-1-6 | Heritage Green | 60 | BG-7-4-5 | Oyster White | 83 | WH-6-4-1 |
| | | | Hippo Grey | 81 | BK-5-5-5 | Pale Mint Green | 63 | GR-1-4-1 |
| | | | Hunter Green | 64 | GR-3-6-8 | Pale Yellow | 16 | YE-4-1-2 |

| Color Name | PG# | TCS# |
|---|---|---|
| Palomino Tan | 72 | BR-1-2-3 |
| Payne's Grey | 50 | BL-5-2-9 |
| Periwinkle Blue | 45 | BV-8-3-4 |
| Persimmon | 28 | RE-3-2-6 |
| Phthalo Blue | 48 | BL-5-1-5 |
| Phthalo Green | 62 | BG-9-1-8 |
| Pigskin | 19 | YE-6-4-8 |
| Pineapple Yellow | 17 | YE-5-2-3 |
| Pine Green | 68 | GR-8-6-8 |
| Pink Angel | 26 | RO-5-3-3 |
| Pink Frosting | 29 | RE-4-3-1 |
| Pink Parfait | 38 | RE-7-6-4 |
| Pink Quartz | 36 | RE-6-5-3 |
| Pretty Pink | 32 | RE-5-2-5 |
| Prussian Blue | 53 | BL-7-2-9 |
| Pumpkin | 21 | OR-5-1-5 |
| Purple | 43 | VI-5-1-7 |
| Purple Dusk | 44 | BV-5-4-6 |
| Putty | 21 | OR-5-2-1 |
| Quaker Grey | 81 | BK-5-5-3 |
| Queen Anne's Lace | 20 | OR-4-2-1 |
| Rainforest Green | 61 | BG-8-6-4 |
| Raspberry | 39 | RV-1-4-6 |
| Raw Sienna | 73 | BR-1-2-5 |
| Red Iron Oxide | 31 | RE-4-6-5 |
| Rose Cloud | 31 | RE-4-4-3 |
| Rose Mist | 37 | RE-6-7-7 |
| Rose Petal Pink | 35 | RE-6-5-1 |
| Rosetta Pink | 24 | RO-2-3-3 |
| Rouge | 28 | RE-3-2-7 |
| Royal Fuchsia | 39 | RV-2-4-7 |
| Sachet Pink | 37 | RE-6-7-4 |
| Salem Blue | 53 | BG-1-3-2 |
| Salem Green | 58 | BG-4-7-8 |
| Sandstone | 84 | WH-6-4-6 |
| Santa Fe Rose | 22 | OR-5-9-7 |
| Santa's Flesh | 22 | OR-6-3-1 |
| Seminole Green | 69 | YG-4-3-6 |
| Silver Pine | 62 | BG-8-8-3 |
| Soft Grey | 81 | BK-6-2-1 |
| Sonoma Wine | 33 | RE-5-6-9 |
| Spice Brown | 74 | BR-2-2-7 |
| Spice Tan | 73 | BR-2-2-4 |
| Spring Green | 63 | GR-3-2-4 |
| Stonewedge Green | 67 | GR-7-9-4 |
| Straw | 18 | YE-5-5-5 |
| Sunbright Yellow | 16 | YE-4-1-3 |
| Sweetheart Blush | 38 | RV-1-2-7 |
| Tangerine | 25 | RO-5-1-6 |
| Taupe | 40 | RV-5-8-2 |
| Terra Cotta | 21 | OR-4-7-6 |
| Territorial Beige | 75 | BR-4-4-4 |
| Tide Pool Blue | 51 | BL-5-7-3 |
| Timberline Green | 72 | YG-9-9-7 |
| Toffee Brown | 75 | BR-5-2-7 |
| Tomato Spice | 29 | RE-4-2-6 |
| Tompte Red | 34 | RE-6-2-7 |
| Trail Tan | 78 | BR-7-4-3 |
| Tropic Bay Blue | 57 | BG-4-1-2 |
| Turquoise | 57 | BG-4-1-4 |
| Ultra Blue | 45 | BV-9-1-8 |
| Vibrant Green | 68 | YG-3-2-6 |
| Village Green | 64 | GR-3-7-3 |
| Vintage Wine | 41 | RV-9-2-8 |
| Walnut | 79 | BR-8-5-7 |
| Wedgewood Blue | 50 | BL-5-5-3 |
| Wedgewood Green | 66 | GR-5-6-4 |
| Western Sunset Yellow | 20 | YO-6-1-1 |
| White | 83 | WH-5-1-1 |
| Wild Rice | 78 | BR-7-6-3 |
| Wild Rose | 36 | RE-6-5-5 |
| Williamsburg Blue | 51 | BL-5-7-5 |
| Wisteria | 40 | RV-5-8-5 |
| Woodland Night Green | 62 | BG-9-6-9 |
| Yellow | 17 | YE-5-1-7 |

## Folk Art® by Plaid

| COLOR NAME | PG# | TCS# |
|---|---|---|
| Acorn Brown | 77 | BR-6-4-5 |
| Alizarin Crimson (PP) | 35 | RE-6-4-9 |
| Almond Parfait | 73 | BR-2-2-3 |
| Amish Blue | 47 | BL-4-8-5 |
| Apple Spice | 31 | RE-4-6-7 |
| Apricot Cream | 23 | OR-6-3-5 |
| Aqua Bright | 57 | BG-4-1-4 |
| Aspen Green | 62 | BG-9-7-6 |
| Autumn Leaves | 25 | RO-5-1-6 |
| Azure Blue | 56 | BG-3-1-6 |
| Baby Blue (Mfg. #442) | 45 | BV-8-3-3 |
| Baby Blue (Mfg. #722–Disc.) | 55 | BG-2-4-3 |
| Baby Pink | 34 | RE-6-3-2 |
| Bachelor Button Blue (Disc.) | 56 | BG-2-4-7 |
| Ballet Pink | 36 | RE-6-5-2 |
| Barn Wood | 80 | BK-3-7-4 |
| Barnyard Red | 29 | RE-4-2-7 |
| Basil Green | 67 | GR-7-9-4 |
| Bavarian Blue | 56 | BG-2-4-8 |
| Bayberry | 66 | GR-5-6-4 |
| Berries 'n Cream | 37 | RE-6-7-4 |
| Berry Wine | 38 | RV-1-2-8 |
| Black (Ivory) (PP) | 81 | BK-5-1-8 |
| Bluebell | 50 | BL-5-5-5 |
| Blueberry Pie | 53 | BL-7-4-7 |
| Bluebonnet | 55 | BG-1-7-7 |
| Bluegrass | 61 | BG-8-6-4 |
| Blue Gray Dust (Disc.) | 48 | BL-4-9-5 |
| Blue Ink | 46 | BV-9-6-9 |
| Blue Ribbon | 54 | BG-1-3-8 |
| Brick Red | 32 | RE-5-5-5 |
| Brilliant Blue | 49 | BL-5-2-5 |
| Brownie (Disc.) | 33 | RE-5-6-9 |
| Brown Sugar | 74 | BR-2-2-6 |
| Buckskin Brown | 73 | BR-1-2-7 |
| Burgundy | 35 | RE-6-4-7 |
| Burnt Carmine (PP) | 37 | RE-7-2-9 |
| Burnt Sienna (PP) | 76 | BR-6-2-5 |
| Burnt Umber (PP) | 78 | BR-7-5-8 |
| Buttercream | 16 | YE-4-1-1 |
| Buttercrunch | 19 | YE-7-7-4 |
| Buttercup | 18 | YE-5-5-5 |
| Butter Pecan | 84 | WH-6-4-9 |
| Butterscotch | 20 | OR-4-7-4 |
| Calico Red | 34 | RE-6-2-6 |
| Camel | 74 | BR-2-4-4 |
| Cameo Coral (Disc.) | 24 | RO-1-3-5 |
| Cappuccino | 74 | BR-2-3-3 |
| Caramel | 73 | BR-2-2-5 |
| Cardinal Red | 35 | RE-6-4-4 |
| Cerulean Blue Hue (PP) | 52 | BL-6-1-4 |
| Charcoal Grey | 82 | BK-6-2-8 |
| Cherokee Rose | 28 | RE-3-5-5 |
| Cherry Royale | 35 | RE-6-4-8 |
| Chocolate Cherry (Disc.) | 33 | RE-5-5-8 |
| Chocolate Fudge | 79 | BR-7-6-9 |
| Chocolate Parfait (Disc.) | 77 | BR-6-4-4 |
| Christmas Red | 32 | RE-5-1-5 |
| Cinnamon | 22 | OR-5-9-8 |
| Clay Bisque | 84 | WH-6-4-6 |
| Clover | 69 | YG-4-3-6 |
| Coastal Blue | 57 | BG-3-4-5 |
| Cobalt Blue (PP) | 52 | BL-6-1-8 |
| Coffee Bean | 78 | BR-7-5-7 |
| Coral Reef (Disc.) | 27 | RO-8-3-4 |
| Cotton Candy | 29 | RE-4-3-1 |
| Country Twill | 78 | BR-7-4-3 |
| Crimson | 34 | RE-6-2-8 |
| Dapple Gray | 80 | BK-3-7-8 |
| Dark Brown | 75 | BR-5-1-6 |
| Dark Gray | 80 | BK-1-7-8 |
| Delicate Rose | 30 | RE-4-4-1 |
| Denim Blue | 51 | BL-5-7-8 |
| Dioxazine Purple (PP) | 43 | VI-5-1-9 |
| Dove Gray | 82 | BK-8-2-3 |
| Dusty Coral (Disc.) | 28 | RE-3-2-5 |
| Dusty Peach | 22 | OR-6-3-2 |
| Dutch Blue (Disc.) | 55 | BG-1-7-8 |
| Earthenware | 76 | BR-6-2-3 |
| Emerald Isle | 61 | BG-8-2-9 |
| Engine Red | 33 | RE-6-1-6 |
| English Mustard | 72 | BR-1-2-4 |
| Evergreen | 66 | GR-6-4-5 |
| French Blue | 46 | BL-3-3-5 |
| French Vanilla | 73 | BR-2-2-2 |
| Fresh Foliage | 68 | YG-4-3-2 |
| Fuchsia | 39 | RV-2-2-8 |
| Georgia Peach | 22 | OR-6-3-1 |
| Gingersnap (Disc.) | 27 | RO-8-3-7 |
| Glazed Carrots | 20 | OR-4-1-5 |
| Grass Green | 66 | GR-7-3-5 |
| Gray Flannel | 81 | BK-5-5-3 |
| Gray Mist | 81 | BK-5-5-1 |
| Green | 67 | GR-8-2-4 |
| Green Forest | 64 | GR-3-5-8 |
| Green Meadow | 66 | GR-6-6-6 |

| Color Name | PG# | TCS# |
|---|---|---|
| Green Olive (Disc.) | 70 | YG-5-6-5 |
| Harvest Gold | 18 | YE-6-4-5 |
| Heartland Blue | 51 | BL-5-7-7 |
| Heather | 41 | RV-9-2-5 |
| Holiday Red | 35 | RE-6-4-5 |
| Honeycomb | 73 | BR-2-2-4 |
| Hot Pink | 38 | RE-7-6-5 |
| Huckleberry | 31 | RE-4-6-8 |
| Hunter Green | 64 | GR-3-6-8 |
| Icy White | 51 | BL-6-1-1 |
| Indigo | 50 | BL-5-2-8 |
| Ivory White | 84 | WH-8-2-1 |
| Kelly Green | 63 | GR-3-2-4 |
| Lavender | 43 | VI-5-1-5 |
| Lavender Sachet | 43 | BV-2-6-1 |
| Leaf Green | 63 | GR-3-5-5 |
| Lemonade | 18 | YE-6-2-2 |
| Lemon Custard | 16 | YE-4-1-4 |
| Licorice | 81 | BK-5-1-9 |
| Light Blue | 49 | BL-5-2-2 |
| Light Gray | 80 | BK-5-1-2 |
| Light Periwinkle | 45 | BV-8-3-4 |
| Linen | 84 | WH-7-3-4 |
| Lipstick Red | 32 | RE-5-1-6 |
| Magenta | 38 | RV-1-2-6 |
| Maple Syrup | 75 | BR-5-1-5 |
| Maroon | 36 | RE-6-5-8 |
| Medium Gray | 81 | BK-5-5-5 |
| Midnight | 46 | BV-9-6-8 |
| Milkshake | 78 | BR-7-6-3 |
| Mint Green | 61 | BG-8-6-1 |
| Molasses | 77 | BR-6-2-6 |
| Moon Yellow | 19 | YE-7-7-3 |
| Mystic Green | 64 | GR-4-6-5 |
| Napthol Crimson (PP) | 34 | RE-6-2-7 |
| Navy Blue | 49 | BL-5-1-9 |
| Night Sky | 44 | BV-5-2-8 |
| Nutmeg | 74 | BR-2-2-7 |
| Old Ivy | 68 | GR-8-6-6 |
| Olive Green | 69 | YG-4-3-7 |
| Orchid | 40 | RV-5-2-3 |
| Oxford Blue (Disc.) | 48 | BL-4-9-8 |
| Paisley Blue | 47 | BL-4-5-6 |
| Parchment | 78 | BR-7-6-1 |
| Patina | 57 | BG-4-1-3 |
| Payne's Gray (PP) | 48 | BL-4-9-9 |
| Peach Cobbler | 21 | OR-5-3-4 |
| Peach Perfection | 24 | RO-2-3-3 |
| Pecan Pie (Disc.) | 21 | OR-4-7-8 |
| Periwinkle | 44 | BV-5-4-8 |
| Persimmon | 26 | RO-5-4-4 |
| Pimento (Disc.) | 25 | RO-5-1-8 |
| Pink | 38 | RE-7-6-4 |
| Plantation Green | 58 | BG-4-7-8 |
| Plum Chiffon | 41 | RV-5-9-8 |
| Plum Pudding | 41 | RV-5-8-9 |
| Poetry Green | 64 | GR-3-7-4 |
| Poppy Red | 28 | RE-3-2-6 |
| Porcelain Blue | 51 | BL-5-7-3 |
| Porcelain White (Disc.) | 82 | WH-3-7-5 |
| Portrait Dark | 23 | OR-6-3-8 |
| Portrait Light | 31 | RE-5-1-1 |
| Portrait Medium | 24 | OR-6-7-2 |
| Potpourri Rose | 37 | RE-6-7-5 |
| Prairie Blue | 50 | BL-5-5-6 |
| Primrose | 30 | RE-4-3-8 |
| Promenade | 26 | RO-5-3-4 |
| Prussian Blue (PP) | 49 | BL-5-2-7 |
| Pthalo Green (PP) | 62 | BG-9-1-8 |
| Pumpkin Pie (Disc.) | 26 | RO-5-4-5 |
| Pure Orange | 25 | RO-5-1-4 |
| Pure Orange (PP) | 21 | OR-5-1-5 |
| Purple | 43 | VI-5-1-7 |
| Purple Lilac | 43 | VI-5-8-5 |
| Purple Passion | 41 | RV-5-8-8 |
| Raspberry Sherbert | 36 | RE-6-5-5 |
| Raspberry Wine | 38 | RV-1-2-7 |
| Raw Sienna (PP) | 73 | BR-1-2-5 |
| Raw Umber (PP) | 79 | BR-8-6-8 |
| Red Clay | 32 | RE-5-5-7 |
| Red Light (PP) | 27 | RO-7-1-6 |
| Red Orange | 25 | RO-5-1-7 |
| Red Violet | 40 | RV-5-2-7 |
| Ripe Avocado | 70 | YG-5-6-6 |
| Robin's Egg | 61 | BG-8-6-2 |
| Rose Blush | 26 | RO-5-3-2 |
| Rose Chiffon | 31 | RE-4-4-5 |
| Rose Crimson (PP) | 38 | RV-1-2-5 |
| Rose Garden | 36 | RE-6-5-7 |
| Rose Pink | 36 | RE-6-5-4 |
| Rose White | 33 | RE-6-2-1 |
| Rusty Nail | 31 | RE-4-6-5 |
| Sachet Rose (Disc.) | 24 | OR-6-7-3 |
| Salmon | 27 | RO-8-3-5 |
| Sap Green (PP) | 67 | GR-7-4-5 |
| School Bus Yellow | 17 | YE-5-1-7 |
| Seafoam | 59 | BG-5-3-7 |
| Settler's Blue | 51 | BL-5-7-4 |
| Shamrock | 64 | GR-3-5-7 |
| Skintone | 23 | OR-6-3-3 |
| Slate Blue | 47 | BL-4-8-8 |
| Southern Pine | 69 | YG-4-3-9 |
| Spice Pink | 24 | OR-6-7-7 |
| Spring Green | 65 | GR-5-4-6 |
| Spring Rose | 37 | RE-6-7-2 |
| Spring White | 65 | GR-5-1-1 |
| Sterling Blue | 45 | BV-9-6-7 |
| Strawberry Parfait | 30 | RE-4-3-6 |
| Summer Sky | 55 | BG-1-7-3 |
| Sunflower | 17 | YE-5-5-2 |
| Sunny Yellow | 17 | YE-5-1-6 |
| Sunset Orange (Disc.) | 26 | RO-5-4-7 |
| Sweetheart Pink | 30 | RE-4-3-4 |
| Taffy | 85 | WH-8-2-6 |
| Tangerine | 20 | YO-6-1-5 |
| Tapioca | 83 | WH-6-3-2 |
| Tartan Green | 62 | BG-9-6-8 |
| Teal | 57 | BG-4-1-7 |
| Teal Blue | 54 | BG-1-7-2 |
| Teal Green | 60 | BG-4-7-6 |
| Teddy Bear Brown | 78 | BR-6-4-7 |
| Teddy Bear Tan | 72 | BR-1-2-3 |
| Terra Cotta | 22 | OR-5-9-7 |
| Thicket | 69 | YG-4-3-8 |
| Thunder Blue | 53 | BL-7-4-9 |
| Township Blue | 56 | BG-2-4-9 |
| Transp. Oxide Red (PP) | 76 | BR-6-1-5 |
| Transp. Oxide Yellow (PP) | 19 | YO-2-1-3 |
| True Blue | 48 | BL-5-1-5 |
| Turquoise | 59 | BG-5-1-6 |
| Ultramarine | 52 | BL-6-1-6 |
| Ultramarine Blue (PP) | 48 | BL-5-1-6 |
| Vanilla Cream | 84 | WH-6-4-3 |
| Victorian Rose | 25 | RO-5-3-1 |
| Violet Pansy | 42 | VI-4-1-7 |
| Viridian (PP) | 61 | BG-8-2-8 |
| Warm White | 85 | WH-8-2-2 |
| Whipped Berry | 44 | BV-6-8-3 |
| White (Titanium) (PP) | 83 | WH-5-1-1 |
| Wicker White | 83 | WH-5-1-2 |
| Wintergreen | 62 | BG-9-6-9 |
| Winter White | 48 | BL-5-1-1 |
| Wrought Iron | 65 | GR-5-3-9 |
| Yellow Light (PP) | 17 | YE-5-1-5 |
| Yellow Medium (PP) | 16 | YE-4-1-5 |
| Yellow Ochre (PP) | 18 | YE-6-4-7 |

## Jo Sonja® by ChromaAcrylics

| COLOR NAME | PG# | TCS# |
|---|---|---|
| Amethyst | 41 | RV-9-2-3 |
| Aqua | 57 | BG-4-1-5 |
| Black (Carbon) | 81 | BK-5-1-9 |
| Brilliant Green | 66 | GR-7-2-5 |
| Brown Earth | 75 | BR-5-1-5 |
| Burgundy | 35 | RE-6-4-9 |
| Burnt Sienna | 77 | BR-6-2-6 |
| Burnt Umber | 79 | BR-7-6-9 |
| Cadmium Scarlet | 29 | RE-4-1-5 |
| Cadmium Yellow Light | 16 | YE-4-1-4 |
| Cadmium Yellow Mid | 17 | YE-5-1-6 |
| Cobalt Blue Hue | 52 | BL-6-1-8 |
| Colony Blue | 56 | BG-2-4-7 |
| Dioxazine Purple | 43 | VI-5-1-9 |
| Fawn | 76 | BR-5-4-4 |
| French Blue | 51 | BL-5-7-8 |
| Gold Oxide | 21 | OR-4-7-8 |
| Green Oxide | 68 | GR-8-6-5 |
| Indian Red Oxide | 33 | RE-5-6-9 |
| Jade | 64 | GR-4-6-5 |
| Moss Green | 71 | YG-9-6-2 |
| Napthol Crimson | 34 | RE-6-2-7 |
| Napthol Red Light | 29 | RE-4-1-6 |
| Nimbus Grey | 80 | BK-4-5-5 |
| Norwegian Orange | 27 | RO-7-4-7 |

| Color | PG# | TCS# |
|---|---|---|
| Opal | 78 | BR-7-6-3 |
| Payne's Grey | 50 | BL-5-2-9 |
| Pine Green | 69 | YG-4-3-8 |
| Plum Pink | 36 | RE-6-5-7 |
| Provincial Beige | 75 | BR-4-4-4 |
| Prussian Blue Hue | 49 | BL-5-2-7 |
| Pthalo Blue | 49 | BL-5-2-6 |
| Pthalo Green | 62 | BG-9-1-8 |
| Raw Sienna | 72 | BR-1-2-4 |
| Raw Umber | 79 | BR-8-6-8 |
| Red Earth | 31 | RE-4-6-5 |
| Rose Pink | 30 | RE-4-3-8 |
| Sapphire | 47 | BL-4-5-6 |
| Smoked Pearl | 84 | WH-6-4-6 |
| Storm Blue | 48 | BL-4-9-9 |
| Teal Green | 62 | BG-9-7-9 |
| Transparent Magenta | 38 | RV-1-2-7 |
| Turner's Yellow | 18 | YE-6-2-6 |
| Ultramarine Blue | 48 | BL-5-1-5 |
| Ultramarine Blue Deep | 48 | BL-5-1-6 |
| Vermillion | 25 | RO-5-1-7 |
| Warm White | 85 | WH-8-2-2 |
| White (Titanium) | 83 | WH-5-1-1 |
| Yellow Light | 17 | YE-5-1-5 |
| Yellow Oxide | 18 | YE-6-4-7 |

## Liquitex® by Binney & Smith

| COLOR NAME | PG# | TCS# |
|---|---|---|
| ACRA Red | 35 | RE-6-4-4 |
| ACRA Violet | 38 | RV-1-2-8 |
| Alizarin Crimson Perm. Hue | 34 | RE-6-2-8 |
| Apricot | 21 | OR-5-3-4 |
| Baltic Blue | 56 | BG-2-4-9 |
| Baltic Green | 58 | BG-4-7-7 |
| Black (Ivory) | 81 | BK-5-1-8 |
| Black (Mars) | 81 | BK-5-1-9 |
| Bright Aqua Green | 57 | BG-4-1-4 |
| Brilliant Blue | 56 | BG-3-1-6 |
| Brilliant Blue Purple | 45 | BV-9-1-8 |
| Brilliant Orange | 20 | OR-4-1-5 |
| Brilliant Purple | 43 | VI-5-1-5 |
| Brilliant Yellow | 17 | YE-5-1-6 |
| Bronze Yellow | 75 | BR-2-5-8 |
| Burgundy | 35 | RE-6-4-9 |
| Burnt Siena | 76 | BR-6-2-3 |
| Burnt Umber | 79 | BR-7-6-9 |
| Cadmium Orange | 21 | OR-5-1-5 |
| Cadmium Red Light | 25 | RO-5-1-8 |
| Cadmium Red Lt. Hue | 27 | RO-7-1-6 |
| Cadmium Red Medium | 33 | RE-6-1-6 |

| Color | PG# | TCS# |
|---|---|---|
| Cadmium Red Med. Hue | 32 | RE-5-1-6 |
| Cadmium Yellow Light | 17 | YE-5-1-5 |
| Cadmium Yellow Lt. Hue | 17 | YE-5-1-6 |
| Cadmium Yellow Med. | 17 | YE-5-1-7 |
| Cerulean Blue | 52 | BL-6-1-4 |
| Cerulean Blue Hue | 52 | BL-6-1-6 |
| Christmas Green | 67 | GR-8-2-4 |
| Chrome Oxide Green | 68 | GR-8-6-6 |
| Cobalt Blue | 52 | BL-6-1-8 |
| Dark Victorian Rose | 36 | RE-6-5-8 |
| Deep Portrait Pink | 23 | OR-6-3-8 |
| Dioxazine Purple | 43 | VI-5-1-9 |
| Emerald Green | 63 | GR-3-3-5 |
| French Gray/Blue | 51 | BL-5-7-4 |
| Green Light, Perm. | 66 | GR-7-2-5 |
| Hibiscus | 30 | RE-4-3-8 |
| Hooker's Green Hue, Perm. | 68 | GR-8-3-9 |
| Lacquer Red | 32 | RE-5-1-6 |
| Light Blue, Perm. | 56 | BG-3-4-3 |
| Light Blue Violet | 45 | BV-8-3-4 |
| Light Magenta | 34 | RE-6-2-4 |
| Light Portrait Pink | 30 | RE-4-3-3 |
| Light Violet | 42 | VI-5-1-4 |
| Maroon | 37 | RE-7-2-9 |
| Medium Magenta | 39 | RV-2-4-6 |
| Napthol Crimson | 34 | RE-6-2-7 |
| Napthol Red Light | 29 | RE-4-2-5 |
| Navy | 49 | BL-5-2-7 |
| Neutral Gray | 81 | BK-5-5-5 |
| Olive | 70 | YG-5-6-6 |
| Pale Portrait Pink | 27 | RE-3-2-2 |

| Color | PG# | TCS# |
|---|---|---|
| Parchment | 67 | GR-7-8-1 |
| Payne's Gray | 50 | BL-5-2-9 |
| Phthalo Blue | 48 | BL-5-1-5 |
| Phthalo Green | 62 | BG-9-1-8 |
| Prism Violet | 41 | RV-9-2-8 |
| Prussian Blue | 49 | BL-5-2-6 |
| Raspberry | 38 | RV-1-2-7 |
| Raw Siena | 73 | BR-1-2-5 |
| Raw Umber | 79 | BR-8-6-8 |
| Real Teal | 58 | BG-4-1-8 |
| Red Oxide | 31 | RE-4-6-5 |
| Sandalwood | 24 | OR-6-7-4 |
| Sap Green, Perm. | 64 | GR-3-5-7 |
| Scarlet | 25 | RO-5-1-7 |
| Soft White | 85 | WH-8-2-2 |
| Swedish Blue | 54 | BG-1-3-8 |
| Taupe | 79 | BR-8-5-7 |
| Turner's Yellow | 18 | YE-6-2-6 |
| Turquoise Deep | 58 | BG-4-1-9 |
| Turquoise Green | 59 | BG-5-1-6 |
| Twilight | 46 | BV-9-6-8 |
| Ultramarine Blue | 48 | BL-5-1-6 |
| Unbleached Titanium | 73 | BR-2-2-3 |
| Venetian Rose | 37 | RE-6-7-5 |
| Viridian Hue, Perm. | 64 | GR-3-5-8 |
| White (Titanium) | 83 | WH-5-1-1 |
| Wisteria | 42 | RV-9-2-9 |
| Yellow Light Hansa | 16 | YE-4-1-4 |
| Yellow Medium Azo | 16 | YE-4-1-5 |
| Yellow Orange Azo | 19 | YO-5-1-4 |
| Yellow Oxide | 18 | YE-6-4-7 |

## NEW COLORS UPDATE—FREE

As new colors are introduced, we offer two different methods to obtain your copy.

**1** *Visit our Web Page on the Internet.*
As the new colors become available, we will add the matches to our page. They can be referenced from the screen or you may print them for future use.

http://www.tru-color.com

**2** *You may request your copy by writing:*
Tru-Color Update, 64 East Marion Street
P.O. Box 496, Danville, IN 46122-0496

Please enclose check or money order (U.S. Funds) for $2.95 to cover postage & handling.

# Tru-Color Comparison Discs

## See for yourself...

Color is visual not verbal! The best way to illustrate basic color hue and value is with a **hand-painted** swatch of actual color. Thousands of decorative painters use the Tru-Color System© for identifying, selecting and comparing the hundreds of different choices which are available.

*The Tru-Color Comparison Disc©* is a collection of **hand-painted** swatches featuring the most popular colors used by the artist. The swatches are painted on circular discs for comparison with corresponding or similar colors. A simple rotation of the discs allows you to compare hundreds of actual paint swatches grouped by color and brand.

## ...Seeing is believing!

# Door/Wall-Hung Paint Rack

## Out of the way, yet handy.

## Paint storage—now there is a better way.

- Easily installs on the inside of any door or mounts on the wall.
- Holds 130 bottles of paint.
- Includes two 35″ modules—ten shelves (19½″ wide).
- Contains complete step-by-step assembly instructions.
- Needs only a hammer and screwdriver.
- Can be decorated and installed all by yourself.

## Quick and Efficient Paint Storage

This unique paint rack is easily mounted on any standard-height door or on a wall. It is built to hold two-ounce paint bottles. It can also be modified to accommodate jars and tubes.

**Paints can be stored by color and brand for easy access. Make it easy by arranging your paint by TCS#.**

Full-door module.........................$33.95 + S/H
Half-door module.........................$19.95 + S/H
(Shipping/Handling: $6.00 U.S., $10.00 Canada U.S. Funds)

**Visit our World Wide Web page on the Internet: Calendar of Events for Decorative Painters**
# http://www.tru-color.com

Tru-Color Systems, Inc.
P.O. Box 496
Danville, IN 46122-0496
(317) 745-7535

# TCS Color Match Software

• Accent® • Americana® by DecoArt • Ceramcoat® by Delta •
Folk Art® Plaid • JoSonja® Chroma Acrylics • Liquitex®

## 2,568 Acrylic colors and mixes with ratios.

• Computer solution to color conversions.
• Find any color, then match to your favorite brand instantly!
• No charts to shuffle, no pages to search.
• Suggested shade and highlight in four brands.
• Includes manufacturer's number so you can easily find the target color on the retailer's rack.

Eliminate the guesswork and doubts since your computer can tell you the color equivalents in the brands you choose to survey. It will print the results and inventory of the colors you own.

# TCS Painter's Library

• **Helps you get organized**...it's easy. This software is designed to help you get your painting books, pattern packets and magazine projects in order—and give you their location.
• **Sorts** your entire library into subject matter so you can choose from flowers, landscapes, santas or any category you choose.
• **Includes inventory listing** of your on-hand painting supplies and creates a personal shopping list of the items you need to buy.

Set up your own filing system, then enter key information about the project or book. Now you can find it by author, title, publication, even location and category (i.e. animals, flowers, landscapes, holidays, etc.). Plus, you can establish your own classifications.

Now, when you see a beautiful wood, tin or fabric item you wish to paint, look in your Painter's Library to find just the right pattern. It's easy to select the best—only the ones you want to paint.

## Download "Free" Demonstration Software
http://www.tru-color.com Windows Versions Only

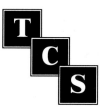

## $49.95 each + $5.00 S/H
IBM or Compatible, for Windows 95 and Windows 3.1

**Tru-Color Systems, Inc.** P.O. Box 496 Danville, IN 46122-0496
Phone: (317) 745-7535; Fax: (317) 745-1886; E-mail: npearcy@tru-color.com

# More Great Books for Creating Beautiful Crafts!

**Priscilla Hauser's Book of Decorative Painting**—Now you can learn to paint Priscilla Hauser's trademark roses—as well as daisies, lilacs, violets, tulips and other beautiful blooms! Over 20 step-by-step flower painting projects will give you endless ideas for using painted flowers to decorate a variety of surfaces. *#30914/$24.99/144 pages/371 color, 22 b&w illus./paperback*

**Easy Airbrush Projects for Crafters & Decorative Painters**—Using the airbrush for crafts and decorative painting has never been easier! You'll get the inside story on getting started in airbrushing and basic painting techniques. Then, move on to 10 step-by-step projects that perfect what you've learned. *#30908/$23.99/128 pages/356 color, 18 b&w illus./paperback*

**Painting Flowers in Watercolor With Louise Jackson**—Master decorative artist, Louise Jackson, shows you how to beautifully render one of decorative painting's most popular subjects—flowers! All you need is the desire to follow 15 detailed, step-by-step projects from start to finish! *#30913/$23.99/128 pages/165 color, 21 b&w illus./paperback*

**Creative Finishes Series**—Explore the world of creative finishing with leading decorative artist, Phil Myer! Each book features a variety of techniques, paint applications and surface treatments in 15 projects complete with detailed instructions, patterns and step-by-step photos.

   **Painting & Decorating Tables**—*#30911/ $23.99/112 pages/177 color illus./paperback*

   **Painting & Decorating Boxes**—*#30910/ $23.99/112 pages/145 color, 32 b&w illus./paperback*

**Gretchen Cagle's Decorative Painting Keepsakes**—Discover a treasury of beautiful projects collected from one of today's most celebrated decorative painters! In her latest book, Gretchen shares 31 of her all-time favorite projects. No matter what your skill level, clear instructions, traceable patterns and color mixing recipes will have you painting in no time! *#30975/$24.99/144 pages/91 color, 44 b&w illus./paperback*

**1,200 Paint Effects for the Home Decorator**—Now you can find the ideal color combination and paint effect for any kind of job! This handy visual guide gives you over 1,200 combinations, based on 25 standard colors. Plus, step-by-step instructions for special finishing effects such as splattering, combing, color washing, marbling, distressing and more! *#30949/$29.99/192 pages/1,000+ color illus.*

**Decorative Painting: Fruits, Vegetables and Berries**—Create a cornucopia of projects with this guide to the secrets of painting luscious fruits, vegetables and berries! Over 40 popular subjects are demonstrated in easy-to-follow detail—including tips on equipment, color theory and preparation. *#30904/$22.99/128 pages/300+ color illus./paperback*

**Making Greeting Cards With Rubber Stamps**—Discover hundreds of quick, creative, stamp-happy ways to make extra-special cards—no experience, fancy equipment or expensive materials required! You'll find 30 easy-to-follow projects for holidays, birthdays, thank-you's and more! *#30821/$21.99/128 pages/231 color illus./paperback*

**Acrylic Decorative Painting Techniques**—Discover stroke-by-stroke instruction that takes you through the basics and beyond! More than 50 fun and easy painting techniques are illustrated in simple demonstrations that offer at least two variations on each method. Plus, a thorough discussion on tools, materials, color, preparation and backgrounds. *#30884/$24.99/128 pages/550 color illus.*

**The Decorative Stamping Sourcebook**—Embellish walls, furniture, fabric and accessories—with stamped designs! You'll find 180 original, traceable motifs in a range of themes and illustrated instructions for making your own stamps to enhance any decorating style. *#30898/$24.99/128 pages/200 color illus.*

**Decorative Painting Sourcebook**—Priscilla Hauser, Phillip Myer and Jackie Shaw lend their expertise to this one-of-a-kind guide straight from the pages of *Decorative Artist's Workbook!* You'll find step-by-step, illustrated instructions on every technique— from basic brushstrokes to faux finishes, painting glassware, wood, clothing and much more! *#30883/$24.99/128 pages/200 color illus./paperback*

**Painting & Decorating Birdhouses**—Turn unfinished birdhouses into something special—from a quaint Victorian roost to a Southwest pueblo, from a rustic log cabin to a lighthouse! These colorful and easy decorative painting projects are for the birds with 22 clever projects to create indoor decorative birdhouses, as well as functional ones to grace your garden. *#30882/$23.99/128 pages/ 194 color illus./paperback*

**Painting Houses, Cottages and Towns on Rocks**—Turn ordinary rocks into charming cottages, country churches and Victorian mansions! Accomplished artist Lin Wellford shares 11 fun, inexpensive, step-by-step projects that are sure to please. *#30823/$21.99/128 pages/398 color illus./paperback*

**The Crafter's Guide to Pricing Your Work**—Price and sell more than 75 kinds of crafts with this must-have reference. You'll learn how to set prices to maximize income while maintaining a fair profit margin. Includes tips on recordkeeping, consignment, taxes, reducing costs and managing your cash flow. *#70353/$16.99/160 pages/paperback*

**Create Your Own Greeting Cards and Gift Wrap With Priscilla Hauser**—You'll see sponge prints, eraser prints, cellophane scrunching, marbleizing, papermaking and dozens of other techniques you can use to make unique greetings for all your loved ones. *#30621/$24.99/128 pages/230 color illus.*

**Creative Paint Finishes for Furniture**—Revive your furniture with fresh color and design! Inexpensive, easy and fun painting techniques are at your fingertips, along with step-by-step directions and a photo gallery of imaginative applications for faux finishing, staining, stenciling, mosaic, découpage and many other techniques. *#30748/$27.99/144 pages/236 color, 7 b&w illus.*

**Master Works: How to Use Paint Finishes to Transform Your Surroundings**—Discover how to use creative paint finishes to enhance and excite the "total look" of your home. This step-by-step guide contains dozens of exciting ideas on fresco, marbling, paneling and other simple paint techniques for bringing new life to any space. Plus, you'll also find innovative uses for fabrics, screens and blinds. *#30626/$29.95/176 pages/150 color illus.*

**The Art of Painting Animals on Rocks**—Discover how a dash of paint can turn humble stones into charming "pet rocks." This hands-on, easy-to-follow book offers a menagerie of fun—and potentially profitable—stone animal projects. Eleven examples, complete with materials lists, photos of the finished piece and patterns will help you create a forest of fawns, rabbits, foxes and other adorable critters. *#30606/$21.99/144 pages/ 250 color illus./paperback*

**Creative Paint Finishes for the Home**—A complete, full-color, step-by-step guide to decorating floors, walls and furniture—including how to use the tools, master the techniques and develop ideas. *#30426/$27.99/144 pages/212 color illus.*

**Paint Craft**—Discover great ideas for enhancing your home, wardrobe and personal items. You'll see how to master the basics of mixing and planning colors, how to print with screen and linoleum to create your own stationery, how to enhance old glassware and pottery pieces with unique patterns and motifs and much more! *#30678/$16.95/144 pages/200 color illus./paperback*

Other fine North Light Books are available from your local bookstore, art supply store, or direct from the publisher. Write to the address below for a FREE catalog of all North Light Books. To order books directly from the publisher, include $3.50 postage and handling for one book, $1.50 for each additional book. Ohio residents add 6% sales tax. Allow 30 days for delivery.

North Light Books
1507 Dana Avenue
Cincinnati, Ohio 45207

VISA/MasterCard orders call TOLL-FREE
**1-800-289-0963**

Prices subject to change without notice.                    Stock may be limited on some books.

Write to this address for information on *The Artist's Magazine*, North Light Books, North Light Book Club, Graphic Design Book Club, North Light Art School, and Betterway Books. To receive information on art or design competitions, send a SASE to Dept. BOI, Attn: Competition Coordinator, at the above address.

8548